Deep Bonds

Raymond M. Simmons

iUniverse, Inc.
New York   Bloomington

Deep Bonds

iUniverse books may be ordered through booksellers or by contacting:

iUniverse
1663 Liberty Drive
Bloomington, IN 47403
www.iuniverse.com
1-800-Authors (1-800-288-4677)

Because of the dynamic nature of the Internet, any Web addresses or links contained in this book may have changed since publication and may no longer be valid. The views expressed in this work are solely those of the author and do not necessarily reflect the views of the publisher, and the publisher hereby disclaims any responsibility for them.

ISBN: 978-1-4401-2935-3 (sc)
ISBN: 978-1-4401-2936-0 (dj)
ISBN: 978-1-4401-2937-7 (ebook)

Printed in the United States of America

iUniverse rev. date: 4/3/2009

Chapter One-
Road Hogs

Lamont planned to be punctual and had allowed himself plenty of time to make his appointment in Richmond. He was up and on the highway at 6AM on this warm May Morning, and as always the interstate traffic was a busy parade of roaring tractor trailers and tourists. It was the busy season for Bush Gardens amusement park in Williamsburg, Virginia, which was the likely destination for the bulk of these early travelers. Lamont guessed that many of them were tourists, who were trying to avoid the rush of the ever present crowds.

He observed a parade of industrial trucks rumbling up and down the highway, carrying assorted cargo and spewing streams of pollution. Such was the messy nature of the buzzing transport business between Norfolk and Richmond. He was thankful that in spite of the busy boisterous traffic, the flow was steady, and at this pace he should be on time for his appointment in Richmond.

The mild weather allowed Lamont positive thoughts while anticipating his scheduled meeting with business tycoon, Jake Cooper. Jake is more than just a business tycoon, he is also Lamont's father, a fact that Lamont discovered three years ago under bizarre circumstances. Those circumstances had created hard feelings, misunderstandings, and resentment at the time.

Unexpectedly, Lamont's focus turned to a blue rusty Cadillac swerving back and forth across the white line just ahead. Lamont was a few short feet behind the Cadillac, and caught a glimpse of its occupants through its dirty rear window. He observed a man and a woman casually laughing while passing something between them. He saw the woman take a puff. "These dumb asses smoking dope," Lamont said aloud with nervous impatience. "Idiots," Lamont muttered angrily, "they're going to kill somebody."

Suddenly an earth shattering loud horn blasted, and screeching tires seemed to surround him. The odor of burning rubber created an unpleasant, nostril opening chemical stench. The Cadillac ahead had drifted into the lane of a huge Mayflower eighteen wheeler, and now drifted back barely in time to avoid a rear end collision. Lamont's palms sweated and his eyes continued to focus intensely on the erratic opera-tion, of the rusty vehicle ahead. His important meeting with Jake and his future with Cooper Industries were the last things on his mind right now. If a collision had taken place he would probably have no future right now. He was deeply concerned that the careless actions of these potheads created potential danger that could affect his future.

He felt nervous and continued to talk aloud to himself. "I got to get away from these fools," he said easing off the accelerator. "Got to keep my distance." He maneuvered his Maxima into the right lane and watched the distance widen between him and the Cadillac. His tension subsided somewhat, as he watched it fade into the foreground. Now his eyes darted across the lanes looking for the unexpected.

Once the Blue Cadillac was finally out of the picture, Lamont breathed a sigh of relief. Now his mind turned back to this upcom-ing meeting, and he tried to anticipated its meaning. Based on all his past conversations with Jake, Lamont concluded that Jake was ready to bring him into the company. He was qualified, and Jake had promised him months ago that he would eventually bring him in soon.

Right now he wasn't feeling as confident as he wanted. After speak-ing with Jake last night, he hadn't felt jubilant because Jake's voice sounded troubled. He wanted to think positive, but after receiving last night's phone call, his paranoia led him to negative second thoughts. Maybe Jake would renege on his promise. Lamont sensed that some-thing wasn't right. Maybe his own insecurities had surfaced because he longed so much to blend in with the Cooper family.

Perhaps he was too anxious to leave his present dead end job, and too eager to move to a new position where hopefully, he could make a difference. On the other hand, he hoped that Jake wasn't going to set him up in a token job, because that would make him feel useless and unprogressive. No, he wanted to earn a job based on his qualifica-tion, not awarded a job based on his relation to Jake, or for saving his younger brother, JJ's life.

Suddenly, he caught sight of the rusty Cadillac recklessly crossing the highway and into his lane again. He saw a stream of heavy smoke oozed lazily from the hood as the Cadillac slowed to a sluggish erratic pace. "Damn," Lamont said frustrated, "I just can't shake these dumb asses." He observed the Cadillac closely and tapped his brakes lightly. The collective horns of angry drivers fill the air and in response, the Cadillac driver stuck his tattooed arm out the window and flipped every one the bird. Lamont tried to see some way to go past him, but the Cadillac hit brakes and slowed to a stop a few feet ahead.

Lamont froze momentarily and weighed his options about whether to hit breaks or switch lanes. He might not have enough distance to stop cleanly, but he could get rear ended if he tried to switch lanes. Instinctively he stomped down on the brake pedal, but he jetted forward so fast that he almost lost control. "Damn you," he yelled to the car ahead, realizing that he wasn't going to stop in time. After a quick glance in the mirror, he maneuvered the Maxima past the rear end of the Cadillac and into the next lane, and stomped hard on the accelerator.

Now Lamont's stomach flipped at the sight of the huge dump truck in his rear view mirror and the vibrations of the rumbling road beneath him. The truck was gaining on him fast, and the Maxima jerked and almost stalled. His eyes froze on the image of the truck, and he said a silent prayer and braced himself. He tensed and pushed the accelerator with so much pressure that sharp pains shot up his right leg. The Maxima wasn't responding instantly and the truck was on his bumper. He felt that there was no way to avoid a crash.

He heard the perpetual squeal of the truck's air brakes, and a ghostly horn shouts a cacophonous eardrum splitting shrill. He was acutely aware of the burnt rubber stench in the air, as his stomach dropped. His heartbeat shifted into overdrive, his senses became numb and his throat was dry. "Oh Jesus," he yelled reverently as the Maxima suddenly burst into another gear and pulled away slightly. Lamont still felt threatened because the truck was too close and it seemed relentless as it continued to gain on him.

He noticed that the right lane was open due to the jam created by the Cadillac in that lane behind him. He didn't want to try and outrun the truck so he jerked the steering wheel to the right to get out of the truck's path, and onto the shoulder of the road. The car fish tailed slightly, but he was able to get out from the path of the truck. He applied breaks and momentarily lost control, and the front end caught a portion of the guard rail, making a crunching metallic sound. Finally Lamont brought the car to a rough stop on the overpass above the small creek that flowed beneath the highway.

Lamont paused, took a deep breath and sat back silently unable to budge. His strength was gone and his heartbeat throbbed inside his, ears and temples. His eyes twitched and he feared that his heart would give out unless he calmed down. That was easier said then done, and it took him a few minutes to pull himself together.

Ten minutes later he was calmer and uttered a silent thank you prayer. "That was too close," he said, glancing about still unsettled. He got out of the car and wobbled around to inspect the damage and pinpoint his location.

There was less damaged than he first thought. The front fender and front grill were dented and the passenger side front tire was flat, but there was little structural damage. He popped the trunk and changed the tire quickly, then prepared to pull onto the highway. He checked his watch knowing that he would be late for his appointment, but that didn't matter now. He was thankful that he was still alive and that those idiots were out of the picture.

The interstate was much busier with traffic now, and he was an hour behind schedule, and he hoped that Jake could still see him today. He hated making excuses, but today he would have to. Even though Jake Cooper was his father, he was also an astute and hard nose business man who hated excuses as much as Lamont did. Nonetheless this was an unavoidable delay. Still, there was little doubt that this meeting was about the job offer and Lamont had to put aside his doubts and hope for the best. If things worked out like he hoped they would, he could start his new career and marry Jane.

He felt like it would work out and that Jake had only made him wait because he wanted to make sure he got the right position. He would certainly do that if he had kids and was in Jake's shoes. He would definitely have kids, and he would have more than one, because being an only child was a cold brush of reality.

His personal experience had ingrained in him a need to be part of a family, which is one reason for his pressing need to bond with his new found family, the Coopers. His need for family is also the reason that he had cast aside his unfounded doubts and agreed to marry Jane. He wanted his own family and he would get started on that as soon as Jake said the right words this morning.

Everything depended on what Jake decided and as much as he wanted to believe that Jake would say the words, he felt that his celebration might be premature. His stomach gurgled with gastric disruption, and his mouth felt like dry powdered cotton as he closed in on his destination. He picked up the cell phone and dialed Jake's private number.

Chapter Two-
The Interview

Lamont stepped off the elevator, and heads into the foyer leading to Jake's office. He was aware of clicking shoes on the highly polish floors, and he inhaled the building's sterile scent. He observed busy employees bustling about on fast forward. His stomach was settled and his mouth wasn't as dry as before. Jake had expressed understanding and concern in their telephone conversation, and in spite of his jitters and tardiness, he tried to remain optimistic.

He smiles at Pam, the pretty twenty five year old secretary, whose eyes locked on him as he reaches her desk. "Hi, I'm Lamont Savage. I'm here to see Jake Cooper."

"Oh hello, Mr. Savage," Pam said in a sultry voice and smiled flirtatiously, while eying Lamont's six foot frame. "Mr. Cooper is expecting you," she replied and purposely looked him up and down before continuing. "You can go right in," she said with a toothy smile.

Upon entering, he saw Jake sitting proudly behind his desk looking through some papers. It was obvious to any observer that the two men were related because of their many similar features. Both men had strong facial features, round firm chins, sparkling dark brown eyes, prominent noses and high cheek bones. They were both muscular men who stood six feet tall, and wore similar short hair styles. Had it not been for the gray in Jake's temples one might think that the two men were brothers close to the same age.

Jake's office was filled with plush carpet, expensive art and looked like a large den instead of an office. A wide screen television was mounted on the wall between a pair of original African paintings, and several small paintings hung neatly in various locations. The earth tone colored walls served as background for the various brilliant color compositions in the paintings mounted on it. Soft music gushed in perfect volume from hidden speakers and blocked all outside noise.

"Hello Lamont," Jake said, rising to shake his hand and give him a hug. "Come in and sit down, son," Jake moved to the large leather couch near the rolling glass bar and sat. "Something to drink?"

"No too early for me," Lamont said, sitting next to Jake.

"Me too. I was suggesting some juice."

"Yeah right," Lamont said slightly awkward. "Cranberry juice is good, if you got it." Lamont suddenly felt nervous again as he watched Jake open the small refrigerator door, and pull out two bottles of cranberry juice. He felt slightly intimidated by Jake for the first time. Maybe it was because he expected something from Jake and he wasn't sure how Jake felt about giving it to him. Such feelings were ridiculous, because Jake was fair, and any initial trepidation was because Lamont didn't think that he could measure up to his father's intensity. No one had helped Jake and Jake hadn't asked any one for anything. Jake was a hot shot, hard working business tycoon who was commercially smart, and he accomplished that on his own. Lamont respected any many who could do that and that respect increased tenfold with Jake, his father.

Lamont shared many traits with Jake and was also hard working, but Jake was an extraordinary go-getter who had mastered business. Lamont was as aggressive and driven as Jake, but frankly Lamont didn't think he could measure up to Jake, no average man could.

He focused on Jake and his heartbeat elevated, because he sensed that Jake was stalling. His internal alarm went off when he noticed Jake's strange expression. That expression fore warned Lamont that he was about to hear bad news as Jake looked into his eyes and sighed deeply. His large ears wiggled slightly and his eyes tighten. "Lamont, I know I promised you an executive position and believe me I want that for you more than you think. And I know from our past conversations that it's what you want too. The problem is that the job I have for you right now is not as an Executive."

Lamont was stunned and suddenly angry by Jakes words. This wasn't how it was suppose to be. He had almost gotten killed today because he was coming up here for some good news. Now he hears this bizarre story. "Oh really?" Without thinking he blurted out his feelings. "What's the real reason Jake? Are you ashamed of me? What is it, I don't measure up? I'm not good enough?"

"What? No, Lamont, you know better, of course not."

"I don't know anything, Jake. You made a promise, and you make me wait for months," Lamont sighed and looked directly at Jake. "But you hired JJ who's an amateur with none of my business experience or sense. Now you sound like you about to break your promise to me. Is it because JJ's your legitimate son and I'm not? Do unskilled legitimate sons trump skilled illegitimate ones?"

"Lamont how can you say something like that. I admit I wasn't the greatest father to you early on, but I've tried to make it up to you. I though we were past that."

"I thought we were too, but apparently my dubious identity still creates problems. You don't think I fit into your world, or maybe you don't want me to."

"Lamont you are so wrong about that. You're as much my son as JJ."

"Yeah sure Jake, but you hired JJ and not me," Lamont said skeptically.

Jake's jaws clenched. "You know why I hired JJ, Lamont?" He continued before Lamont could speak. "To give him some responsibility and to keep him out of trouble. He can't screw anything up where he is." Jake sighed and turned to Lamont with a serious expression. "Lamont I respect you and your skills too much to give you a meaningless token job."

"But you don't respect JJ enough to do the same for him? Come on Jake, that's kinda hard to swallow."

"Lamont, JJ is immature and irresponsible and I thought a job would instill," he stopped himself. "Look, this isn't even about JJ, or the girls for that matter. This is about the future of Cooper Industries and how you could help me preserve it."

"The future of Cooper Industries," Lamont shot Jake a puzzled glare. "What has the future of CI got to do with this job you're offering me?"

"Lamont, listen to me. The job I got for you is the most important job here, and that's no BS." Jake paused and sighed as if ready to deliver sad news. "I know it's not the job you expect, but please believe me it's the most critical job at Cooper Industries, and I'm offering it to you."

Lamont listened in silence, obviously disappointed. "The bottom line is that you're the only trustworthy person I can think of to do this."

"What about your legitimate children," Lamont said harshly, with no plans to apologize.

"Lamont you need to understand that I love all my children, but love is one thing and trust and competence is another. I wouldn't trust any of them to attempt to do the job I want you to do. Cheryl is a reckless spendthrift, Ann is afraid of her shadow, Ruth has a drinking problem and JJ thinks a party and a woman makes the world spin. They're all over twenty one and they continue to act like irresponsible adolescent teens instead of conscientious grownups," Jake said, with a brief pause. "I know that's my fault, but the damage is done. I spoiled them and that's why I can't entrust any one of them to do this."

Lamont was confused at Jake's startling revelation. "So are you telling me that of all your children, I'm the only one who's trustworthy?

"Yes," Jake said eagerly. "Ironic isn't it?"

"It is," Lamont said aloud. And sad if it's true, he thought to himself.

Jake sipped silently from his own bottle of Cranberry juice then continued. "So will you listen to me and at least think about it? If things work out you'll eventually get the job that I promised you."

"Eventually, that's such an indefinite word. It could be four days or forever."

"It's the best I can offer at this time, Lamont, because this is more essential." When Lamont remained silent Jake continued. "Lamont, the bottom line is that a hostile takeover, by the mob is in the making and I need you to get proof on the man I think is behind it. I need you to pick up information that can nip this thing in the bud."

"You mean be a snitch," Lamont said, obviously more disappointed now than he had been before.

"Not a snitch, undercover security," Jake insisted.

"If you have your suspicions, why not just fire the guy?" Lamont asked.

Jake gave him a silent gaze and moaned. "I can't fire some one based on suspicion alone, even if I am the boss. Even though he's been with me for years, I'm sure that he's working with the conspirators. Mysteriously large blocks of stock are being made available and some one is secretly buying them up. No doubt the buyer is getting inside info first hand, which I've narrowed down to one source with access to vital information."

Lamont listens attentively, and in spite of his present disenchantment, he respected Jake, because his comportment revealed his obvious class. His jovial exuberant and easy congeniality charmed strangers and friends. However Jake was also a hard nose business man who was successful in business because he used various methods to close deals.

That's why Lamont doubted Jake's conspiracy story, questioned his honesty, and doubted if the job that Jake offered even existed. He wasn't going to even humor Jake by taking his make believe job. "No Jake I don't think I'm interested," Lamont said with obvious sadness. He was sad because he felt like this classy congenial and astute business man had nothing but bullshit for his Bastard son.

Chapter Three-
Letdown

When Lamont Savage left Jake Cooper's office, his positive energy was thoroughly deflated, because nothing had turned out like he expected, and he could only focus on his disappointment. He had expected too much, taken some things for granted, and been over confident because of his outstanding qualifications, and personal relationship to Jake.

Maybe he shouldn't have expected to receive anything based on the fact that Jake Cooper was his father, but he sure didn't expect to be penalized for it. So far being Jake's competent son wasn't enough. Perhaps his illegitimate birth weighed more than Jake was willing to admit. Life would be different had he grown up in the Cooper household.

Lamont imagined that growing up as a Cooper must have been joyous without worry, work, school or money. Life wasn't just good for the Coopers; it was sweet, delicious, and luxurious. They were like celebrities with permanent financial security and free will to spend as they please. Lamont sighed depressed and a bit jealous because he and his siblings were from different worlds. He wanted to be a part of their world, but mainly he wanted to learn about Jake's world. However, today Jake's words and attitude had thrown up detours to prevent that from happening.

In the end it had all come down to take-it-or-leave-it, business as usual with no options or compromises. Sure he could go along but why waste his time? What could he expect in the future? Forthcoming promotions would remain an illusion. He couldn't help thinking that this was Jake's imaginative way of rejecting him.

He felt defeated, and his legs were heavy as he climbed the stairs of the parking garage. He reached his car and slid behind the wheel trying to shake off his disappointment. He fought back sad memories of isolation that he had faced growing up as an only child. He always hated the idea of being unconnected to another sibling in the universe. That's why he had been so elated and filled with anticipation when he discovered that he had an entire family.

He felt a strong need to connect with them, even though they didn't seem to share those desires. He wondered if they perceived him as an opportunist looking to cash in on the family treasures. That wasn't true, but he understood how they might think such a thing. After all brother or not, he was a stranger.

Even though he was a stranger, everyone except Ruth, the baby girl, had been polite and tolerant. Ruth was resistant and openly hostility from the start and she obviously had a chip on her shoulder. Her presence always made the situation awkward and she never treated Lamont with the same reasonable civility as the other family members. At first Lamont thought that Ruth was a wild card who didn't count, but then it crossed his mind that perhaps the others might feel as Ruth did. Perhaps their kindness was really gratitude, which wasn't what he wanted. He needed to be a part of this family in spite of their dysfunction and selfishness.

They had all refused or made some excuse as to why they couldn't help JJ. Eventually he had been asked, and at first he had refused, but once he saw JJ, he couldn't let his only brother die. It cost him a kidney, but he had gained their reluctant acceptance because he had given something precious in time of crisis. He wanted more than reluctant acceptance; you could get that from an enemy.

Now that no crisis existed, he wondered if his new family felt anything genuine for him now. He sensed that they didn't feel the slightest need to connect to him. Sure Ruth was openly hostile, obnoxious and rude, but at least he knew exactly where he stood with her. Ruth voiced her opinions loud and clear and made it known that she didn't like him. Every one else seemed to make an attempt to be gracious, but he never got a sense of warmth from their attempts. Lamont hoped that they didn't all feel as Ruth did and wanted to remain strangers.

His mind shifted from siblings to thoughts of what he had to do next. What did Jake really want from him? Why had he come up with this bogus position? Lamont realized that he was farther than ever from the job that he sought.

His position as director at the Center, and his handling of such a controversial government agency was evidence of his competence as a responsible administrator. Jake on the other hand seemed to have an agenda that excluded him regardless of his outstanding résumé.

Lamont pulled from the parking lot and drove onto the high-way heading east, away from Richmond. He had taken the day off and Marcia Dawson had covered for him. He trusted Marcia and he had neglected his duties today because he anticipated giving his two weeks' notice today. Now there would be no two weeks' notice because the job he wanted at Cooper Industries wasn't available. His attentions must now turn back to the drudgery of his current dead end job at the Center.

Lamont started to call his fiancée, Jane Curtis but she was busy at the station and besides he wasn't in the mood. He planned to call her later, but after picking up some fast food he went to his apartment and fell asleep still thinking about his horrible interview with Jake. Today had not been a good day for him

The next day Lamont arrived at the office and as expected every-thing was in order thanks to Marcia. She wasn't just his assistant, she was also his sounding board and as they sipped coffee and did mas-sive paperwork, Lamont purged his feelings about his interview. "You know Marsh, I was so sure that I had that position. I thought he was ready to accept me finally," Lamont said without thinking.

"Who Mr. Cooper? Accept you how?" Marcia asked puzzled. She wasn't aware that Jake Cooper was Lamont's father.

"Well he did promise me, but apparently that didn't mean any-thing."

"I don't understand, Lamont, if he wasn't going to offer you a job, why did he call you?"

"Oh he offered me a job, but it was some BS job and I left his office without accepting it. I told him no but he asked me to think about it. I'm not taking such a job." Even as he said this, Lamont remembered how stressed Jake had seemed. What if someone was trying to steal the company and he refused to help? He wouldn't be able to bond with any of the family if the company fell into the hands of the mob.

"Wow," Marcia said eying Lamont, "So you think he just lied to you? Why would he do that, Lamont?"

"I don't know. I like Jake and up until now and I thought the feeling was mutual, but after he fed me that story about a takeover, I guess he doesn't like me, or for that matter respect my intelligence," Lamont said. "How could I be the only person he can trust?"

"Yeah, that puzzles me? Why would he trust you and not his own flesh and blood?"

Lamont realized that he had said too much and he didn't want to reveal any more about his relationship with Jake. "Who knows? I say he's backing out of his promise."

"But what if he's telling you the truth, Lamont? What would happen?" Marcia asked playing devil's advocate. "You know, Lamont, he could be testing you."

Lamont smiled, realizing that Marcia was on the wrong track because she didn't have all the facts. To him the most important thing was being a part of the Cooper inner circle, and feeling that connection through business and blood. Being in the business and on the job was icing on the cake. He had said too much already and he wasn't going to talk about Jake Cooper and the job that got away.

"In any case I'm not going to be leaving here no time soon I guess. I can forget about giving that two weeks notice and start thinking about the headaches I'm going to be facing for so little money. I'm catching hell juggling the money around to keep every program up and running, but the budget gets smaller every year."

"I know, the writing is on the wall," Marcia said crossing her legs and brushing back her brown hair. She tried to keep a professional relationship, but Lamont always got her switches going. His gorgeous dark eyes and sexy baritone made her nipples hard. She imagined his full lips ravishing her stiff nipples. She forced herself to think of business now. "It's getting too political around here and I don't blame you for wanting out, but still I like having you here." She was usually shy about approaching men, but made no secret about her feelings for him. She smiled showing perfect teeth and looked yearningly at him through smoky dark eye makeup.

"Well I guess you're stuck with me," he said with a smile.

"I think I can live with that. Besides, no one can run this place like you do." Marcia cast him a look of admiration and blinks her eyelashes playfully. "But seriously, Lamont you're doing a terrific job here even with the budget cuts you've managed to keep this crew employed and most of these shaky programs running."

"It ain't easy but I do try."

"And you do a hell of a job here. I'll bet you do more work here in a month than some executives at Cooper Industries do in a year."

"Maybe I should have you go talk to Jake for me, since you're making such a case for how great I am."

"Not a chance. I couldn't bear the thought of losing you, I'm sure not going to help you leave."

"Point taken," he said eying the pile of paper work, then turned to her. "Shall we?"

"Might as well." They went through the paperwork together and began the tedious task of separating and analyzing the various requests for the many social programs sponsored by the down town Center. Now that he wouldn't be leaving the Center, Lamont felt even more drudgery about his presence here. The decision had been made but he wasn't sure that he could live with it.

After leaving the Center, Lamont arrived at his apartment and kicked off his shoes, grabbed a beer and picked up the telephone to dial Jane's number and ask her to come over. He got her voice mail saying that she was on some assignment in Washington. He hated her job sometimes. She was always out of town covering some story. Sometimes he wondered if she liked going out of town playing Lois Lane. On the other hand he was against living together and had refused to submit to her wishes to do so. He would be giving up his freedom soon enough.

Suddenly he needed to get out of his apartment and he picked up the phone and called his buddy, Hal then headed out. They met at Eddie's Bar to have a beer and shoot pool. Lamont was back in Eddie's good graces after being banned from the place two years earlier for fighting. Even though the fight took place outside the bar, Eddie had banned him anyway.

Hal, unlike Marcia, knew about Jake Cooper and Lamont's relationship to him. Hal had played a key part in establishing that relationship. Once Lamont met up with Hal he started venting non stop about his interview with Jake.

"Man, I wouldn't worry about it."

"I ain't really worried, Hal, It's just that I can't push Jake from my mind right now. I mean that thing about the mob sounded too dramatic, like something from a bad melodramatic movie," Lamont said as he took a shot and missed. "JJ's my brother," Lamont started, "but his only qualification is that he's Jake's son. I'm his son too, and with more skill and qualifications and I'm still excluded. I don't buy Jake's excuse for hiring JJ, Hal. It doesn't make sense to reward one son for his shortcomings and penalize another son for his skills."

"Think about this though, Mont," Hal said, lining up his shot. "I mean suppose he's being straight with you, Man? What if the mob really is out to get his company? The mob do that kinda shit all the time and Cooper Industries is in the money."

"I ain't saying that it's not possible, but even if it is, I don't believe that I'm the one who can stop them. Jake's just backing out of his promise," Lamont said, pausing and sipping his beer. "Jake just didn't come through for me, Hal."

"Well the choice is yours to make man. You know what's best for you," Hal puffed on the cigarette and put it down to line up his pool shot.

"I thought you quit smoking," Lamont changed the subject abruptly. "That's why your little narrow ass can't pick up any weight. That nicotine is in your genes."

"Well that is my option," Hal lined up the next shot. "Eight ball in the corner," he blurted, bending to take the shot. He made one long stroke and the ball dropped. "You got some options too, Mont."

"Yeah I can take the job that Jake offered and hope for the best. The only thing about that is it might be a waste."

"And it might not be," Hall shrugged his bony shoulders and twisted his mouth into a comical expression. "But like I say that's your choice to make. You can't get fat on what I eat or get drunk on what I drink."

"Yeah, you're right. Frankly it would be a relief to get the hell out of Dodge. That place is always got some constant time consuming drama, and I feel like I'm overdue for a change. I wanted that change to be Cooper Industries, but now I have to consider submitting my resume elsewhere. Being a company snoop just ain't me."

"Wow, you're not gonna consider it then? That's sure a negative attitude."

"No, I'm just going to move on, and that means revising my plan. The world won't end if I go to work some place else."

"But ain't that defeatin' the purpose?" Hal asked with a puzzled expression. "Ain't this supposed to be about you getting close to the family, or have you changed your mind about that?"

"No, but."

"It's probably gonna be hard to bond with your family if you ain't around them," Hal chose his words carefully. "Look, man I know how you feel about bonding with your family, so I'm gonna just say this." He paused and breathed deeply. "I think you ought to just go for it. But like I said what I eat…."

"Yeah, yeah," Lamont interrupted, "what you eat won't make me fat. I get it," Lamont said, and then silently stared at the tall skinny frame of his friend. He hated the fact that he was being lectured by Hal of all people. He was a friend, but he was in no way qualified to give him advice when his own life wasn't in order. Hell he was still living with his mother and two sisters and seldom held down a full time job. "With all due respect Hal my relationship with my family is now of your damn business, so just but out."

Hal's eyes stretched and he froze, and gave Lamont a concise curious stare. "Well excuse the hell out of me but listening to you moan about your old man and your hard life is annoying. I'm just trying to help."

"I didn't ask for your help. I was just venting, man. You need to keep your mouth shut about things you don't understand."

"I'll keep my mouth shut if you'll keep yours shut. And whether you like it or not Jake really don't owe you shit. It's every man for himself in this world, you of all people should already know that," Hal screeched, now visibly upset. He threw the pool cue on the table. "And you know what; you ain't got it so bad. Hell I'd kill to be in your shoes and you're bitchin' and moanin' and thinking about blowing it off." Hal paused briefly then threw up his hands. "I gotta go Mont, see ya," he said headed for the door. "I don't have to take this shit from you," he said, storming out. Within seconds the familiar whirring sound of Hal's old beat up van rattled out of the parking lot.

19

Lamont could only manage to say, "Damn." He realized that he was pissed off because Hal was right. "Damn it," Lamont said as he too stormed out of Eddie's bar, bumping into several patrons on the way out and not bothering to apologize or even look back.

Chapter Four-
Decisions

Lamont hadn't slept after his argument with Hal last night, and now that he realized that Hal was right, he couldn't pretend that he wasn't concerned about the validity of Jake's story. If there was any truth in what Jake said then maybe he should reconsider the job offer. Maybe his expectations were unreasonable, because he didn't know what to expect from his long absent and neglectful father.

Lamont once believed that Jake Cooper didn't owe him anything, nor did he have anything to prove. Now he believed that Jake at least owed him a chance, because he was well qualified and anxious to work at Cooper Industries. He only wanted what he earned and he wasn't looking for favoritism.

He wanted Jake's love as a father and his respect as a strong man and that was a tall order. It was hard to impress a powerful man like Jake Cooper, and being his bastard son made that task more difficult. Maybe Jake wasn't impressed with him, and that's why he hadn't given him the job that he wanted. Jake's words had seemed sincere, but how could Jake think that he would be better working as a snoop than an executive? He had so many questions about Jake's decision.

He recalled parts of his conversation. *"I can bring you in as an apprentice exec just like I did with JJ, but in reality you'll be keeping your eyes open,"* Jake had said. *"Everyone will accept the fact that I simply hired my other son for a token position. It's perfect."* Now Lamont wondered if maybe this really was a token job and Jake saw him as a potential failure. On the other hand it could be a test as Marcia had assumed, but why should he be tested? He had the credentials and he should be judged on them, and not treated like an irresponsible rookie. He wasn't looking for a token job and he refused to accept handouts even from his own father just to ease his guilty conscience.

Lamont wondered how Jake felt about being his father, and if he would ever act like a real father to him. How did real fathers act? Was it the way Jake acted with JJ? Of course it was unrealistic to expect

Jake to be as close or treat him the same as he did JJ. He's been there for JJ all his life and they were close. However, Lamont believed that Jake loved him in some small capacity. Lamont believed that Jake was the kind of man who loved all of his children, in spite of prevailing circumstances.

The Cooper clan was a dysfunctional collection of misfits and brats as Jake had aptly pointed out. Yet, Lamont wanted to be part of the family. The problem was that, in spite of their kindness, the family seems to treat his existence with opposition, confusion, and awkwardness. This always made him feel uneasy, because he didn't know the motives behind their display of kindness and tolerance.

He sometimes wondered if Jake's show of kindness was a guilt reaction to compensate and atone for his past neglect. That was unsettling because if that were the case, he would never bond with Jake the way JJ had. Perhaps he was a foolish dreamer, because no one in this family seemed to be interested in who he really was, nor were they making any effort to find out. So how could they care for him when they knew nothing about him? That's why he assumed that Jake and the rest of the family were simply tolerating him, perhaps even hoping that he would go away.

Jake certainly hadn't sought him out until JJ needed his help, so conceivably he was expecting too much from a family whose life style was as extravagant as the rich and famous. He had only met them for the first time three years ago, at the age of twenty six. He knew then that bonding with this family might be as impossible as balancing the budget and fixing the economy. It's possible to bond with Jake if they were to work together, but with the rest of the family, nothing would change. He would always be a brother by default, who was conceived from loin lust, and never fully accepted.

Lamont hated his obsession to become part of this family. He had always been independent and strong, never craving any one's respect or attention until he met his new family. Family ties were something that he had longed for but had only imagined in the past. Now he liked the idea of family. The thing he liked was that there were traces of himself in every member of his family. They must see it too. In any case, anything was better than being alone.

At first he had only wanted to impress Jake, the head of the family.

It was only later that he felt the need to impress the others and show them that they were all the same. He wanted to prove that they were all cut from the same cloth because of Jake. Presently, he hadn't really impressed any one including Jake. This was a tough crowd to please and they never stopped trying his patience.

Is that what Jake was doing now? Trying his patience? The more Lamont recalled his meeting with Jake the more he wanted to believe Jake's haunting words: *'I trust you Lamont not because you're blood but because you're a good man, and I know that you can help me stop this plot to steal my company.'* Lamont asked himself if trust was the same as love or respect. If Jake loved and respected him he wouldn't have given him some bogus story about a mob takeover. That part about Lamont being the only one who could save him was over the top. After all Lamont was no super hero.

Still Jake's sad serious eyes had seemed so sincere, and his voice had cracked at one point when he talked of how hard he had worked, and how some one wanted to take everything away. Right now Lamont did feel some guilt and wondered if he was being selfish. Yes he was, but didn't he deserve to be?

He turned back to the work on his desk and tried unsuccessfully to drown out Jake's voice. *'Help me save my company, Lamont. Lots of people will lose their jobs and their pensions.'* Jake's words still reverberated inside his head. "Even if the company was in danger, it is not my responsibility," he murmured under his breath, looking over the budget.

In spite of his determination to forget about Jake's offer and remain independent, he weighed the advantages of working at Cooper Industries in any capacity. He wanted to believe that Jake really did need his help. On the other hand if this was a fake job he would feel foolish and duped upon discovery. Would Jake do something like that to him? He couldn't answer that, but what he did from now on depended on how he answered that question. This whole conspiracy thing could be all in Jake's mind, but if it wasn't, then Cooper Industries was in a lot of trouble. Besides that, would it be such a bad thing to work with a company that pays well and has great benefits? He had an important decision to make and he had to do it soon.

Chapter Five- Crisis

Lamont evaluated reports and concentrated on the task at hand along with his able associate, Marcia Dawson. He tried to forget about Cooper Industries, but this rainy wet day seemed extra dreadful, and he felt trapped with the mundane mind numbing routine of this job.

Everything changed abruptly when a series of loud screams and murmurs filled the air, coming from the lobby. Lamont gave Marcia a brief look as they both dropped the report on the desk and dashed towards the source of the commotion. Lamont almost ran into Greg Jones, another associate, who also headed towards the lobby. Now they focused on the tall husky Caucasian man standing in the lobby clutching a large gun and pointing it at his throat.

Lamont and Greg moved slowly towards him. "Oh Man! This is just what we need," Greg said, sighing impatiently. "Wish I had taken off today, like I started to."

Lamont looked intently at the large man's scary eyes, attempting to gauge his action and suddenly recognized the man who had come in for depression counseling. He had given his name and Lamont remembered. "Butch," Lamont said. Butch's wife of ten years ran off with their two boys last month. Until then Butch was a dedicated family man, and he had gone into mild shock upon returning home from work and discovering an empty house.

Right now, Butch seemed on the verge of committing self destruction. "Why here and why now?" Lamont murmured, while studying the big untidily dressed man whose eyes seemed too large for their sockets. Butch wore a twisted scowl on his pale round face, which made him appear deranged.

"Where the hell did this big ass psycho come from?" Greg asked Lamont in a tight hushed whisper, not moving his lips and staying close behind. Lamont and Greg were karate black belts and their goal was to get closer and disarm Butch.

"Greg, is everyone out?" Lamont whispered to Greg from the side of his mouth, still inching closer. Greg looked around to see that every one, including other members of the staff was out the door with the rest of the crowd. Only Lamont, Greg and Marcia remained inside observing Butch standing on the wall wearing a blank expression. With his black hair slick to his scalp, and his dark glazed eyes, he appears trancelike and scary.

The only noise in the room was Butch's heavy breathing and the ceiling fans' humming. Marcia had insisted on staying and now she stood watching Lamont feeling anxious and unsteady. "Lamont be careful," she said a silent prayer for him as tears welled in her eyes.

Lamont moved towards the big nervous man. "Butch, put the gun down, Man. Let's talk."

"Stay where you are, Lamont," Butch said suddenly and moved the weapon higher and grasped it more firmly. Suddenly he pointed it at Lamont.

"Shit, Lamont. We need to wait for the cops, Man," Greg whispered nervously.

Lamont was oblivious to Greg's plea. His heartbeat was hard and he felt the throbbing in his eardrums and had difficulty swallowing. He didn't need this, but he had committed himself and now he had to follow through. "Come on, Butch, this ain't the way."

Butch looked around as if his surroundings were odd. His brow wrinkled intensely and he blinked rapidly with robot-like motion. "No. It ain't," he slurred.

"Okay then, put down the gun, Man, and we'll get you some help."

"Can't nobody help me. Angelina and the boys are gone. I got nothing to live for now." Suddenly he turned the gun to his own head. "What's the use man? Tried to be straight and honest, but Antonio was right. Honesty sucks." Butch rambled on unable to finish his sentences. "I'm a failure. That's why she left me. She'll make the boys hate me. I got no job. I got nothin'." He pointed the gun to his head.

"Wait! Please, Butch, think. Please, man. Why don't you give me the gun?" Lamont stepped closer.

"Stay back, Lamont! I like you, but if you keep comin' I'm gonna' stop you. I'm gonna do this. I wanna die."

"Why, Butch? You're a religious man and you know it's wrong to die like this. All I ask is that you wait one more day. If you can hold on for a day, and you still want to do it then I'll help you."

He pointed the gun at Lamont again and Marcia let out a frightened gasp. "Hey, don't gimme that crap," Butch said glaring angrily. "I know you ain't gonna help me die. You don't do suicide assistance here. You think I'm stupid," he said with increased volume that bounced trembling echoes off the twirling ceiling fans. "Don't try psychology on me cause you ain't talkin' me outta this," he said in an uneven voice, and looked to be in a daze.

Greg spread out a short distance from the disturbed large man who stood only three feet away. Once again, he wished that he had taken off today, but he dismissed the thought of evacuating now. Besides if he left now he would be acting like a punk, and Lamont would play the hero and take all the credit. All he could do was hope that things didn't get gruesome and bloody.

Suddenly Greg's heart was in his throat when he saw Lamont moving rapidly towards Butch. Lamont had seized his chance and now sprang forward when Butch lowered the weapon slightly. He grabbed Butch's left hand and began wrestling for the weapon. Greg reacted as well and closed in a split second later and both men struggled to retrieve the weapon from Butch's clutches. Marcia's high pitched scream filled the air as two shots rang out, and landed harmlessly in the ceiling.

Butch stood six feet four and weighed two hundred sixty pounds, and was incredibly strong. The combination of his size, strength and adrenaline surge rendered him almost superhuman and beyond control. Still, it wasn't enough to dissuade Lamont and Greg from holding on and wrestling the weapon from Butch's hands.

Butch transformed into a pitiful mass of hysterical tears, once he was subdued. "Oh God, what am I doing?" Butch's eyes stretched in wonderment, and his words were followed by body wracking sobs. He had apparently been shocked to reality and the raging bull had become a sobbing timid calf. "Easy, Butch. It's gonna be okay," Lamont said soothing Butch, but he knew that this wasn't over.

Lamont and Greg ushered Butch into his office and Lamont put the gun safely away in his desk drawer. "Man they don't pay me enough money for this shit," Greg said with an angry scowl and rapid shake of his head. "You got this under control, Lamont?" Greg asked, seeming anxious to get back to his office.

"Yeah, man," Lamont said giving him the thumb up sign, "Butch is okay now."

"Okay then you got it," Greg said then went to his own office.

Now Lamont and Butch were alone in his office, and he assured the curious staff that the danger was over. Several of them looked on and listened outside the door anyway. Lamont's small office consisted of paper thin walls, and a noisy ceiling fan. Butch ceased sobbing and regained his bearings. "Lamont, man thanks for saving my life. If I had pulled that trigger," he darted for the trash can in the corner, bent over it and spilled the contents of his stomach.

Shortly, he was apologetic "Sorry, about that, Lamont, I…"

"Don't worry, Butch," Lamont said, while moving the can to the far side of the office and covered it with some old newspapers. Marcia appeared seeming from no where, wearing a nervous smile. "You okay," she said with concern.

"Yeah, I'm just gonna be sore from all that wrestling," Lamont said.

"I'll take care of this," Marcia said as she removed the messy can.

"Thank you, Marsh," He said.

She just smiled and made a gesture as if to say 'don't mention it.'

"I'm gonna get my life back. I swear on my mother," Butch said, suddenly commanding Lamont's attentions once more.

Lamont noticed Butch's strange expression and wondered if he needed more help than the Center could give him. "I think you mean that, Butch," Lamont said nodding his approval, but frankly he didn't know this man's capabilities or limitations. He was just being professional.

"I do. Nobody is gonna walk on me again, Lamont, I swear."

Lamont noticed two uniformed officers coming his way. "Oh boy," he murmured. "Damn," he wanted to keep this out of the news, but that was impossible since gunshots were fired.

He turned to Butch. "Butch, listen to me. The cops are heading this way so just go along with me and maybe you won't be arrested, but if you are arrested I can make arrangements to get you bail."

"What?" Butch turned his head to see the two officers inquiring at

Marcia's desk and looking towards the large inter office glass window next to the door. "They're coming for me? You called the cops on me?" He seemed hurt and not angry.

"No, Butch I didn't, but they had to be notified."

"Okay, Lamont," the big man said seeming reluctant and timid, but fully understanding what was happening.

The older of the two officers entered after a brief knock. "Lamont Savage, you in charge here?"

"Yes, officer," Lamont said moving to close the blinds on the huge window. He turned and focused on the officer's name tag. "Officer Butler, you're here about that little disturbance we had earlier."

"That's right. I understand somebody discharged a firearm inside this place. That's a violation of a city ordinance 339-116A."

"Yeah, I'm aware of that. Lucky for us no one was hurt and he came to his senses."

The older officer suspiciously eyed Butch, who was sitting quietly and attentive. Now he pointed towards Butch and moved to within six inches of where Butch sat. "Isn't this the guy? He fits the description we got. Tall husky Caucasian male with slick black hair, dressed in dirty jeans, old black sneakers and a ratty Redskins' jersey," said the officer whose eyes were on Butch.

Lamont' wanted to help Butch but he wasn't going to lie and be arrested for obstruction of justice. They'd probably grill him for being a smart ass. He recalls suffering such an ordeal in the past at the hands of Jesse Thompson, the racist cop who arrested him for Mack Courtney's murder.

The point was moot because, Butch stepped up and admitted being the suspect. "Lamont I appreciate what you did for me. You and Greg saved my life. That's more than enough to ask. I don't want you to get in any trouble on my account. I understand that you had to call the cops because of so many witnesses. I accept the consequences of my actions," he paused then added, "Thanks man, you're a real friend."

"You're sure you'll be okay?" Lamont asked still concerned.

"Yeah. Don't worry; I'll be okay thanks to you. I don't take that lightly." He continued wearing a strange expression. "I know what I have to do," Butch said over and over, while staring blankly into some middle distance, pondering regretfully. "I just have to."

The officer glared at Lamont as if he were about to say something, but he didn't pursue it any further. "Okay, Savage, you come down to the station and fill out a report sometime within the next couple of days."

"No problem, Officer."

Officer Butler turned to his partner and nodded. "Cuff him Doyle," he grunted then turned to Lamont. "Where's the weapon?"

Lamont opened the desk and handed him the gun. "Do you have to handcuff him?" Lamont asked.

"Don't interfere, Savage," he said irritated, holding his index finger three inches from Lamont's face. "Say anything else, I mean anything at all and I'm taking you down with him for obstruction of justice."

"Please officer, he was trying to help me. He didn't do nothing," Butch pleaded.

Butler looked at Butch than back to Lamont, and then nodded to his partner again. "Move 'em out, Doyle. Let's get outta this shit hole." The officers look straight ahead and never bothered to look back as they ushered Butch out the door past the curious onlookers.

Lamont watched the officers accompany Butch out the door, and the only thought that crossed his mind now was how this incident would reflect on him and the Center when it eventually leaked. The Downtown Center was constantly under a spotlight and when this made the Six-O-Clock news all the politicians would take notice.

The incident would give politicians and adversaries of the Center more reasons to tear it down: as if they needed more. The politicians had their eyes on this site for waterfront condos and riverboat gambling, so of course they were looking for any justification to promote their greedy ambitions. They have painted the Center as a haven for the scum of the earth and claim that it does nothing to help those who seek it. This incident might just be the last nail in the coffin that will be used to bury the Center.

In his first days here at the Center, Lamont had been starry eyed and ambitious about things he could do, but the cold reality dawned on him with all the dead ends that materialized because of budget cuts and restrictions. Slowly, he lost interest in improvements and started thinking more and more about working for Cooper Industries. Today he had lost another measure of interest and he was sure that his time at the Center was limited no matter what happened with Jake's job offer.

Chapter Six-
Second Thoughts

Lamont was giving more thought to Jake's offer, even though it wasn't exactly the job he wanted. He had to consider taking baby steps for now, because his options were lousy and any job was an improvement over this one. The one good thing about taking the job is that he could get close to Jake. Jake wasn't blind and Lamont was no fool, so Jake would recognize Lamont's competence, talent and ability to lead.

Under Lamont's leadership the Center had maintained organizational effectiveness, even though his outstanding work never earned him any praise. Surely Jake knew that he had skills, and this puzzled Lamont. If Jake knew that he had skills, why was he so reluctant to allow Lamont the opportunity to use his skills?

The only possible logic was that Jake really is sincere about his beliefs in a conspiracy and his trust in Lamont. Lamont wanted to believe it because he knew that trust was very precious to Jake. It would make no sense for him to lie about trust. He had no recourse but to give Jake the benefit of the doubt until he found out something different. Jake had too much to think about without making up elaborate lies to tell him. The bottom line was that there would be no jobs for any one if Jake's suspicions were right. Even Lamont couldn't deny that Jake's mind was sound, so he could rule out delusion and paranoia.

Looking back now he felt a little ashamed about the way he acted. He had proved himself to be just as much a brat as the others. Jake's words hadn't been the words that he wanted to hear, so he decided that there was a conspiracy against him, and had come just short of a temper tantrum. Was he going to start acting more like a brat now that he had a rich father and a possible inheritance?

He had changed since discovering his relationship to Jake Cooper. Lately, he had developed the same attitude and expectations as his siblings, in spite of being denied the contents of the family's silver spoon. As much as he claimed that money would never change him, he realized now that people with access to wealth instinctively dared to dream of more elaborate goals.

He always thought that access to lots of money wouldn't change him, but it had. Lately he felt special knowing that his future is secure. However, he hasn't turned into a rich brat thus far, nor has he gone through any drastic changes. Strangely he was trying not to be like his siblings and yet, he didn't blame them for their dependency and belief that their life style was something that they deserved.

They only cared about what they wanted and how much it cost. They never worried about the cost because there was always enough money to cover it. They were the poster children for spoiled brats and yet, they weren't responsible for the circumstances of their birth any more than he was for his own.

Unlike his siblings however, Lamont was focused and well adjusted enough to handle the idea of inheriting riches. However, he had as much right as the others, since none of them had earned it. If entitlement is a birthright, than he, as first born, should be the main heir. His goal wasn't to be the main heir, or to take more than he deserved. He didn't need it all because he had never been much of a spendthrift. He didn't understand how some people wasted so much money. Perhaps it was because they had so much access to excess without earning it.

Unlike his siblings, Lamont knew what it was to work and earn money by being competent and worthy. He wanted to be valuable in his father's company, and he wanted Jake to give him a chance to prove himself worthy. That was the difference between himself and his siblings. He knew how to earn money and was no stranger to the work place. His siblings could never measure up to him in the workplace even if they wanted.

He had to admit to himself that he did expect his father to show favoritism and provide him with what he wanted. He wasn't being a hypocrite; it was just a perk that he looked for because he was Jake's son. Asking for a chance to earn is a hell of a lot better than standing around asking for some one's earnings. Besides, hiring him would be justified because he would do a great job.

He sighed and looked around. Anything would be better than this place. Now he suddenly focused on a known troublemaker about to cut the line. Lamont recognized the husky black youth. It was Carl T, a twenty year old, wearing long dreads and a tight old tee shirt, with an image of a black fist punching the air.

Carl T was a loud mouth wanna-be gangster, who bounced up the line listening to his I-pod. Lamont had thrown Carl out twice this month, and he was prepared to do it again. He stood at the back door focusing not only on Carl, but on the collective diverse misery contained among these hapless souls. He fought back his rising pompousness and his anxiety to leave and never see these miserable sad creatures again.

Lamont wasn't intentionally looking down his nose, or finding comfort in his new link to money. His money problems weren't over and he wasn't suddenly immune to financial distress. Things can and do change and people sometimes have a reversal of fortunes, almost overnight. He was painfully aware that bad things can happen to anyone, because bad things had happened to him.

He had been luckier than many of these people, because he had been rescued by money power. These poor souls were victims of continued unfortunate circumstances beyond their control. Sometimes those circumstances work favorably, and other times they didn't. Any of them could have been in Jake Cooper's shoes.

He watches Carl T march up past the long line filled with short tempered people. That was definitely a NO-NO, especially when people discover that they've been waiting in the wrong line, and have to go to the back of a different one. "Hey man, you can't just cut the line," a skinny young White male about twenty five addressed Carl T.

"Oh keep your shirt on, Whitey. I gotta ask this lady a question. So just calm your pale ass down," he spoke, giving the White male a fleeting angry glance then purposely brushed hard up against him as he moved past.

"That's no excuse. You still suppose to wait in line like everybody else," the White youth offered timidly, batting his eyes nervously.

Before Lamont could intervene, Carl T got his information and left. Lamont knew that something was always about to boil over in this place. Conditions were about to get even worse, because there was no more money forthcoming, and all the remaining programs were about to be cut. Now he felt overwhelmed, because he was required to put forth so much effort for such meager rewards. Even he had to admit, that some of the people here didn't deserve help. Many of them had refused jobs and would rather take hand outs.

Lamont didn't understand how anybody could take a hand out. Maybe it was because he had always been willing to work and had spent most of his life earning money. He was a perfectionist about work, which sometimes frustrated and annoyed people who worked with him. Had he not been a perfectionist, he would never have done such an outstanding job at the rundown, marked-for-death Outreach Community Center. Still he had to give some credit to Marcia who had always been a loyal associate. Marcia constantly volunteered to help out and often performed duties not required of her.

Their main interest in common was the Center, but there was a subtle fire of passion that also burned between them. Lamont fought it because he was engaged, but mainly because he thought that work place relationships caused too much friction. Even if he hadn't been dating Jane, it would have been awkward to date a co-worker.

She would obviously feel pressured because of it. He could be accused of sexual harassment, a breach of trust, and misusing his authority as a supervisor. That hadn't stopped him from noticing how much prettier and sharper she seemed every day. She was a gorgeous lady with a body and a personality to match. That was rare and it was what sane men dreamed about, but she was off limits to him. His goal up to now was to keep things professional between them.

However, there was one night when he almost yielded to his temptation, and in one unguarded moment they shared a very long passionate kiss that almost turned into a sexual encounter. He didn't have a condom at the time, and had backed off and apologized. It never happened again after that, but he was always tempted, especially on those nights when he and Marcia worked late, and she treated him to those voluntarily massages. Marcia had taken a course in massage and she knew all the right spots. That night, the touch of those fingers, the smell of her perfume, and the image of her filled him with wild fantasies that took massive will power to resist.

He shuddered to think how awkward it would have been to work together with his lover all day. Lamont forced himself to think of Jane and their upcoming marriage. He felt like he was cheating on her when he slipped into such pleasant memories of Marcia. His mind was still on her in spite of his efforts to conjure up images of Jane. Marcia was sweet and sexy, and those big eyes were always watching him with anticipation. She was sexy, but they had to remain friends.

In spite of his convictions, Lamont unconsciously compared Jane to Marcia. Marcia was an easygoing lady who was fun to be with and Jane was sophisticated and classy. Marcia and Jane both had great bodies and phenomenal curves, but there the similarity ended. Marcia had a hysterical infectious laugh that made grumpy men smile. Jane was the serious type and laughed with guarded subtlety. Any time but now, and with any one else but him, Marcia would be competition for any woman. She was fun and sweet but she worried too much. Jane was sexy, hot and knowledgeable, which was what he needed. She was the type of woman who presented a solid social image and he considered her the perfect role model. She's a gorgeous, talented local television celebrity with a great body and a bright future. Lamont admitted that Jane's personality was sometimes stiff and haughty, but even with her flaws she wasn't a witch. She was a sophisticated lady and Lamont was sure that she would impress the Coopers.

Lamont realized that he was daydreaming about the two women and turned back to his desk to try and get the paperwork done. Some of it was paper work that Greg had failed to finish due to constant absence. Greg was knowledgeable and smart, but he was just marking time on this job and didn't try to accomplish anything. It was clear that Greg was job hunting on those days when he took off. Lamont couldn't blame him for job hunting, just for doing it on company time.

Greg had a tremendous ego and considered himself irresistible because he was tall and very handsome, with short cut hair and a diamond ear ring in his ear. He had bachelor's degree in black studies but his specialty was harassing the ladies in the office. The staff welcomed his frequent absence because it seemed like more work got done when he wasn't around.

In spite of his attitude and poor work ethic, Lamont had to work with him because nobody else wanted the headache of working at the Center. Lamont avoided altercation with Greg, but on a few occasions he had confronted Greg about fraternizing with female coworkers as well as females seeking services. Greg would just joke about it and continue to do the same thing. He shrugged Lamont's reprimand off and pretended that he didn't know what he was talking about. He would then mumble under his breath that Lamont wanted all the "pussy" for himself. He was convinced that Lamont and Marcia were having sex and he considered Lamont a hypocrite.

Their philosophies were miles apart, and the only thing they had in common was their Karate skills. Lamont suspected that Greg resented him, and he hadn't missed the subtle eye rolling and strange glances Greg shot him on occasion. Lamont thought it was because Greg saw him as an establishment figure and therefore the natural enemy. Greg would sometimes jokingly refer to Lamont as "bossman" or "massah, Lamont." There seemed to always be tension between the two men and whether he wanted to or not, Lamont sensed that sooner or later he would have a violent confrontation with Greg Jones.

Chapter Seven-
The Offer

Marcia Dawson knocked on the door and entered Lamont's small office. "Hi, handsome. That was some excitement yesterday, huh?"

"Yeah, it was."

"Need some help with those reports?" She came up to his desk and looked over his shoulder.

"Naw, I'm good," Lamont said, hoping to sound nonchalant but he was stirred by her nostril invading perfume. He tried to ignore her sexy body, clad in the short black skirt, exposing her sculpture perfect legs. He instinctively cast furtive glances in her direction when he thought she wasn't looking.

Marcia sensed his reluctance to talk about yesterday's event, and was about to change the subject when the telephone rang. "I'll get that for you," she said reaching for the phone and moving to the front of his desk. Her low cut pink blouse exposed cleavage that threatened to break free from the tiny bit of material. "Just a moment," she said covering the receiver. "It's Bob Pierce from the regional office," she said with a wide seductive smile. "He might have some good news this time."

"I wouldn't bet on it. I wouldn't be surprised if this is the call to warn us that the demolition crew is coming to tear this place down."

"You can't think that way Lamont. You gotta think positive." She held up her hands with crossed fingers. "Here's hoping for the best." She checked to see if he was still noticing how great her outfit looked on her curves. She was being wicked right now, and was only here to watch his reaction to her figure in this outfit. She still nursed the hope that Lamont would throw her on his desk and screw her brains out. She wasn't a bad girl, she just wanted what she wanted and she wasn't totally innocent in the sack.

She thought that she was a good catch as well. She was an intelligent, perky well toned, tight body twenty seven year old. She constantly received numerous compliments from everyone except Lamont.

She suspected that he felt like he had to be loyal to that diva bitch, Jane Curtis. Still, there was chemistry between them, whether he admitted it or not.

She almost smiled as she remembered the night he had gotten excited and almost made love to her. If she could wear him down like that just once more, she could take his mind off of Jane completely. She knew that he noticed her figure and she had seen his occasional covert glances towards her. Jane wasn't the girl for him any way. She was a phony, cold, stuck up, career minded, serious no fun bitch from what she observed. Jane was probably much too selfish to adequately fulfill Lamont's sexual needs. He needed some one like her to do that for him. There weren't too many things that she wouldn't do for Lamont Savage, and she sensed that Jane Curtis had no such ambitions. Still, Lamont apparently couldn't see through Jane's performance. Marcia had predicted that that relationship wouldn't last six months, but it lasted a year and they were now engaged. Regretfully, she could do nothing about that because he thinks that she's what he wants.

They weren't married yet, and even though she couldn't purposely try to break them up, she could purposely wish for it. That was evil. However, if that did happen and Lamont came to his sense and pursued her, she would be there for him. Between the late hours and the volunteering, she already spends more time with him than Jane does. She liked being there for him, making coffee, ordering sandwiches, finding files, and boldly giving him back rubs.

She relished the feel of his muscular body during those back rubs. Her whole body seemed to have multiple orgasms as she engages in her own husband-wife sexual fantasies. Her sister, Eunice and so many women might see her as a dreamer and a doormat. She didn't think like Eunice who claimed to know so much about men, and yet always picked the wrong one. As far as Marcia was concerned, her sister's opinions were null and void as long as she continued to deal with trash. Eunice had never known a man like Lamont, who had ambitions, goals and respect for women. Sometimes Marcia wished that Lamont would lose some of that respect and ravish her.

Maybe he preferred girls like Jane and if he did dump her, he would find someone just like her. Good men were attracted to bad girls unfortunately for her. She had always tried to be a good girl, but apparently the world was twisted because good girls got penalized, and bad girls got the good guys. Maybe Lamont thought that Jane was more exciting because she looked like a slut. Some men were attracted to slutty women like Jane and Eunice. Lamont probably didn't think that she was exciting, but if she ever got the chance she would show him just how exciting she could be.

Lamont listened to Bob Pierce, expecting to hear bad news, unaware of Marcia's intense gaze as he motioned for her to leave. Marcia was reluctant to leave and felt hurt that Lamont was treating her like the help. She had a right to share the news with him instantly. She went straight to her own phone, and listened in. She had earned the right to know what was going on the instant that Lamont did.

"Look, I'm gonna get right to the point," Bob Pierce's voice crackled on the other end. "I looked over your reports, and I like your ideas," he hesitated.

"But," Lamont said anticipating Bob's next words.

"But it's not feasible at this time," Bob said. "Lamont, you gotta know that the budget is tight and there's barely enough money for basic things. Funding for Home Land Security and this economic crunch has put us in a bind. You understand."

"What's to understand? We both know the deal. It's politics as usual."

"That's not necessarily so," Bob Pierce said with obvious irritation.

Lamont didn't care about stepping on his feelings. "Look, Mr. Pierce I know that the tycoons have their eyes on this place, and my efforts are kinda like pissin' in the wind. We both know that money is available, but this Center will never see a dime of it. It's all politics, and I won't pretend that I don't know that. The real goal is to shut down this place and get moving on that building project so those millionaires can stuff their pockets.

"Sorry you feel that way Lamont. You've done such a great job with that place that you earned a promotion," Bob said in an upbeat voice that blasted into the receiver.

"What did you say about a promotion?" Lamont asked, puzzled. He was expecting to hear about plans to evacuate the place, not about a promotion. Bob Pierce's next words cleared it all up.

"Yeah, there's an opening in DC tailor made for you."

Marcia's heart beat raced and she almost dropped the extension. No, she thought Lamont couldn't leave her now.

"A promotion? Move to Washington?" Lamont didn't pretend to be interested, and he thought it was ironic that he actually dreaded being promoted. That was the second impossible thing that has happened recently. First not jumping at the opportunity to be with Cooper, and now not jumping for joy about the possibility of making more money

"Yeah, we want you to head the DC branch of the Center. We like your insight and imagination, and the speed at which you've restore order to that place. We're convinced that you're the man for the job."

The flattery didn't sell Lamont, because he wasn't ready to make the sacrifices. He had no intention of packing up and moving away to play nurse maid to a larger population of the same unfortunate misfits. It was bad enough seeing the neglect and chaos here, he didn't need to see it spread tenfold in Washington. In the long run he would beat his brains out and no one would even twitch. He realized that a job well done was sometimes dull and unnoticed.

Still, Bob Pierce's offer put him under pressure to tell him something sooner rather than later. If he didn't go to Washington he would have to set his pride aside and accept Jake's offer because he had no other prospects. He could hope that Jake's offer was for real. It would be great if Jake wasn't lying to him.

Now he was forced to lean towards taking Jake's offer because he wasn't about to relocate. He was already well briefed on how Cooper Industries operated, and he was aware of their priorities and all of their major business decisions. He had studied Jake's life story after their revealing first meeting, when they faced the reality of their common flesh. Jake had started his company from scratch and made it into a powerful corporate entity.

Lamont had always been good at business, perhaps a trait that he had inherited from Jake. He would never be as good as Jake, because he couldn't start from scratch the way Jake had. He didn't mind the hard work or the risks, because he thrived on those things. However, his job as supervisor at the Center and the constant pitfalls, headaches and struggles for adequate financing and competent help, occupied his every conscious moment. Soon procrastination about personal goals became habitual.

He felt that his business skills would serve him better with his father's company, and knew that his future there would be secured. He wasn't different from any one else, he wanted to feel secure. Maybe he wanted it even more. At first he had felt as if his father was rejecting him with his job offer, but what right did he have to expect anything? Now he realizes that that offer might be all he has left. It was either go with Jake's offer or be left to contend with the turmoil of a thankless dead end job in a thankless chaotic city.

Lamont's thoughts were interrupted by the sound of Bob Pierce's voice "Think about it, Lamont I need your answer soon, like next week. I don't mean to rush you, but DC needs you. The good news is you will be given a much larger budget and a salary increase of five grand. I'll meet with you in a couple of days and we can discuss it then."

Lamont already knew that the increase in budget wouldn't be enough to do any of the things that needed to be done. He also suspected that whipping that place into shape would be a nightmare. Bob didn't have to say anything about the condition of the place, because Lamont already knew how public facilities operated in the big cities. He had little desire to trade one set of problems for a larger set. "I don't know Mr. Pierce; I'd have sacrifice quite a bit to take this job."

"We all make sacrifices Lamont. You're not thinking about turning it down are you?"

"I might be. Yes. But I'll sleep on it"

"Lamont don't talk nonsense. Why would you want to turn down a promotion?" Bob Pierce's voice reflected disappointment, while Marcia sat in her office saying a silent thank you with her fingers crossed.

"Well there are a number of reasons. Like moving, for one thing. Pulling up roots and going to a strange place with strange people."

"It's all a part of advancing your career. And we will pay for all your moving expense. This could lead to something even bigger for you. I thought you would be pleased, Lamont. The job offers a substantial increase in opportunities and pay. You could go further up the ladder."

"You know Mr. Pierce, five grand is nothing, and it would be sucked up by the more expensive cost of Washington. And I also know that a promise of a raise is not a guarantee."

"Think about this Lamont," Bob paused then added, "I pulled

43

some strings for you boy. You need to address this," Bob said, sounding more irritated.

"I said I'd sleep on it, Bob," Lamont said increasing the level of his voice, obviously irritated at Bob Pierce.

"Do that and I'll call you."

Lamont still held the phone realizing that Bob had hung up. He was definitely not moving to Washington. He had a fiancée', and he wouldn't think about asking her to consider moving. Jane was established here in her job as a promising television news journalist. She now had a shot at news anchor position and no way was he about to ask her to give up her dream. That was settled and now that he wasn't going to Washington, he had only one option left to consider. He decided to leave for the day and do just that.

Shortly, Marcia felt panic as she watched Lamont leave the center, and the idea of him leaving permanently had her stomach turning flips. To make things worse, she was stuck here for the remainder of the day with Greg, the lecher.

Even though Lamont had talked to Greg, he was still constantly harassing Marcia and Rosa, and flirting with some of the other women applying for programs. No one said anything to Lamont, because no one wanted to see a confrontation between the two. Marcia saw Greg as untrustworthy and insensitive to women, but she could handle herself. Greg wasn't the first jerk that she had ever dealt with. She was always elated when he called in sick, which was often.

At times, she did get fed up with his constant sexist remarks and references to her breasts, legs and rear end. Still, she didn't see the need to go running to Lamont like some cowardly little wimp. Most of the time, she had managed to shrug Greg off by ignoring him.

Marcia felt partially responsible for Greg's lewd behavior because she liked to dress provocatively, to impress and tempt Lamont. Ironically, it was Greg who was tempted and impressed. He was constantly watching her with his sneaky eyes, stealing glances, grabbing his crotch and making lewd gestures with his tongue "That's what happens when you roll the dice," she sighed to herself. "Sometimes you just get crap. Why the hell didn't they offer his sorry ass a job in Washington?"

Chapter Eight- Bon Voyage

Lamont took a ride on the highway to clear his head and think as always. He knew for certain that he could count on Jane's support of any decision he made to leave the Center. Jane often spoke harshly about the Center and its people, and openly told him that he was wasting his time and talent on such a dreadful place. Jane hated everything about the Center, the location, his coworkers, the people seeking help, and Lamont's hours. At times this caused some friction between them.

She wanted him out of there so bad that she was sometimes overzealous about taking action. She once set up an interview between Lamont and her father, without telling Lamont until the last minute. Lamont rejected that interview and an impending argument resulted. She claimed to support his decisions, but she continued to try and persuade him to work with her father. He had accused her of being pushy, and she had said he needed to show more ambition. That bothered him because he had always strived and worked hard. Jane seemed to want to choose his goals, but he refuses to fall in line with what she wanted for him.

Right now Jake was it for him since he wasn't going to Washington. He definitely wasn't about to work with Dan Curtis, even if Jake's job wasn't what he wanted. Dan Curtis was a condescending, loud, arrogant blow-hard, who loved to hog the spotlight and put people down with sly wicked subtlety. His bold beady eyes seemed as if they could pierce human skin, and often scanned people with merciless scrutiny. Dan bragged too much and wore more bling than rap stars. Lamont was reluctant to tell Jane that he felt uncomfortable around his future father-in-law.

Once he left the Center, he wasn't about to put himself in another negative situation. He hoped Jane wouldn't push it because there was no way he would deal with Curtis' drama. He wasn't a great pretender, but he could put up with Dan and show respect on a personal level because he was engaged to his daughter. However there was no way he could exist in the same work place with this man.

Dan, like most fathers, was critical of his daughter's choice of a mate. He was more of a doting father than most, and Lamont constantly felt the scrutinizing lenses of Dan's microscope. He never doubted that Daniel Curtis resented his relationship with Jane. Daniel especially liked irritating him.

In previous meetings, he always managed to steer the conversation towards Jane's past boyfriends, praising them and boasting about their accomplishments. It was obvious that the snobbish and flashy Daniel Curtis looked down his nose at Lamont, and his subtle back-door insults were endless. What would he say if he knew that Lamont was heir to a fortune? In Daniel Curtis Lamont saw just another fool with no class but who was lucky enough to be successful in spite of it.

Daniel was so different from Jake because even with his money, Jake wasn't flashy or crass. Jake would never wear so much jewelry and flash it that way, it was obscene. Lamont remembered something his Uncle Johnny had once said about Jake: *"Jake ain't special because he's rich, he's rich because his special."* Lamont hadn't seen it then but he saw it now. His father was indeed a special man and he was a class act all the way. That's why it was important for Lamont to make an impression on Jake that was so outstanding that Jake would never regret accepting him. That's what he really wanted more than anything else, including Jane.

He thought of Jane right now. He wanted to contact her, but her cell phone wasn't ringing now and he suspected that she probably forgot to charge it again. One reason he had left the Center early was to spend time with her. He hadn't been sure about getting married in the beginning. Actually, Jane had talked him into it, but she agreed not to press him for a wedding date.

Lamont cared for Jane and she excited him. He hoped that was a strong foundation for marriage, because he still had doubts. He didn't doubt Jane, he just didn't know if marriage was right for him. Suppose he was no good at being a husband. What would he do then? On the other hand, if he and Jane really cared about each other, didn't they owe it to themselves to try? Perhaps he had his doubts because he had always seen marriage as something that would happen years from now, and after he had built a solid career. Now all that had changed because Lamont didn't have a career, and he might not have a job. In spite of that, Jane Curtis was his future wife.

Before he met Jane Lamont had dated briefly, but never got too serious with any one girl. Jane's good looks and movie star persona dazzled him, and altered his future plans. She had that sweet way of whining in his ear when they made love, and she'd top that off with a voice that sounded like the actress, Vivica Fox.

He wanted to resist and tell her to put their engagement on hold, but she had worn him down with her sweet nagging and sympathetic pleading, followed by hot wild love making. She was his weakness and she knew it as much as he regretted it. As sweet and wonderful as she was, she was always so perfect about her treatment of him. The bedroom was her domain, there could be no doubt. Admittedly he wasn't that wise when it came to women like Jane. Her caring attitude towards him had been the thing that sent him a step past his burning lust. No woman has ever treated him this good. The girls he had dated after his brief encounter with Felicia Courtney had all been causal things that he never took serious. He hadn't lived the life of a playboy, but he dated frequently before meeting Jane. He never dated two girls at the same time, and had become sympathetic towards women after the way he had dogged Felicia Courtney. That wasn't his finest moment. He had used her and been so diabolical about it. He was sorry about that and he wished that he could make it up to her.

It was different with Jane. Sure they argued, but it was too petty to even press the issue. Frankly he liked a little argument between them because that was the only time he felt as if she was real. Ironically, it took a touch of anger to bring out the true Jane Curtis. Strangely, he liked the slightly angry Jane Curtis much better than the sweet perfect caricature. She seemed more down to earth when she showed anger.

There were times when he got a strange sense that she was an actress on stage. She was loaded with etiquette and opinions, spoke perfect English, and bragged about her coworkers proclaiming that she speaks like a 'white girl'. He didn't mean to be so critical and paranoid, but sometimes it seemed like their relationship was a play in which she was the lead actress, and he was a guy from her audience. He didn't even know himself anymore, because the fantasy of this perfect relationship was so dazzling that he wasn't seeking a way out. Who would want out of this, he thought.

She was the perfect sex partner who knew tricks that made it impossible to deny her what she wanted. She knew what a man liked and gave it to him before he asked, and sometimes before he even knew he wanted it. Sex with Jane was a thrilling adventurous ride that was always different and exciting, with novelties along the way. He was addicted to her fiery nature and deep passion. She had so many weapons and once you were in her fold, she knew what you wanted before you could make up your mind. He had thunderous orgasms that made him tremble and speak in tongues it seemed. He liked that with her.

As a consequence he agreed to get married even though he wanted to wait. As a compromise they became engaged which wasn't marriage and in the meantime, he'd still preserved their relationship. Even though he wasn't sure about getting married, he was sure that he didn't want to lose her, so he abandoned his plan and got in step with her. He added new definitions to the words *pussy whipped,* and he hated himself for becoming one of those guys whose penis became the center for determining his actions. He used to look down his nose at guys like that, but now he was in the club.

On the other hand Jane was so sweet, and frankly she had taught him a few tricks with her exotic love making. If he had to get a few wimp points because he wanted to hold on to her, then so be it. He often blocked out the times that she's moody and cold, and smiled when remembering her sweet nature at other times. Sweet trumps grumpy, and he often overlooked her dark side and pictured her body in sexy lingerie, while recalling her soft sexy voice.

She brought him so much bliss that sometimes he didn't think that he was a worthy mate. He always felt that something would go wrong and he would lose her. Even though they never discussed it, maybe she didn't think he was high profile enough for an up and coming news journalist such as herself. That was dumb, he thought. If that were the case why would she want to marry him? Besides, he reminded himself that he was not just any guy; he was heir to part of the Cooper fortune, at least he still had that.

Now, Lamont arrived at his apartment door wondering where Jane could be. He had called the television station after trying her cell phone, but he failed to reach her. He felt tired and anxious, so he went home, took a shower, and tried to relax. He would try to get in touch with her later.

As Lamont opened the door, he was aware that some one was there. However he wasn't alarmed because Jane had her own key. He entered, the apartment now conscious of the soft jazz coming from the speakers, and the aroma of spaghetti sauce drifting from the kitchen. No doubt Jane was here, because there were also traces of Jane's familiar perfume in the air. He suddenly felt uplifted knowing that Jane was here preparing dinner.

Suddenly he was anxious to embrace her. "Jane!" he called.

"Hi, hon," she appeared in the doorway wearing a small apron tied around her tiny waist, giving Lamont sexual urges. The outfit gave her a new air of sexuality that didn't escape Lamont's grasp. The dress hugged her curves and the tightly tied apron bow strings gave her hips a sexual air. The four inch black peep toe pumps and black fish net stockings accented her gorgeous legs. "I must have done something right today because I came home to a super model," he said wearing a wide smile.

He reached out and pulled her even closer and kissed her hard. He instantly found and fondled her tongue, stabbing, thrusting and circling it and reveling in the oral glee. He was hard and he grabbed her wrists and pulled her arms up and pinned them to the wall where they stood. He moved closer making sure she felt his unmistaken hard penis grind ever so slow against her. "Suh AAah. I missed you."

"Me too," she moaned pushing up against him and placing her crotch where she could feel his hot and ready manhood. She had to laugh. "Damn what a nice surprise," she teased as she stepped back and purposely eyed his crotch. "I like it."

He embraced her, squeezing her tight, holding her for what seemed a long time. "Oh, Lamont. You're all wound up," she said smiling with a naughty glare.

"Want some of this," she teased and humped against him.

"Damn right," Lamont said breathlessly.

She pushed him away playfully. "You can get some of that later. Tell me about your day.

He was stunned. "Are you kidding me," he stood there looking at her in disbelief. She never refused to have sex with him before.

"No I'm not. You got a serious look in your eyes. Did something happen today?" She sounded concerned, as she stepped to the couch and sat.

"No not really. Same ole same ole," he said moving to the couch, and sitting beside her.

"Lamont, don't keep anything from me. I'm going to be your blushing bride in a few short months, so you have to tell me everything. Those are the rules," she said batting her lashes.

"There's nothing to tell. I was a little stressed earlier, but I'm much better now. It means a lot to me that you're here," he said pulling her close.

"Baby, I'll always be here for you," she said dismissively. "But you still haven't told me what happened?" Her eyes stretched. "Lamont did another lunatic go berserk down there? Those people in that place scare me, Lamont. I don't want you to get hurt baby," she said stroking his jaw softly.

Lamont was ready to drop this conversation. "Oh baby that doesn't happen daily. This was one isolated incident. The guy wasn't a lunatic he was depressed. He'll get treatment and he'll be fine. You'd be surprised at what depression does to people.

"Then what's the matter baby? You still sweatin' about the job at Cooper's"

"No it's not that." He almost mentions the offer of a promotion, but decides to stay with his plan to remain silent for now. "Just your typical mad Friday." He turned and kissed her on the lips again, and cupped her breasts. His tongue explored inside her hot mouth and he reeled from the euphoric delight of her precious warmth against him. "I don't want to talk about work anymore. You're here and I'm here," he said while struggling to get the short dress up over her head.

Suddenly Jane pulled back. "Down boy, Desert comes after the main course," she said playfully, pulling her dress down and gently pushing him to arms length. "But remember where you left off and we'll continue this later," she said while easing away, walking slowly and seductively towards the kitchen.

He had to get his mind on something else. "How did you know I would be coming home early?"

"I'm, psychic," she teased. When he didn't reply, she continued. "Actually, I called the office and your secretary, Michelle, told me that you had left for the day."

"You mean Marcia," he corrected. "She's an associate, she's not my secretary."

"Anyway," she continued, ignoring his statement. "I took off from work, stopped by the store and picked up some wine and some stuff for dinner. I was expecting you to be here when I got here, but this worked out better I think."

"I would have been here but I ran some errands," he lied. No need to tell her that he was trying to clear his head. Then she would want to know why.

"And dinner is all done. I made your favorite; spaghetti and meatballs and garlic bread," she said smiling proudly, showing perfect teeth. Dan Curtis had made sure of that his daughter's smile was perfect.

"Oh. Smells good," Lamont said. This wasn't his favorite. Jane only adapted it as his favorite because it was the only thing that she could cook without fouling up. Boiling water, opening a jar and tossing a salad are the cooking skills that Jane has acquired in her 30 years. Her main tool for food preparation was the telephone, and she was great at using it to order take-out.

"You sit here, Lamont, I'll bring you some wine to sip on while I toss a salad." She handed him the remote for the television automatically. She flashed him a smile and sashayed towards the dining area and poured him a glass of red wine and brought it to him. She noticed his eyes watching her and smiled inwardly. That was good, she thought smugly. He wanted her, and he would be nice and horny later. That's when she would break her news.

Lamont sipped the wine and tried to make small talk. "So how has your week been going?"

"Not too shabby, but I'll tell you all about that later. We said we wouldn't talk about work, remember?"

After dinner, and a few glasses of wine they make out on the large comfortable sofa. "You smell so good, baby." Lamont commented while covering her with passionate kisses. "Make me wanna bite ya."

"I'm counting on it. I got a nice surprise for you." She smiled as she slipped away and disappeared into the bedroom. Her surprise would doubtlessly be to model some sexy new expensive lingerie, and dance for him. She had a natural wild sexual imagination, and a carnal knowledge of ways to turn him on.

"Lamont honey, could you come in here a minute please," she called out from the bedroom. Lamont didn't hesitate, and he was pleasantly surprised and turned on by the outfit she wore. She moves like a stripper, and he moved quickly to where she stood. "You look like a sexy milk chocolate goddess," he said staring into her eyes.

She went to his arms draped in a transparent tight short black nightgown that made her breast look more luscious, and her legs longer. She teased him now, moving back and spreading her legs apart with her hands on her hips. "You were saying something about biting me? Well baby come bite me because you're gonna love my flavor," she giggled.

"You're not afraid you'll get rabies," Lamont said teasingly.

"With you handsome I'm tossing all caution to the wind. You can bite me any where you'd like," she said shaking her 36 c cups. "But I hope you start right here."

Lamont had never seen her so playful and uninhibited. "You might like me mad wild and all over your luscious body, with foam at the mouth," he said, pulling her to him.

"I think you're right. I've never been screwed by a mad man."

"You're freaky, and scary, and sexy as hell right now."

She reached out and wrapped her arm around his neck and pulled him even closer, kissing him hard and aggressive. "I want you." Her eyes sparkle at the sight of his bulging manhood. "I guess you want me to, Baby," she said playfully. Now she was serious. "Oh, Lamont, you make my mouth water right now," Her hand found his crotch. "I missed you." She said looking down between his legs directing her words to his penis.

Lamont pulled her to him and planted baby kisses on her shoulders, neck arms and face. He knew her sexual fantasies, and all her hot spots. He started kissing her passionately and hard on the lips. Their tongues engaged in some random fencing maneuvers and filled them with blind random passion.

He pulled her arms from around his neck and separated his lips from hers. They both undressed, but Jane left her panties for him to remove. He stood there nude ogling her and observing her hungry expression. He silently moved closer and pulled the panties slowly down to her ankles. He lifted the sheer top to gain access to her enhanced breast, but did not take it off completely. He moved closer, caressing and kissing her breast with skillful passion. He was aware of her tender high pitched moans, as his hands touched her known hot spots and amplified her passion.

"Ooh, Lamont, that's it. Now babee, now," she begged as she spread her legs and tugged at him. "Give it to me, dammit."

Lamont lowered himself down to her neatly shaven triangle of womanhood and nestled the tip of his penis inside. She whimpered slightly as he inched inside and filled her void. "OOOH yes, yes, yes, yes. You feel so good baby. It's so perfect," she cooed. "Give me all of it," Her husky musical voice added to his mounting passion, and threatened to send him to the edge. He thrust deep inside of her, suddenly impatient to fill every inch of her.

Their lovemaking had started cautiously, as if they were probing and exploring, randomly, but intense reckless pounding soon replaced light cautious probing. They matched strokes with uncanny precision in their pursuit of ultimate satisfaction. Their movements and words were a perfect orchestration of tremendous mutual sexual energy and sweet random surges of lust.

Such intense mind boggling lust had to end and they both felt themselves moving to that wondrous realm. Jane began to curse shiver and vibrate. Lamont could only grunt like a cave man in a language that defied translation, and yet clearly expressed the state of his exploding passion. Jane's sexy voice in his ear spurred his passions even more, prolonging his violent gushes. His moans were louder as Jane's inner vibrations sent new intense sensations of pleasure throughout his entire body.

He had no will of his own as he spent his liquid passion slow and deep inside the condom. "OOH God, baby, you so damn sweet, shit," he cried out at the height of his momentous climax. "That's it, right there."

"OOH Shit, OOOH Lamont, fuck me, fuck me babee yes,"

Jane screamed, shuddered and spurted out of control with passion. "Daaaaayam, that was sensational," Jane shivered and cried out when she finally returned to sanity. "Damn baby, you are so powerful and I think I'm still having mini climaxes. Not that you ain't always good," she said cautiously now. "But Dayam. That was special, "she said smothering him with baby kisses. "Oh baby you really did it to me good."

"Yeah it was special." Lamont said still holding her, but he was wondering why she was going overboard with all the praise. Tonight she was more melodramatic than usual. He was horny tonight but he didn't consider himself a great stud, and he hadn't done anything special. He didn't object to a little ego stroking, but Jane's compliments seemed patronizing and he had the feeling that she wanted something. Was she flattering him now because she wanted something? Did she want to push up the wedding?

Jane was such an actress sometimes, and he figured that it was because she spent so much time facing the cameras. That was something that he would have to put up with if he was going to be with this woman. The obvious perks were, that Jane was gorgeous, sexy, and a great sexual partner. He wasn't about to find fault in her minor flaws. They cuddled together, kissing, spooning and enjoying the after math of their love making. "You know maybe it was so good because..." She paused.

"Because what?" He felt her tense up.

She hesitated as if she didn't want to say what was on her mind. "Maybe you got a sixth sense."

"Sixth sense, I don't think so. What does a sixth sense have to do with anything?"

"Well, maybe you sensed that our session tonight would have to last for a while and..."

"What are talking about?" He propped up on one elbow. "Are you dumping me?" He said playfully, but still thinking that was a possibility. That would be the perfect bad end to a bad week. He had faced a maniac, a job rejection, possible unemployment, and now the possibility of getting dumped.

She gave him a patient smile that one gives a dim-witted child. "NO, silly", she said with a dismissive half frown.

"Well, what then?"

Now she wore a guilty expression. "I was gonna tell you earlier, but you said not to talk about work. Then we got so involved and." She paused batting her eyes at him.

"For goodness sake, Jane, just say it." Lamont was curious and impatient with her reluctance, and he saw through her coy act.

"Okay. Remember I told you that I might be getting to do a feature for the network?"

"Yeah, I recall that," he lied, half the time he didn't listen to her rattle on with all that gossip about the station and her coworkers.

"Well, the good news is that Grover, the station manager, came through. He promised me that doing this story would make me the top candidate for the anchor position."

"That is good news. So what's the bad news?"

"Well, the bad news is that I have to go to Atlanta for a week to do the feature.

"Atlanta? Georgia?" Lamont sighed deeply and tried to maintain his composure. "So when are you suppose to be there?"

"Well I'm due to meet the crew and get started Monday morning." She paused and shot him a guilty glare. "I booked a flight for 7:20 tomorrow morning."

"What? Tomorrow? 7:20 AM? " He wanted to scold her for not telling him sooner, but instead he said. "That's some short notice."

"Yes." She studied his face. "You're upset, aren't you?"

"Frankly, yes. Can't you take a later flight?"

"No, that would get me there a day later."

"Why didn't you tell me before now? I know I said we weren't going to talk about work, but you could have told me this."

"I was going to, but then we got into it and that was the only thing on my mind. I was concentrating on just pleasing you." She felt as if that was a good enough reason, but apparently Lamont didn't.

"Oh for goodness sake, Jane, I have voice mail on all my phones. You could have left word for me to get in touch with you. Even if I was busy, you could have let me know."

"I know baby and I'm sorry. It was thoughtless of me. And you know I can never remember to charge my damn cell phone."

Lamont was surprised that she was apologizing, instead of trying to have the last word. That wasn't like her. Then again, she was getting what she wanted. "Yes it was and..." He started.

She stopped his words with her mouth, and her tongue darted in between his lips. "Will you please just let me make it up to you baby, and I promise I'll never do anything like that again. Say you forgive me. Please, please please," she said, clasping her hands together as if she were praying.

Lamont realized that it was senseless to argue about it now. She would go regardless, so he might as well quit his futile protest and concentrate on more fruitful things. He became aware of her sweet scent, and was reminded of their recent torrid sex.

Jane continued to plant baby kisses on him as she spoke in her most seductive and pleading voice. She was proud of her unique strong sexy voice, that men like Grover and Lamont found irresistible. That's why she was so confident that she would get that anchor's job, and that's why it was easy to manipulate Lamont Savage.

Lamont called a truce because he didn't want them to part in anger. Besides, her actions right now abolished all lingering anger and forced his attention to her.

"I'll only be there for a week, and if I do a good job, I'm a shoe in for Miles' job when he retires in a few months. Then I'll be an anchor and I won't have to leave ever again."

"You're sure you're going to get the job?"

"Positive. They're looking for a woman for that job and Grover assured me that it's mine, if I do a good job in Atlanta. Then nobody can yell foul. Or accuse me of taking short cuts."

"Short cuts?" Lamont was stunned. "Short cuts, like what?"

"Nothing, it's just that...Well, you know how some jealous sluts start rumors when an attractive woman gets a promotion over them. They never believe that she earns it."

"You mean they might say you slept your way to the top?" Lamont asked thinking for the first time if that was possible. It was crazy and he wouldn't mistrust her without a solid reason.

"Exactly. Honey, you know how some of those bitches can be. That's why I don't have anything to say to them."

"Yeah, I know what you mean." Lamont knew that Jane was ambitious from the day they met, and now he wondered how far she would go to get what she wanted. That job was very important to her and he took second place next to her career. He accepted that because there was a chance that he might do the same thing, if he became a Cooper Industries executive.

He wanted to spend the whole weekend in bed making love and ordering take out, but that was impossible now. He would have to make the best of these few hours that they had left. He cuddles close and concentrated on what she was doing to him. Suddenly her head popped up. "Gotta pee, Baby. Be right back." She was up and heading for the bathroom.

He watched her until she went inside and shut the door. Now that his time with her was going to be short, he suddenly needed to make love to her again. Knowing that she would be leaving, he was feeling an extra surge of passion. He wanted that eager sexy woman that Jane had become tonight. Perhaps it was because she was so eager, receptive, and responsive. That was probably because everything was going the way she wanted.

Still, he wished that she would put this trip on hold, but it wouldn't be fair for her to lose this opportunity. It bothered him that she had waited until after they made love before she told him. He felt as if she had used sex to manipulate him. He warned himself that such pathetic need for her was that dangerous, but what could he do?

He didn't want to think about that so he turned his attention to the bathroom door with a smile. He watched her step out of the bath room, and he smelled her sweet scent. He observed her wicked expression. "You look real sexy baby, and there's no doubt in my mind that you're gonna get that job. It a great opportunity and I'm glad it's coming together for you," he said, pulling her down on the bed and hugging her tight.

"Then you're okay with it?" She sounded elated.

"Oh course I am. I wish you were staying in town so that we could spend some time together, but if this is going to help you get that promotion you're seeking, you have my blessing."

"Oh, Lamont." She showered him with baby kisses on his face and neck. "You're the most wonderful man in the world."

"Yeah that's me, good ole Lamont."

Jane wore a devious smile as she felt Lamont instant respond to her touch. She was good, and thus far she had Lamont under her sex spell. She officially owned him body and soul. Even though she appeared to be pushing her career, it was just part of the game she was playing. As soon as they were married, she would kiss this whole career thing goodbye. In fact, once they were married she didn't plan to work again ever. Why should she when she had hit the lottery? Very soon she would be collecting her winnings.

Chapter Nine-
Hanging Out

Lamont returned to his apartment disappointed and drained after taking Jane to the airport. He noticed the answering machine's light blinking and realized that he hadn't checked his messages the day before. He hadn't thought much about anything after the abundance of bad news that he received the day before. His one positive hope was to spend time with Jane, but that disappeared when she broke her bad news.

"How much worse could it get from here," he asked himself. He found out when he hit the play button and listened to Jake Cooper's voice. *"Hello Lamont, I just wanted to discuss what we talked about. I'm anxious to know your decision. I also wanted to know if you feel like getting some fishing in with JJ and me on the boat this weekend. Hope you can make it. Give me a call when you get this message or meet me at the pier; you know the spot, number twenty four."*

Lamont checked watch to see that it was almost nine. "Damn," he said, wishing that he had checked his messages yesterday. Jake liked to get an early start so no doubt they had already cast off, but he would call anyway. Had he known earlier that Jane was leaving; he would have made plans to join them. Even though he loved to fish, he didn't care about catching fish today. He just wanted to relax quietly on Jake's boat and have a few beers. This week end would have been perfect for it, but circumstances had made it impossible. He added that on to his list of bad news for the week, and was reluctant to listen to the next message. However, curiosity overcame fear.

The next message was from Hal. *"Hey buddy, I just wanted to holler at you."* He hadn't spent much time with Hal since their argument at Eddies, but they were still friends. This hadn't been their first argument and he knew it wouldn't be their last. He would call Hal later and invite him to drink some beer and play a game of pool.

Lamont picked up the phone and dialed Jake Cooper's cell phone. Jake answered after the second ring. "Hello"

"Hey Jake, It's me."

"Lamont, how you doing? Sorry you couldn't make it. I've caught two beauties already and it's only eight thirty AM."

"Yeah, I'm sorry too. I'm just checking my machine now."

"So have you decided what you want to do about my offer?"

"I'll have to discuss that with you in person. It's too complicated to get into, so let's skip it," Lamont said and changed the subject now. "So you caught some nice ones huh?"

"Yeah I did," Jake said quickly. He was curious about Lamont's decision. "Lamont, I know you got your own problems," he said, "and I don't mean to be pushy, but I really need to work on my plan right away, and I need your answer like yesterday. This matter is top priority and I'd like to see you as soon as possible."

"About the spy job," Lamont said listlessly.

"Don't make it sound so demeaning. Believe me when I say that it might be the most important position in the company right now. I know how that sounds, I'm not stupid. Of course you might doubt my judgment," he said with a pause then continued. "I know it sounds like it's over dramatic, but I need you to trust me, Lamont. Maybe I don't have the right to ask you that, but you're my only child who has proven himself," Jake said. "I hope you don't have a problem with working for me, Son," he added.

"No, it's not that Jake." Lamont wanted to say that he was ready to work for him, but in the position that they had discussed in the beginning. He was sure that he would better serve the company if he was doing the job that Jake had promised him. He expected Jake to fulfill that promise. Instead Jake was offering him something that had nothing to do with what they discussed. Still he had no choice but to accept Jake's offer with great reluctance and slender desperation.

"If you don't have a problem working for me, then you shouldn't have a problem with the job that I give you. If you trust me you know that my instincts are good. When I say that I believe a conspiracy is taking hold, you can believe me about that, Son. Do you?"

Lamont couldn't say the words. "I want to Jake, but I don't know what to believe." He was suddenly aware of his own whining and paused. Hal was right; he sounded pathetic and was acting more like a brat everyday. The accident of his birth hadn't earned him an elite status, and he had to shake any such idea. A man still had to earn his own rewards, not have them handed to him by birth right.

"Look Lamont hear me out. I tell you what, come to Richmond tonight and have a nice dinner with us, and let's discuss it. I would really appreciate it."

Lamont pondered briefly. "Look, Jake I think I know what you're gonna say and believe me I ..."

"I didn't want to say this over the phone," Jake cut him off, "but you're not giving me a choice. I'm desperate, Lamont, and there are things going on here that could send Cooper Industries into a crisis. Things are worse now than they were when I first told you. Share holders are being intimidated into selling, and that sure smells like the mob to me. The board and the department heads are," he paused before finishing. "Look, meet with me, please. I'll send a helicopter to pick you up. "

"No Jake, that won't be necessary. I'll drive to Richmond and meet with you, I need to clear my head and do something to keep me occupied," Lamont said, recognizing the grave concern in Jake's voice. Jake sounded so concerned that Lamont now wondered if Jake's fears were founded. There was but one way to know for sure.

"That's great my boy. Let's make it around seven. We can have some dinner and some drinks. Then I want to discuss a strategy with you," he paused then added. "No pressure, just talk, for right now. And Lamont, everything is negotiable."

Lamont responded to the last statement, thinking that perhaps Jake threw it out there as a life line. Was it possible? "Okay seven it is." Lamont said with less enthusiasm than Jake had expressed. He wasn't fond of visiting Jake's estate. He had called it '*Cooper Castle*,' because he felt displaced and uncomfortable in the huge mansion. His discomfort came as a result of seeing so much waste in the name of luxury. He was acutely aware of waste, because he constantly observed much scarcity and poverty. Jake's place was huge and impersonal, and came across as a vast and vague museum lobby, and not a warm cozy home.

Nevertheless, he respected Jake and did not judge his taste, or measure his waste based on his fallibilities. Money didn't exempt any fallible man from the need for security. Jake was always such a gracious and hospitable host, and Lamont enjoyed spending time with him, even in the gigantic mansion.

Lamont arrived at the Cooper house in the ritzy Henrico County section, just outside the city limits. He entered the premises after checking with the guard at the gatehouse. Jake greeted Lamont with a hearty hand shake and a brief hug. "Come on in," he said and moved towards the long dinning table filled with a variety of entrees.

Lamont spotted Candace standing in the doorway of the dining room, wearing a very tight low-cut satiny black dress. Her smile matched the sparkle in her diamond necklace and ear rings. As she glided towards him, he scanned her entire body, taking in the full rounded feminine hips that tapered into a tiny waist. Her legs looked incredible in an expensive pair of black velvet peep toe pumps, and black sheer stockings.

Lamont realized that he had fallen under her spell for a brief moment and guilt made him shift his concentration. He wasn't supposed to lust after his father's wife. He almost panicked when she came directly towards him with outstretched arms. "Hello, Lamont. Good to see ya," she said giving him a brief hug and a peck on the cheek.

"Good to see you too, both of you," Lamont replied awkwardly. He ignores the subtle urges that threatened to erupt as her exciting intoxicating fragrance dance inside his nostrils. How was he going to get through the night with her here, smelling sweet, and wearing that dress?

"Wish I could stay and chat, but unfortunately I have a meeting with my charity organization. So I'm going to miss dinner with you two handsome devils," Candace said, wearing a saddened expression as she prepared to leave.

Lamont realized that he should feel relieved now that he wouldn't have to go through the torture of her constant presence. Now he didn't have to carry the burden of guilty feelings about his lewd fleeting glances and slow rising lust. Candace wouldn't be here to tempt him, and that should be a relief, but he felt a sense of loss.

"You two will have the place all to yourselves," she said, flashing a wide smile. "Lamont you just got to come again real soon and we can all have a nice visit." She widened her smile, exposing glowing white teeth.

"That sounds like a plan," Lamont said trying not to sound disappointed. Now, he hated to see her leave. He watched her with vague remorse and a sense of undefined longing. She kissed Jake's lips, and then headed towards the door. Lamont realized that he was staring and quickly diverted his attention elsewhere.

"Take care, guys," she said in a sultry half whisper, then strutted to the door with a subtle sexual walk and was gone in a few short strides.

Lamont turned to Jake, feeling a bit awkward because of his disappointment at Candace's departure, but now he was jolted to reality. "Where's JJ," Lamont said hoarsely.

"Had a hot date, as usual. I haven't seen this one yet. He's keeping her...." Jake sighed and stopped his words, deciding not to say anymore about it.

"So it's just you and me?" Lamont asked, while trying to block Candace from his head.

"Yeah, that's the way I wanted it."

"I already know what you're going to say, but first tell me what are we having for dinner? I'm hungry," Lamont said hoping to put off the business conversation until after dinner.

Jake had gone along and remained silent about the business during dinner. However, after Dinner, Jake wasted no time trying to convince Lamont to accept his offer. They went into his study to further discuss business. "Son, I think together we can weed out that snake and I need you with me."

It was obvious to Lamont that Jake was sincere about his beliefs, but Lamont couldn't decide if those beliefs were real or imagined. If some one was trying to steal the business, it was probably some CEO from another company. This Mob business couldn't be for real could it? In any case he had already decided that he would take Jake's offer, but with some compromises of his own. "I tell you what, Jake. I will come to work for you, but I want to propose some conditions." If Jake wants him bad enough, he will accept Lamont's compromise to customize this job for him.

"Like I said, Lamont, I'm willing to work with you within reason," Jake said. "What's on your mind?"

"I want access to business matters."

Jake smiled. "Lamont, that's the beauty of this whole thing. You don't even have to ask, that's all part of it. You'll be learning the business, while we weed out this crook. That way, nobody suspects a damn thing and that gives us the edge," The two men sat back in the high back chair in the study. "So yes you definitely got that and you'll have access to confidential matters as well."

"If that's true, then I'm ready to come in as your undercover Jr. Executive."

"Great, I'll say that you have experience with some fictitious company similar to Cooper Industries. That way, you won't be treated like a green rookie, and it won't look suspicious that you have access to more info than rookie's usually get," Jake said. "And, of course, you could even help out with the accounts. I'll create some phony special assignment that will allow you access to loads of information," Jake said and smiled with relief. "It will work, and with you and me together, there's no way anybody is going to hoodwink us."

Lamont felt a twinge ripple up and down his back seeing that Jake felt the same excitement that he felt about the two of them working together. Maybe he had been looking at things through cloudy glass. Maybe Jake does want the same thing he wants, and maybe some one is out to take his company.

"There just one thing left to discuss. How soon can you start?"

"I'll give my two weeks' notice at the center, but I can take my vacation and start studying up on your personnel, and take the tour right away. Once I do that there's nothing keeping me from spending time at CI."

"That's great. I'll get you that info you'll need. Like I told you before, there's only one man that I suspect, and that's who you'll be working with. I'll give you a profile of all the department heads and local board members as well," Jake said, seeming to beam for the first time now.

"Lamont, I know you got the Cooper genes. You catch on quick, that's a Cooper trait. I wish my brother, Johnny had your patience and business sense," he said, with a strange expression. "What you did at that Center was a major task."

Lamont shrugged. "Well, it's too bad it was all done in vain. They're going to close the place down real soon. Too many people losing money on those proposed condos."

"That doesn't change the fact that you did an excellent job in spite of such negative commotion. That will all work in our favor because you know organizational structure."

"I didn't do anything that spectacular. And I had help," Lamont said modestly.

"Oh don't be so shy about taking credit, Lamont. You showed a leader's spirit, and you inspired those under you. You're a good leader who leads by both example and action," he said then paused before continuing. "Together, we're gonna get to the bottom of this conspiracy."

Although he struggled to keep his euphoria hidden, Lamont was elated at receiving praise from Jake face to face. This was a major breakthrough tonight, because now he knew that Jake saw his real value. There was a real chance that Jake would make good on his promise, and this job could lead to more responsibility in Cooper Industries once the mission is accomplished. He was done with stressing about why he hadn't been chosen to be an executive. What mattered now was that his foot was in the door, and his skills would be discovered soon enough.

After their discussion and agreement, Lamont swept aside all invasive thoughts and relaxed. Tonight, he wanted to enjoy hanging out with his father because such moments were rare and hard to come by.

The following Monday, Lamont notified Bob Pierce and submitted his resignation. Pierce didn't hide his expression of anger and disappointment "Okay, then Lamont if you want to leave like this I can't stop you," Pierce had said. "I just hope it all doesn't turn to shit and you have to come running back," he said with a mean growl. "I think you're making a fatal career mistake."

Lamont now saw Bob Pierce as the enemy who would do whatever was necessary to dissuade him. Pierce had proven to be a company man who gave bad advice, and lied to promote his own interests. Lamont felt relieved to be through with him as well.

Chapter Ten-
The Affair

Lamont assumed that Marcia would replace him temporarily because of her qualifications. However, Marcia declined the position and Greg had the unofficial temporary position by default. Lamont pushed aside his concerns about the confusion that might ensue with Greg in charge. Temporary in this place could mean a year or more. He didn't care because the Center was no longer his problem and he shifted to more pleasant thoughts.

Jane was due back tonight and he anticipated her arrival, and imagined ways they would make up for lost time. He had the whole weekend free, his mind was clear, and he was ready to spend some indoor quality time with her. He wondered what new item of lingerie she had bought especially for the occasion. His energy level soared when he thought about all the physical things he wanted to do to her.

Unfortunately, Lamont's elated mood and plans changed abruptly when Jane called to say that she had to stay in Atlanta for another week. "They screwed up some of the tape, and I'm gonna have to re-shoot," she said to Lamont over the phone. He didn't think about even mentioning his new job. He hoped that the demands of their careers wouldn't keep them separated too much in the coming weeks. That would no doubt make their relationship difficult.

He didn't know exactly where his career was headed, but he was planning on being at Cooper Industries permanently. Business and finance had always fascinated him, and he planned to use his imagination and intellect to build a solid reputation. He admired Jake and cherished the rare times that they got to talk business, because it was a learning and bonding process all in one. However, they didn't get to talk as much as he wanted because of Jake's concentration on work and family.

Perhaps now that he would be working closer, he would get more quality time to discuss business matters. He also felt that he would get to see more of the family as well. To a person who never had a family, a connection even to a dysfunctional family brought forth some sense of solidarity. He wanted that as much as he wanted to be an executive. Sure they were a bunch of misfits, but that didn't matter. He didn't care about Cheryl's promiscuity, Ann's constant aloofness, JJ's womanizing or Ruth's ever present meanness and rudeness.

He cared only about focusing on, and doing a good job. The job at CI came with a big salary, many perks and fringed benefits thanks to Jake's generosity. Such generosity told him that Jake was making the attempts to fulfill his promise. Even his fake position allowed him access to privileged areas and information about the company's operations.

In the mean time, he would press to seek some credence in Jake's instincts and theory. Jake is too sane and logical to be shrugged off as eccentric rich and delusional. He planned to look hard and long at the situation and if there was something foul in the mix, he would find it.

He would start at CI next week and he could hardly wait. Tonight however he had to find a way to spend his free time. He met with Hal for a game of pool and some beers before heading to his apartment alone. He couldn't help but wish that Jane had returned as planned. He had even secretly hoped that she would say that she was joking about staying in Atlanta another week, but that didn't happen.

****

It was so quiet when she pulled into his parking space, and looked around to see if any one was milling about. She slid out of the car and sashayed purposely towards the door of his apartment, inserted her key and stepped inside. He was out, and she felt excited about being here to prepare for his return. The thrill of exciting clandestine meetings always filled her with excitement and impatience to sin. She felt highly stimulated by role playing and staging surprise encounters. Each one was pleasure filled and greatly rewarding.

She moved about quickly, changing into new sexy lingerie, and studying the mirror with an admiring glare. She wore a pleased smile and understood why men ogled her so much. She pulled her taunt stomach even tighter and studied her body up and down. Surely men could see what she saw. "Stop it girl, you just too damn sexy." She smiled and pushed out her breasts and squeezed her nipples. "That feel's so sexy I don't want to wait."

Her pouty lips held a florescent glow and formed into a perfect valentine, and she smiled at the thought of tonight's expectations. She turned on the night table lamp, and a red glow softened the mood and made her white outfit look sexier. She touched herself while thinking about him. She couldn't think of the words to describe him, and she shivered each time she remembered their most recent encounters. It was always extra good, but that was because their meetings are secret and taboo, and they were stealing lust.

Their time together is always well spent because it is never wasted on ceremony, which gave them complete sexual freedom together. With him, her sexual versatility had no limits, and she could be everything from a lady to a whore. They could make conventional, tender and passionate love, or they could have tainted, rough, perverted sex, depending on the mandates of their extemporaneous urges. Tonight she was prepared for something kinky and different, preferably rough, aggressive dirty love-making. She knew he would oblige her anything she wanted, because she was in control.

She swished over to the cabinet, smiling as she scooped the Champagne bottle from the ice and opened it. He had instructed her to open it just minutes before his arrival, and it was time. She was ready for him to bring out her dark perverted side. She cautiously juggled two lovers who both gave her maximum sexual joy in different ways. It was important to her sense of fulfillment to have the attention of two men. To her, one man was only half of a man and it took two men with different techniques to give her what she needed.

She trained her eyes on the mirror, while sitting on the bed and sipping from the long stem glasses, her birthday present to him last year. She turned her head to different angles, trying to decide the best face to present. She pinched one nipple lightly and touched her patch of womanhood. She twisted her face into a huge passionate scowl and uttered throaty moans of ecstasy. She smiled and talked to herself. "Honey, you better get here or I'm gonna do myself."

Tonight she wanted it rough, hard, aggressive, and kinky. She wanted the master at pushing all the right buttons to satisfy her kinky cravings. Little miss sweetness has gone back into her shell. Now it's MS. Bitch's turn. That's why she was here instead of across town.

Ten minutes later, she heard him step inside the apartment and, close the door. She had sprayed on perfume and it filled the air. Now, she hears him tramples towards the bedroom.

"I know you here, Baby," he whispered in a voice filled with anticipation. "You sure smell good," he said, whiffing the perfume and moving closer.

"Is that you Honey," she said.

"Who else," he replied. "I'm so glad you made it."

She sat patiently on the bed in a seductive revealing pose that exposed her long lovely legs, which were clad in stockings and accented by spike heels. She reclined slightly, pushing her breasts out for maximum cleavage. "This turns you on, Baby," she said pushing his breast out and batting her eyes. She knew him well enough to know that it did. His fantasy was to find her waiting in flimsy lingerie, smelling sweet, and being slutty.

Nothing has changed, and now he stood speechless at the sight of her reclining on the bed with her legs crossed. Her magnificent breasts were exposed, even though they were enclosed in the transparent white lacy gown. "Damn! Sexseee! I love that outfit. And you're actually here at last."

"I told you I would be here," she said, pretending not to notice his eyes scanning her. "Did you doubt that I would show?"

"No, it was just that I was looking forward to it so much that I figured something might screw it up. I thought you were staying another week."

"Yeah, that's the word I put out. I'm supposed to be out of town still, so I'm totally free to spend the night if I want to."

"This might work after all," he said then kissed her hard.

She turned away, teasing him. "You really thought I wasn't coming, huh?" She asked skeptically. "Then, why was the champagne on ice?"

"Well, I was still hoping."

"Kiss me," she said, but then she kissed him before he could respond.

"So glad you got back, Sugar," he said, between deep heavy breaths, while hugging her tight.

She pulls back now. "Did you really miss me, or was it this?" She looked down to the crotchless panties. "Want some of this?"

"Come here and let me show you, you sexy little bitch."

"Oh, so you want to do it dirty tonight, huh? Well I'm in the mood, you Neanderthal asshole. I'm gonna screw your brains out tonight." She smiled wickedly, then licked her bottom lip and bit it gently.

"Not if I screw yours out first, Slut!"

"Bring it on big boy! Cause I got what it takes," she paused and touched herself. Now she leaned over and touched his crotch. "To handle all of that. And every time you get it up, I'm gonna put it down," she said with a gleeful squeal.

They locked in a tight ardent embrace, both excited by their dirty talk and mutual anticipation of the tawdry pleasures ahead. Their French kisses were wet, noisy, and filled with wolfish hunger. The long, hungry kisses produced a heat stream that flowed quickly to the bloodstream. "OOH, Jane baby, I'm so glad you're back. How was Atlanta?"

"Like you give a damn," she said between hungry kisses. "Just shut up and be real. You better keep your mind on what's here between my legs. You're just lucky I'm horny enough to let you have your way."

"No sugar tits, you're lucky," he smirked now then paused and wrapped his hand around his penis and shook it at her.

"You're so crass and vulgar," she said with a mischievous glare and a half smile.

"And tonight this crass and vulgar cock is all yours," he scowled playfully and came closers. "This is the prize you've won by showing up here tonight.

"Then bring it here and stop talking me to death," she said huskily and pulled him on top of her. "The time for talk is over. Take care of momma, Greg honey. Take care of momma. Now!" After some brief fore play, she centered herself beneath his crotch and felt him slowly eased inside her. In the midst of her passion fits, she blanked Lamont completely from her mind. She only cared about now and what Greg was doing to her at this moment. "Oh, I'm such a bad little bitch," she cooed breathlessly as she matched him stroke for stroke.

"No baby. You're such a good little bitch," he stressed the last, plunging inside her, and thinking that this was so perfect. "A damn good little bitch," Greg said, sinking deep inside her and lost himself in bliss.

"Oh fuck me you dirty bastard. Harder. Give it too me. Don't you want it?" She egged him on.

It was late when Lamont left the bar, but he was still sober and making plans to hang out with Hal and JJ the next day. He thought about inviting Greg along as a friendly gesture, but Greg would likely find some excuse to decline, so he wouldn't waste the effort. Besides, neither Hal nor JJ liked Greg, and he didn't need the tension right now. On the other hand JJ just might be busy as well. He recalled that Jake had mentioned JJ's new female interest and Lamont assumed that his brother might have other plans. Knowing JJ, he's probably planning an expensive party as usual. JJ just couldn't seem to get enough of parties and women.

More than likely it would just be Hal and himself hanging out and doing something boring. He really wished Jane was here right now and he needed a distraction. Hal was definitely a distraction because he always made Lamont laugh and take himself less serious, which he needed. He cleared Jane from his mind briefly, and enjoyed Hal's corny jokes and jovial disposition. Hal was more than just a comical side kick; he was also a trusted friend. Hal had actually helped uncover information that had led Lamont to Jake and his recently discovered family. Hal was a comfortable friend to be around, and Lamont trusted him in spite of his flaws and bad habits.

Lamont did become annoyed and irritated when Hal brought up his personal business, like his relationship with Marcia. Hal was sure that Lamont was having sex with Marcia and he would throw hints from time to time. "You telling me you ain't hittin' that?" Hal had asked rather crudely on occasion. Sometimes he just wouldn't let it go. "I know yall work late sometimes, and all that behind and those legs, she just your type: pretty big eyes, honey coated chocolate skin," Hal often said. "She got the prettiest lips you ever saw and perfect teeth," Hal had said insisting that Marcia was the girl for Lamont. "Hal you just don't get it do you?" Lamont asked patiently. "I'm with Jane, and I'm not about to two time or dump her just to be with some one else. That not my way," Lamont said firmly.

"Okay Montay," Hal said, casting Lamont a skeptical expression and looking as if he was about to burst out laughing any minute.

"Okay you think it's a joke, but I believed that you reaped what

you sow I don't have to tell you about that. You remember what happened with Felicia Courtney."

"Yeah but I'm just saying bro, don't put all your eggs in one
baske…."

"Hal I don't want to hear it." Lamont put his hand up. "Look you
don't have to believe it, but Marcia is like a sister." Lamont felt like a
hypocrite because in reality, his thoughts about Marcia weren't always
as pure as he would have Hal believe.

Chapter Eleven-
Exposed

At 5:30AM Saturday morning, Marcia was awakened from a deep sleep by the incessant ringing of the phone. She hopped from her comfortable bed to answer it only to discover that it was her helpless and needy sister, Eunice. Marcia knew right away that Eunice was either having man trouble with a boyfriend, or wanting to borrow some money. Marcia was fed up with being asked to do these unreasonable favors for Eunice, and then taken for granted.

In spite of her constant griping, Marcia always came to her sister's rescue, because Eunice would lay a guilt trip on her if she refused. More than likely she would refuse to let her see Annette as well. Eunice was a burden and a nuisance, but Marcia felt a family responsibility and couldn't break away from her.

Eunice had committed despicable and dirty acts and constantly justified her actions. Eunice loved having sex and has stooped to prostitution without remorse or guilt. "Girl it so cool that a woman could have so much fun and get paid," Eunice proclaimed.

Eunice was addicted to men and swore that she was smarter than the average man. In spite of this claim she seldom outsmarted them, and often ended up the victim. Her history with seedy men continuously put her at a disadvantage and kept Marcia on standby.

She wanted Marcia to be more like her and had taunted Marcia about being picky. "Girl you letting all the hot studs get away while you dreaming about Mr. Right," Eunice often said. "You're so particular because you think no man can meet your standards. You better stop being a loser," Eunice had said. Actually Eunice hated Marcia's successful career and wanted to see her fail at something, because she felt like a failure.

On the other hand, Marcia felt only disappointment at how her sister had turned out, and secretly wished that some miracle would change her for Annette's sake. Eunice's poor judgment and lack of discretion didn't end with the men she dated. Eunice was everything that a mother shouldn't be. She was a poor house keeper, lousy mother, notorious slut who slept with multiple sex partners, and poor unfortunate Annette was stuck with her. She was the worst possible role model as a mother, having fewer morals than a poop slinging Baboon.

Annette was a hostage to Eunice's immoral life style, and unfortunately in the process Annette had become a replica of Eunice. Marcia loved her niece, but the poor girl was tainted with the curse of Eunice and she wore her mother's unnatural lust and promiscuity like a birthmark.

Without guidance, the young and impressionable Annette was hanging out, doing drugs, and sleeping with older guys. Marcia had heard rumors that Eunice had forced Annette to sleep with her male friends for money at a very young age. The idea appalled her, and she hated to think such things, but Eunice was indeed capable of such deplorable actions.

Marcia was thankful that Annette didn't have a baby of her own, but she suspected that was the result of either a miracle, or an abortion. Abortion was the best bet, since Annette was sexually active and not always so careful about it. Marcia didn't advocate abortions, but in this case it might be merciful. Annette was following faithfully in her mother's footsteps, which was sure to lead to tragedy.

Marcia hated Eunice's careless indiscretions, and desperately wanted to be strong enough to disown her sister. Instead, she constantly ran to her rescue, knowing that she had no sincere regard for her. Marcia was just the dependable one, who is always on standby and ready to assist with no expectation of appreciation.

This morning's rescue was no different from any other. Eunice voice whined from the other end. "Marcy, I hate to call so early but I'm stranded. That creep and I had a fight and I'm way over across town at the Golden Peacock. I need a ride." Marcia was furious but she wasn't going to give Eunice another lecture. She would still end up picking her up any way. Eunice was taking her for granted and assuming that she would be available. It's true that Marcia wasn't dating right now, but that didn't mean that she should spend time coping with her sister's negative life style. Yet here she was, early Saturday morning, heading to some sleazy bar in a very scary neighborhood.

Thirty minutes later Marcia was parked outside the bar watching a scary looking woman coming towards the car. The women stumbled and Marcia's heart rate increased as she checked to be sure her doors were locked. No doubt this was a crack addict coming to put the pinch on her for some money. The woman's hair looked like birds had fought their way out of it. She wore a soiled black dress and hobbled rapidly towards the car on broken spike heels. The woman tapped on the window, and only then did Marcia recognize her sister and unlocked the door.

Marcia spotted the bruises on her sister's arm when she reached for the door. Obviously, Eunice had been in a physical confrontation with her beau, who had beaten her up. "Do you like getting your ass kicked and purposely go out looking for these bullies," Marcia said as soon as Eunice got inside the car. "Or do you purposely piss men off to the point of no return?"

"Don't start Marcy, I got a headache Eunice said defiantly. "And that ain't your business no way."

"I had to get my ass up to come get you, so it's my business," Marcia said looking her up and down. "Picking abusive mates is a regular pattern for you ain't it?"

She ignored Marcia's scolding just like she always did. "What took you so long, Girl? Damn my legs are killing me." She didn't look at Marcia as she wiggled in the seat and took off her shoes, sighing loudly. "Done broke my damn expensive pair of spike heels and ruined my pretty black dress. Shit."

Marcia held back her comments and gave her sister a long look. Eunice looked like an older slutty version of herself. They had the same facial features and they both stood at 5'6", but there all similarities ended. The lines on Eunice's face were obvious and her face was always slightly bloated. In spite of that she was attractive and even conceited. "You're welcome," Marcia said sarcastically, and gave her sister an acid side long glare.

"Oh yeah thanks, Sis," Eunice said matter-of-factly, and quickly changed the subject. "I like your ride, Sis. This a Lexus? Old mellow yellow could turn some heads in this thing, I'll bet. And it's red too." Eunice skin color was a shade lighter than Marcia's and she referred to herself as mellow yellow even though her complexion was milk chocolate."

"No, Eunice, it's a Nissan," Marcia said, unenthusiastically, knowing that Eunice could care less and was only talking because she liked the sound of her own voice. She felt tortured in the presence of her sister. Was she being uppity like Eunice had often said?

"Oh, you know you gotta get to the waterfront and pick up Annette too." Eunice said as if to remind Marcia.

"Are you asking me or telling me," Marcia sighed loudly and showed obvious anger at her sister. "Why you always do that shit, Eunice?"

"Doing what? Marcy, you acting all funny and shit," Eunice said eying Marcia with a curious glare. "Oh excuse me," she said with a dramatic show of outstretched arms. I guess Queen Marcia Dawson is too good to help her sister? Well, I ain't gon' beg you," she said, suddenly defiant. "I ain't gotta kiss your ass just 'cause you got a job and a car? You don't wanna take me then don't. Shit, you can take this Japanese beetle and ram it in your ass. And I can get out at the light, and take a cab."

"The problem is that cabs want money," Marcia said impatiently. "And since we both know that you're not taking the bus, let's face it, if I don't take you home you sure can't wobble there in those broke shoes, smelling like reefer."

"Fuck you Marcy, you uppity black bitch, I'm grown. You ain't momma. Shit."

"Act like it then, and stop all that damn cursing. I'm doing you a favor."

"Stop this car I'm getting my ass out. I don't have to take no shit from you cause you got a little red car and an..."

"Oh Eunice, just cut the shit please. I already told you that your lazy ass ain't walking no where, and ain't no cab gonna pick your broke ass up smelling like pot and looking like a crack whore. So just tell me how to get to where my niece is and let's get this over with."

Eunice started to speak but stopped herself, realizing that her dire circumstances left Marcia with the upper hand. "Go up here and make a right on Westover," Eunice said submissively. Marcia felt bad about being so harsh, but she wasn't going to take anything back.

Marcia had mistakenly thought that Eunice's actions could no longer shock her. However, Marcia was shocked to discover that Annette had spent the night at her boyfriend's apartment. Nothing was ever going to change with Eunice, because apparently she didn't care. Eunice was so self centered it was unbelievable and Marcia wanted to shake her. Marcia never understood that someone as self centered as Eunice hadn't aborted the pregnancy as soon as she found out. Surely she didn't have a baby for the sake of nurturing.

Now that innocent baby wasn't so innocent any more, and was thrust into a seedy life and forced to become an adult too soon. Of course Annette didn't mind. The apple didn't fall far from the tree and she too was addicted to men. At seventeen, Annette passed for twenty one and knew all of Eunice's tricks and philosophies about men. Annette bought alcohol and went to adult night clubs because she looked so mature. Marcia didn't doubt that she shared the same raging hormones as her mother and was willing to bet that her niece was involved with multiple sex partners.

After Marcia finally collected Annette they made some small talk, but for the most part the conversation was non-existent because the situation was awkward. Marcia detected the odor of sex on the two women as she drove them home. Afterwards she said a thank you prayer, and then quickly pulled from the curb with a sigh of relief. She felt depressed about her closest relatives being a duo of promiscuous and reckless mother and daughter sluts, and she feared that they would some day become tragic victims of some crazy boyfriend or john, whatever the case may be.

At this moment she wanted nothing more to do with either of them. Suddenly, she admonished herself because she remembered that Annette was powerless to resist her mother's influence. Marcia was powerless, because she couldn't discard Eunice without affecting her relationship with Annette. So for Annette's sake she couldn't simply break ties with Eunice.

The more distance she put between herself and Eunice the better she felt, and for now she would forget her sister and think positive. She would go home, take a hot shower, relax, and enjoy her weekend. She would play cards with her neighbor Cindy and a few girls; maybe they would go to a club later. She'll go shopping and do something for herself and not worry about Eunice. Eunice had the same opportunity to finish school, but chose to become educated about other things and had gotten herself knocked up.

She wasn't going to feel guilty anymore. It was ironic that Eunice had so many men and she didn't have one. It wasn't that she couldn't get men, she had gone on dates, but they all fell short. Maybe she was setting the bar too high. Too bad she couldn't spend this time with Lamont. "NO," she said aloud. "I'm not going down that road again. I have to get over him." She took a deep breath and looked straight ahead.

Marcia was concentrating on the road ahead when she came to the intersection. A car sped buy, running a stop sign. Marcia had been startled and as she paused to catch her breath she spotted a couple, in a small apartment complex, standing on a stair way, kissing passionately. Their intimacy stirred her and she observed closer. The man wore a robe, and stood there grinding against the fully dressed woman, pushing up against him. Marcia assumed that the lady had concluded an all night booty call and was about to head home.

Suddenly the scene lit up as beaming bright headlights flashed from a car pulling out the driveway, and Marcia couldn't believe her eyes. She recognized the couple. The man in the doorway and the female on the threshold were none other than Greg and Jane Curtis. "No, that couldn't be," Marcia muttered while trying to get a better view. She had to be sure that she hadn't just imagining this because she hated Jane so much.

It wasn't long before all doubts had been erased from her mind. As they broke their embrace, Marcia saw Greg's glimmering diamond ear ring, and recognized Jane's arrogant slutty strut. Now she was sure.

The sudden honk of horns startled her and she realized that there was traffic behind her and some cars had even started to come around. She pulled slowly away to avoid being spotted by Jane. She circled the block and drove back down that street once more. Upon circling the block she spotted the big beige Acura with the personal tags that read JC10. Seeing Jane's car and personal tags erased any remaining doubts.

Jane and Greg were having an affair. It hit her so hard that she couldn't focus on the road or stop her body from trembling. "She's cheating on Lamont with a scumbag," she said with disbelief. "That dirty phony bitch." Why would she do something like that to him? God if she were his woman, there was no way. And with Greg, that creep of all people. They were both scum to do something like this to Lamont. She always knew that Greg and Jane were two sneaky bastards, but she never imagined that the two of them would get together. Some one had to tell Lamont.

Marcia drove home on radar, because her mind was in deep concentration on her options. She would not allow Jane to go unpunished for her deception of Lamont. Some how Lamont's fate had just been put into her hands and she had the hard task of exposing Jane, and rescuing him.

She wanted to be objective and to make the right decision. However, her subtle inner jubilation about Jane and Lamont's possible breakup, made her real motives dubious. Jane's cheating would hurt Lamont, yet she considered that it might be a blessing for her. It was selfish, wrong, and probably even sinful that she might find some delight in the looming misery that Lamont would eventually face. Yet the seed of elation remained strong.

She felt a sudden sense of impending yet guarded freedom, as she held on to the possibility that Jane might be history. She no longer cared if such feelings made her a bad person. She couldn't be nearly as bad as Jane, and it was time for Lamont to know. It was time for Jane to fade out.

Chapter Twelve-
Apprentice

Marcia studied the cheerful expression on Lamont's face and from first appearances, everything seemed okay. She knew different, but she couldn't say anything about what she had seen, because her revelation would cast suspicion and disbelief on her motives. Without proof, she would be perceived as a jealous woman who was out to sabotage Lamont's relationship. Her feelings for Lamont were obvious, so naturally there would be doubts about her negative comments about Jane. She wished that she had thought to use her camera phone to take pictures, but the unexpected shock had numbed her briefly.

Lamont pack after saying his office good-byes, and Marcia watched him, wishing that she could tell him what she knew, but she didn't know if that was the right decision. On the other hand, being forced to remain silent about Jane's treachery depressed her. She had been right to suspect all along that Jane was conniving, sneaky, selfish and calculating. Now she had to prevent Lamont from getting into a disastrous marriage. Why couldn't Lamont see through her? Was it some unwritten law that all the good men were blinded by Jane-like bitches? Still he couldn't be so blind that Jane could get away with cheating on him forever.

Right now she hopes for a miracle to trip Jane up, because she dreaded breaking the news to Lamont herself. She sensed that if she were to divulge that information, she would lose more than just his friendship. The only alternative was to let Lamont find out for himself, but Jane was slick and that might happen too late, and by then his life would be ruined.

Marcia suppressed thoughts of Jane as she mulled around with Lamont making small talk and watching him clean out his desk. She felt isolated and empty, knowing that he was leaving and that she wouldn't have too many chances to discuss Jane with him. She would have to eventually, but not today. She would put it off for as long as possible, but she would step in to prevent him from marrying Jane.

She observed Greg smiling crooked and acting friendly, and now more than ever she wanted to expose him and Jane, regardless of the consequences. Greg was laughing at Lamont to his face and Jane was probably laughing behind his back. She was infuriated at the thought of Lamont being duped by a jerk like Greg, and a slut like Jane. Lamont couldn't be left in the dark, he had to know. That must be top priority. She longed for the pleasure of wiping that smug look from Greg's face. "Why are you so blind," Marcia blurted out unintentional and suddenly, before realizing it.

"Blind? About what Marsh?" Lamont asked puzzled.

"What," she said looking at him strangely, just realizing that she had spoken her thoughts out loud. "Nothing, just thinking. You got an apartment too huh?"

"Yeah," Lamont said studying her closely. "Are you alright?" Lamont asked and guided her to a nearby chair.

"Yeah, I'm just sorry to see you leave."

Lamont felt guilty now for being so elated about leaving. "It's not like I'm going far. I'll be just up the road on the outskirts of Richmond. I'll still drop by and hang out," Lamont said.

"Yeah, yeah, that's what you say now, but you'll soon forget everything about this place, and everyone in it."

"Not everyone," he said, smiling and facing her. "How can I ever forget you, Marsh? You've been my right hand, my left hand and my conscience." He held her soft hands but let go quickly when the brief tingling sensation passed between them. Now he remembered Hal's words: *"That's a lotta woman you're ignoring partner."*

Marcia was crying and he moved closer and wiped her pretty brown eyes, staring intensely into them. "I guess I didn't really expect you to go," she said and started for the door. "I have to go," she said as she rushed out the door.

After Marcia left he felt a sense of lost and couldn't shake the feeling that Marcia had something on her mind. She looked so sad and he had fought the urges to pull her close to him. He wasn't supposed to feel that way about her. Yet those eyes, those sculpted cheekbones, and cute smile haunted him now. He realized that her beauty was inside as well as out. Even with her vulnerability she had stood proudly and attempted to make a cheery smile, but it was haunting and sad.

He wished now that he had something encouraging to tell her. Now he realized that she wouldn't be there for him and suddenly he couldn't think of working anywhere without her there with him. He was going to have to make an adjustment. He knew it all came with the new territory, but still he had to ask Jake for one more favor.

****

The following Monday Lamont arrived in Richmond and attended special meetings with Jake Cooper, and his personal lawyer and advisor, Lawrence Preston. He was introduced to Board members and Cooper Industries key employees, including Peter Vel Haus, Jake's personal assistant. Peter was the target of Jake's suspicions. Lamont tried to forget Jake's suspicions and give the partially bald, gray haired associate, the benefit of the doubt. After all Peter was gracious and sociable, like an eager wife trying to make peace with her husband's hated in-laws.

Peter smiled good naturedly and eagerly welcomed Lamont into the company. He outlined the operation, Lamont's duties, and made sure that Lamont got his coffee just right. He promised Lamont that he would be moving on to more responsibility according to his work. Lamont played along but he knew that his apprenticeship under Peter would only last until Peter was exposed.

He was actually evaluating Peter, and not the other way around as Peter believed. Still, Lamont wondered how much he could do with such limited knowledge of the company's intricate mechanism. He had run the Center and knew about organization, procedure and finances, but things are much larger and different here.

For a brief moment Lamont wondered if he had the ability to handle the massive responsibilities of his complex secret job, but he fought back the urge to become overwhelmed. He'd try to absorb information that would help Jake and make him a valuable asset.

After one month on the job, Jake called Lamont to his office for a progress update. Lamont hadn't uncovered any information at the time and in the midst of their business chat about Peter's actions, the intercom buzzed. "Mr. Cooper, Miss Cheryl Cooper to see you," Pam's voice sounded from the speaker.

"Okay, Pam send her in. I know what she wants," Jake said, with a knowing expression.

"Well I'd better be getting back," Lamont said as he stood to leave.

"Nonsense, you can stay a few more minutes. Say hello, I'm sure Cheryl will be happy to see you."

Lamont sat back in the chair facing Jake without protesting. "Okay I got a few minutes and you're the boss," he joked, but he was glad Jake had made the gesture.

"Knowing Cheryl she's coming for some money, but I can't gripe because I spoiled her more than I did the others. At least she's trying now. I know that going back to school wasn't easy for her, but she finished two semesters already," Jake said with a pleased expression.

There was a knock on the door and Cheryl stepped onto the thick rich brown carpet. She seemed reluctant at first, but now her features softened and her grim expression turned to a smile. "Hi Daddy, I know you're running a business and this is during business hours," she said as she walked towards Jake's desk and gave him a peck on the cheek. "I don't think Pam like's me too much," Cheryl commented about Jake's secretary. She wants you all to herself. As if you wo." She didn't finish her sentence because she was aware of Lamont's presence. He had been sitting in the high back chair unseen by her when she first arrived. "Hi Lamont, what are you doing here?" She asked impulsively and moved closer, kissing his cheek.

"Hi Cheryl," Lamont said, standing and giving her a hug. "Jake didn't tell you?" He looked towards Jake, who sat smiling behind his desk.

"Oh," Jake said, "did I fail to mention that Lamont joined us here at CI last month?"

"Yes you did fail to tell me. That's wonderful Lamont. I'm glad you're on board," Cheryl said mechanically.

Lamont wondered if she might perceive his presence in the company as a threat to her, and wondered if she might envy his new status as the oldest sibling. He asked himself if she possible thought that he had taken something that she felt belonged to her.

"How do you like it so far?" She asked but before he could answer she added, "I know I ain't smart enough to be a Cooper Industries executive, and I don't think I'd want to be. But I'm glad for you. It couldn't have happened to a nicer guy."

Lamont thought that Cheryl was over dramatic and he wondered how he would feel if he were in her shoes. He assumed that it wasn't an easy task to take a back seat to a newly discovered older brother. Thus far he couldn't see any visible changes in her attitude towards him. "Thanks Cheryl," he said with a brief pause. "Well I'll leave you two for now, I got work to do." he turned to Cheryl and smiled. "Good seeing you again, Sis. We gotta get together more often now that I'm living in Richmond," he said giving her a hug.

"That sounds good, I'll call you and maybe we could do lunch. It's always good to see you," Cheryl said with a smiled.

Lamont left office feeling good vibes from his encounter with Cheryl. Next to Jake, she was the main Cooper that he needed for support. She seemed sincere, but he knew that his sister was a master manipulator of men. There were so many way that women like Cheryl could manipulate men, even their brothers.

There was a brief silence after Lamont left the room, but Jake, being an efficient user of time, broke the silence. "So to what do I owe this visit? Or do I already know?" He eyed her suspiciously, but good naturedly and pulled out his checkbook. He was sure that she wanted money. He didn't mind her spending, since she was attending school as he had suggested. She couldn't spend it all.

"Daddy, this is so hard." Cheryl wrung her hands.

"Well just spit it out, Cheryl."

"A friend of mine is in trouble and..."

"Wait, wait wait. Come on honey. If you need some money just say it. We don't need these false scenarios about good friends being in trouble any more, do we?"

"You think the money is for me?" She asked with visible anger.

"Look, just tell me how much money you need and I'll either say yes or no." Jake wasn't about to go into any deep drama with Cheryl. He had learned when to choose his fights with her.

She was about to protest and plead with him. She didn't want him to think that she wanted it for herself, especially such a large amount. "Okay fine then, but I swear to you it is for a friend, who has come upon some hard luck. Her business just burned down and the insurance money is delayed and." She paused and looked into his eyes. His expression was a combination of disbelief and amusement. "Okay so you don't believe me."

"Honey, just tell me what you... What your friend needs and I'll consider it." His voice was one of a man humoring an enchanted child.

Obviously Jake didn't believe her but it wasn't important. It was only important that she got the money. "Fine then. My friend needs seventy five thousand dollars."

"What!" Jake looked at her concerned. "Cheryl, are you in some kind of trouble?"

"No Daddy, I'm not in any trouble. But my friend is."

"Your friend again huh?"

"Why can't you believe me for just this once? Can't you at least give me the benefit of the doubt and...and...Oh never mind." She started crying and heads swiftly to the door.

"Cheryl, wait."

"Forget it daddy. I should have known that you wouldn't believe me. It's not your fault. I understand." She turned as she reached the door. "I'm the girl who cried wolf so many times that no one believes that the wolf actually showed up." She wiped her eyes with some tissue from her purse and left his office.

Cheryl was aware of Pam's icy curious eyes focused on her, but she didn't care what that glorified secretary thought. To Cheryl it seemed as if it took a million steps to reach the safe haven of the elevator and descend to the ground floor.

Jake stared at the door after Cheryl left and wondered if she might be telling the truth. She did seem more sincere this time. Had he just blown it, by showing her that he didn't trust her? She said she understood, but did he understand? Instantly the telephone was in his hand. "Pam, get me Lucas Sheppard," Jake said into the telephone, but now he hesitated then said, "Pam, never mind," he grumbled and hung up. He wasn't going to put bloodhounds on his own family. He was either going to trust her or not.

Lamont had watched Cheryl rush out of Jake's office and he wondered why the meeting had been so short, and why Cheryl had dashed towards the elevator in those high heels. He almost bumped into one of the girls and suddenly stopped short. "Oops, sorry, wasn't looking where I was going," he said with an apologetic smile to the 23 year old office worker assistant.

"Oh that's okay Mr. Cooper, I wasn't looking either."

The girl headed rapidly towards the exit, before Lamont could correct her. Most of the employees noticed his resemblance to Jake and the Cooper family, and they knew that he was related. Some office workers didn't know his last name and assumed that it was Cooper.

Lamont entered his office and sat behind the large desk, observing the plush space. Apprentices didn't get such nice offices of their own, and Lamont had told Jake that he didn't want to be treated special, but Jake had insisted. "We want this to look as if I'm pampering you to avoid suspicion," Jake had said. "That way my enemy doesn't take you as a serious threat."

It wasn't a secret that he was related to Jake, and any internet surfers could confirm his connections as a Cooper relative, because it was made public record three years ago. However, Lamont had tried to hide it rather than flaunt it because he didn't want that kind of recognition. Once people realized who he was, they assumed that he was born with a silver spoon in his mouth. He found that amusing, and sensed that he would meet with constant resentment from those who believed this. No doubt collective gloating would come with his every miscue.

However, his main concern was to gather incriminating information against Peter in the course of his work, and not worry about such pettiness. So far he hadn't detected anything out of order, and he wondered if maybe Jake was wrong. On the other hand, maybe he wasn't as good a spy as Jake thought he would be, or maybe Peter was too slick.

Still, Lamont played his role by reading through the company's financial structure and the sales reports that Jake had provided. Cooper Industries made everything from electrical appliances to airplane parts, and the paperwork was massive. There was a myriad of interconnections, balance sheets, financial statements, sales projections, and revenue reports. Lamont faced the dual task of learning the business, while uncovering the conspiracy.

Jake knew the task wouldn't be easy and he had recently hired Lucas Sheppard's private detective agency as extra insurance. Still, it would be up to Lamont to get the hard core facts. Lucas Shepherd could do regular detective work, but this was a special case and Jake felt that Lamont was perfect for this particular job. Mainly it was Lamont's job to secure guarded information about underhanded suspicious tactics. However, he had not uncovered anything significant thus far.

Lamont's fight wouldn't be with Peter, but with the mean spirited human forces dedicated and determined to see him fail, and who planned to use the miscues of Jake's dysfunctional family to gain control.

Chapter Thirteen-
Groundwork

The next day Lamont received a telephone call from Cheryl "Hey you, how about meeting me for lunch?" She asked over the phone.

"Sure," he agreed. He liked the Idea, and whatever he was working on could wait. Perhaps after seeing him yesterday, she wanted to hang out more just like she said. Around eleven thirty, he began to anticipate having lunch and spending time with his smart savvy sister.

Lamont arrived at the restaurant just before she did, and she spotted him when she entered. She smiled and went to the nearby table where he sat, and he sensed her nervousness. There was something different about Cheryl, and in spite of her smile she looked tired and seemed far away.

Lamont was stylishly dressed in an immaculate blue pinstripe suit, tan shirt and blue and tan pattern tie. His black hair was cut close and neatly trimmed. She was impressed with his fashion sense as were several other ladies who eye her with envy as she approached her handsome brother.

"Hi Lamont," she said as she sat facing him.

"Hi, Cheryl. Good to see you again. You hungry?"

"I could eat a nice salad," she said seeming less nervous now.

He smiled and nodded as if he knew a secret.

"What's that look?" She asked defensively.

"Nothing, just that I knew you were going to say that?"

"What?"

"People who don't need to watch their weight are always watching it anyway," he said smiling amused.

"Well thanks; I think that was a compliment. And I'm not really watching my weight, I'm just not hungry."

They placed their order and chatted while they waited. "So how's school?" Lamont asked, trying to make conversation. He sensed that she wasn't at ease. Cheryl didn't seem eager to talk so he came to the point. "Cheryl, why did you want to meet me?"

She cast him a submissive glance. "To tell the truth, Lamont I need your help," she said pausing briefly, giving Lamont a guilty glance then continuing. "I have to convince Daddy to loan me some money to help my friend."

"Oh," Lamont said as he breathed an unhappy disappointed sigh. "That's why you wanted to see me?" Lamont asked with obvious disappointment. He thought that Cheryl wasn't interested in hanging with him, she just needed his help.

"Yes that's one reason, but also to have lunch and catch up," she said with a waning smile. She noticed his grim expression. "What's wrong, you're in a sour mood all of a sudden?"

"Nothings wrong," he said looking around impatiently.

She didn't believe him. "Something is wrong. What is it Lamont?"

Lamont decided to get it off his chest. "The truth Cheryl," he said without giving her a chance to reply. "I thought you wanted to hang, and I was hoping that we could talk and maybe get to know each other," he said without thinking. In spite of those feelings, he continued. "Look, I know this family still hasn't accepted the idea of a newcomer joining the flock. I'm sorry that you don't trust me."

"Whoa boy, you got the wrong idea. I never said that," she said stretching her eyes.

"No, you haven't said it with words, but your actions say it. You all treat me like an outsider and that's okay because I am, but I'm not the enemy, Cheryl. I'm your blood brother, but I guess that don't mean much because I'm a stranger."

"Don't be so damn sensitive, Lamont," Cheryl said impatiently. "Shit, I know you're my damn brother and I accept that. Have I ever said that we weren't blood, or that you weren't my brother, or that you were an outsider?" She glared at him and insisted on an answer. "Well have I?" She asked, raising her voice slightly in volume.

"No, but like I said actions speak louder."

"Actions my ass," she said annoyed. "I like you. I liked you from the start. Just because I ain't all over you don't mean shit. Everybody doesn't jump for joy when they hit the lottery. Some people just ain't into all that emotional stuff. Hell I don't kiss nobody's ass," she said then paused before adding, "well maybe daddy's some time, but that's my boundary."

Lamont couldn't help but be amused and he smiled at Cheryl's antics right now. He believed that she had spoken truthfully in spite of her crude self expression. She did keep it honest even though she could be disagreeable. "Well I liked you from the start too, and I still like you," Lamont said awkwardly. Now there was silence between them, broken by the unharmonious buzz of the small crowd and the piped in music.

A tall thin Spanish waiter brought their orders and left. Lamont looked up at Cheryl as she poured the low fat dressing on the salad. "Cheryl, you know I'm here for you if you need me?" He touched her hand.

"Yeah, I know," she said forcing a smile and patting his hand. "I'm here for you too but I can't be here for anybody right now because I'm messed up and frustrated." She shook her head. "Got one damn friend and can't help her."

"Just one, huh? That figures," he said playfully.

"Shut up, smart ass," she said lightheartedly. Now she turned serious. "It's a shame that I can't help her though."

"Why do you think Jake would listen to me and not you?"

"I don't know. Maybe he wouldn't. Sorry to get you all hyped up asking you to do things you can't," she said with a deep sigh. "It was selfish of me to ask, so forget it."

"Hello," he said holding both hands palm up. "In case you haven't noticed, I'm a big boy and I can make my own decisions," he paused then added, "Though it is touching of you to care. Seriously though if I can help you, Cheryl you know I will."

"I know, but you can't. Daddy wouldn't believe you any more than he would me, even though he does have great respect for you."

"Really, I hadn't noticed," Lamont said, beaming beneath his cool exterior.

"I have," she looked into his eyes and continued, "but forget it, I got to make him believe me."

"So there really is a friend?" Lamont asked, taking a bite from his steak.

"Of course there is. Why would I make that up? Daddy would give me money if I ask. I don't have to make up stories to get money," she said, with an annoyed half scowl.

93

"Hey don't bite my head off. I'm just trying to get the facts. Jake is the one who doesn't believe you, I'm keeping an open mind." After a brief silence Lamont said, "Do you really think he would listen to me though?"

"Lamont, just forget it okay? I said I'll find a way and I will." She gave him a hopeful expression suddenly. Still it wouldn't hurt if you were an ally."

"What good is just being an ally if I can't help? You must see something that I don't."

"Believe me, the more I think about it, the more that I think he would listen to you. And not just because he's grateful for what you did to save JJ. Even though you could use that to help persuade him too." She stopped abruptly, detecting a disapproving look from him. "You think I'm a bitch to think about using something like that for leverage don't you?"

"Like I said Cheryl, I'm not judging you."

"Yeah you say that, but," she paused briefly. "I don't mean to be selfish or sneaky; it's just that I want desperately to help my friend."

"I understand, believe me," Lamont said, rubbing his chin. "I only wish that I could believe that Jake thought as much of me as you seemed to think. If that was the case, I'd be glad to help," he said looking into her sad eyes. He sensed that she wasn't as tough as she pretended to be. She played hardball but she was just a Barbie doll.

"Well, I ain't frettin' it no more," she said digging into her salad now. "This is good," she said ready to change the subject.

Lamont wasn't ready to drop it because he wanted to help. "Mind if I ask how much she needs?"

"Seventy-five thousand."

"That's quite a sum."

"Yeah but it's nothing to daddy, as long as he doesn't thinks it's for a shopping spree. I guess I can't blame him."

"I got to admit that I have heard about your legendary shopping campaigns, but I believe that it's different this time."

"Thanks for the vote of confidence anyway," she said without emotion.

Lamont watched as she dug into the salad. In spite of his limited personal knowledge about her, he instinctively believed her. "Ask him again, Cheryl and tell him the whole story."

"I plan to, but I don't think it's going to matter. Knowing daddy he'll probably give me a couple of thousand, thinking that would soothe my shopping fever, as he calls it. Don't you think it's funny that the one time I want to be unselfish, I can't?"

"This is the only time huh?"

"What?" She realized that he was joking. "Shut up," she said clinching her teeth and playfully pointing the fork at him, "or I'm gonna stick this fork between your eyes, Mr. Smart ass." They both laughed and momentarily the tension was erased.

Lamont pursued the subject once more. "Cheryl is it urgent that you have that amount or could?"

"Yeah, it is," Cheryl interrupted. "She needs it for the contractor. It's a long story but she had a fire and she needs to rebuild. She got me out of a jam once, and if I had the money I'd give it to her. But I don't, and she might lose her business."

"She has a business?"

"Yeah. Well not now. She had a business. It got burned to the ground."

"That's different Cheryl," Lamont said half smiling.

"What?" Cheryl stopped eating and stared at him now. "How is that different?"

Lamont was focusing in some middle distance deep in thought. "Maybe I can help you after all. I think that there might be something that we can do to help your friend."

"Really," she said smiling. "What, how?"

"Don't worry about that. Just tell me the details, I have an idea."

"Lamont don't bullshit me about this," she said with in an elated vibrating voice, then anxiously explained the situation in detail. However she purposely left out one particular important fact because she knew that it would possibly ruin any chance of getting the money.

She knew that eventually all the facts would have to be revealed, but if she could postpone it long enough, maybe that revelation won't affect the loan. Timing was everything and right now wasn't the time. That one detail had to remain undisclosed, while she waited for Lamont to talk to Jake and get back to her like he promised. Cheryl left the restaurant feeling overwhelmed, empowered and hopeful; thinking that having a smart big brother was shaping up to be a good thing right now.

Chapter Fourteen-
The Split

Lamont had planned to catch Jake and plead his case for Cheryl, but Jake had meetings with politicians and CEO's and was not available except for emergencies. He made plans to catch up with Jake the next day so he could pitch his idea about Cheryl's friend.

Jane had called and asked him to meet her at the station. "Lamont honey do me a big favor and you won't be sorry," Jane cooed from her end.

"Who do you want me to kill," Lamont joked.

"Nobody right now, but I'll take a rain check. Anyway I'm having some work done on my car, so I need a ride."

Later Lamont left the office and went to pick up Jane at the television station. He smiled, remembering the wild sex between Jane and himself that morning. He spent last night at her place and he would spend tonight there as well. Even thinking about her right now brought on a craving for intimacy with her. They had been spending more time together since she returned from Atlanta.

Lately she had been so attentive and concerned that he was ready to accept her as his soul mate. He had to stop worrying about impending doom and start encouraging the positive. He had positive memories of Jane's first time visiting the Center. They had been drawn to each other. She had been there to do a feature on the homeless, but she had switched her interest to him.

They flirted overtly, which led to their dating and eventually their engagement. That was over a year ago, and he had just about convinced himself that it would be hard to find a better mate. She was smart, gorgeous, ambitious, and classy. With all those positive traits, there was no way that marrying her was not the right thing to do. He was getting over his doubts and starting to accept the idea of being with Jane for a long time.

Lamont arrived at the television station, parked the car, and walked inside to the huge lobby, beaming prideful and slowly scanning for Jane. He spotted her standing in the doorway, wearing a form fitting burgundy dress and four inch black pumps. He was pleasantly stunned at how gorgeous Jane looked, but then again she was a television personality who got paid to look good. Their eyes met and they both smiled instantly.

His smile lingered and she moved closer and kissed him quickly casting stolen glances for any witnesses. Lamont had long ago accepted the fact that Jane liked to show off. Now she pretended to protect him from the girls who stood watching. Lamont thought that it was strange how Jane's co workers treated the two of them as if they were red carpet celebrities.

"Get back bitches," Jane said playfully, "he's taken, so keep your slutty paws off." Lamont thought it was strange that Jane was so aggressive with co-workers. Maybe that was why Jane had very few girl friends. She turned now and gave Lamont a wink.

"Let's blow this pop stand, honey."

"Let's do it." Lamont replied and tried to walk swiftly towards the exit. Jane however purposely walked slow, and drank in all the attention she was getting. "Baby you look extra good today and these bitches can't take their eyes off us," Jane whispered as they moved to the exit. "This is so much fun, flaunting my handsome stud and making these bimbos jealous."

Later that night their intimacy reached new levels and Lamont cast aside all doubts. In the midst of their lovemaking, Lamont began to anticipate their wedding day, because at that moment she was the only prize that he wanted to hold forever. He planned to take off early the next day after his talk with Jake on Cheryl's behalf. Then he would spend the rest of the day with Jane.

However the next day he had to cancel his plans right after he spoke with Jake. Jake had asked him to work late with Peter and keep an eye on him. "He's going to make a slip sooner or later," Jake said, "and I want you to be on the scene to bust his ass. I know he's been working late and he's up to something."

Lamont dreaded the task of calling Jane with the bad news almost as much as he hated to miss being with her. Jane on the other hand took it quite well.

"Don't worry about it baby," she said good-naturedly. "Your sexual dues are paid up for at least one night so do what you gotta do, but don't make this a habit," she said with a chuckle.

Lamont was elated that she understood, but sad that he couldn't get next to her right now. His positive attitude about the upcoming marriage was reinforced by the sound of her voice. Maybe his fears and uncertainty had just been pre wedding jitters. He promised himself that he would think more positive and that he would have more confidence in her and this upcoming marriage. It would work itself out, he thought.

****

"I hate it when you lie to me, Gregory." Jane said, looking angrily over at Greg. She moved from the bed where he sat. "I can't believe you." She was gathering her things. "I only came over tonight because you insisted that you had something urgent to tell me. You had me worried and thinking that Lamont had busted us. Then you damn near rape me when I get here. All you wanted was a booty call and I told you to never do that. That's cheating, Greg. You know that. You had your time. Remember?"

"Well I'm not satisfied with my skimpy proportions of time." He made quote mark gestures with his hands. "It's not enough, and yes I cheated. Besides, you didn't put up much resistance. You weren't complaining a few minutes ago. Hell, you were moaning and groaning like you needed pain killers."

She gave him a pitying look. "Oh that's so damn clever, Greg," she said with a scowl and spit his name out as if it were a nasty piece of phlegm. "I can't believe you're so damn childish."

"Oh so suddenly I'm childish, huh? I guess that means you're gonna run to Monty Mont? I know he don't put it on you like I do. I know you and him don't have the same wild sex that we have." She dressed quickly, but made no comments. "So I guess you're not considering my earlier offer to eliminate Lamont from the picture?"

She sighed impatiently and shot him a contemptible glare. "Greg your demands are outrageous, silly and unattractive. Are you forgetting our arrangement?"

"I'm sick of hearing about that damn arrangement. I was hoping that you would forget that arrangement once we really started getting busy."

"We both agreed to those terms, and a deal is a deal," she said pulling on her panty hose and adjusting the tight skirt.

"Forget the deal. I want you Jane and you need me, not Lamont. You're too much of a bad girl for Lamont, but just bad enough for me. I know I'm a better lover than "Mr. Nice Guy or you wouldn't be cheating on him." He paused because Jane looked at him unimpressed.

"Greg you knew from the beginning that I was engaged to Lamont. You and I are just temporary."

"I know that, but things changed for me Jane."

"But not for me, Greg. I still feel the same way about Lamont.

His attitude changed suddenly. "How could you? Why can't we cancel that arrangement and just be together? You know you want to," he paused briefly then continued, "but I should have known that you were just a materialistic bitch. You'd sacrifice your personal feelings for money."

Suddenly she focused her full attention on him. "What are you talking about," she said pretending that she didn't understand his words.

"Cut the shit, Jane. You know exactly what I'm talking about. I know why you're so anxious to be with Lamont. I can read and do research too. You ain't the only one who can find out about people. I know Lamont's related to Jake Cooper that Millionaire that he went to work for. Looks like daddy is looking out for his boy."

Jane was stunned at first, but now her expression reflected indifference. "So you know. What do you plan to do about it?"

"I don't know."

"Expose me? That won't win you any points, that's for sure," she said dressing more quickly now. "If you did that, you could kiss all this goodbye," She said holding her arms out spread eagle.

"Baby, we've had some pretty wondrous times." He came closer and swiftly grabbed and held her tight, cupping her buttocks and attempting to kiss her. "Now I know you ain't gonna tell me that you don't get wet when I do all this."

"Greg, please." She pushed him away and gathered the rest of her things and quickly put them into her large handbag. "You need to brush your teeth."

"So now you can't stand me, since you got what you came for, huh?"

"What *I* came for? Listen to yourself," she said with an intolerant sigh and a look of disbelief. "First of all, Buddy Boy, you called me, and lied. And now you're sounding paranoid and that's unattractive."

"Well excuse me if I ain't cold blooded like you. I don't have a standby waiting for me. I was hoping that..."

"Come on Greg. You knew that I was with Lamont when we started this, remember? And since you know the whole story, why do you think that I would back out now that I'm engaged to be married to him? I thought you understood that sex was all we had between us. It doesn't mean anything, and you're free to be with someone else."

"Yeah but didn't you think that things might change and that somehow...."

"No, never. Understand that, Greg." She blamed herself for lacking the foresight to see that this might happen. What real man could give her up, and what could he look forward to after sharing her scorching passion? Still, that wasn't her problem because she sure wasn't going to give up Lamont for a few hours of passion with this pauper.

Lamont was the son of a millionaire, and that trumps studs even if Lamont was a dud in bed. Sure she knew the whole story about Lamont. She had found a story about Jake Cooper's illegitimate son, while doing unrelated research. Her curiosity led her to gather all available information about him. She knew all about his kidney, the white girl he had dated, and his murder trial.

Once she discovered that he worked at the local Outreach Center she had been determined to meet him face to face. Once she did, she became determined to marry him, and began setting her traps. Fooling men always came easy for her, because they all thought with their penis' and she was always willing to give them a nice warm place to think. She thanked God that she was pretty.

She wasn't angry that Lamont hadn't told her the whole story. She suspected that he wanted to be sure of her feelings before revealing his connection to impending wealth. Ironically, that worked in her favor because Lamont had no reason to suspect that she was after his money.

He had no idea that she knew about his connection to Jake Cooper, and she would pretend to be so surprised when he finally did tell her. Now she hoped that Greg would keep his mouth shut.

At thirty Jane was a year older than Lamont, and felt that Lamont was her timely pot of gold, and she would never give him up. Once she became Mrs. Lamont Savage, all her worries about the hustle and bustle of a busy career were over. She planned to resign as soon as she got married. She would get on the wealthy Mr. Jake Cooper's good side and call him Dad from the start.

Up to this point, Greg had been a delightful distraction who faithfully served her dark side, but she wasn't dumb enough to choose him over Lamont. She had little remorse about cheating because she believed that a woman with her sexual appetite required two men. How else could explore all sides of her self?

"So what about you and me?" Greg asked distantly.

She was annoyed at Greg's out of place, low pitch whine, which invaded her fantasy with a rude drone. She needed to get away from him before she blew her chances with Lamont. Suddenly her sympathy for Greg turned to impatience. "You and me? There is no you and me," she said, then after thinking briefly, "in fact, this arrangement must end. You've lost focus and we should chill for a while."

"No baby, don't say things like that," Greg said, with a panic expression. "Look, I got a little carried away, but I'm back now. I won't be a nuisance. You and Lamont belong together and I think…"

"Look, I'll call you okay?" She walked fast and stepped quickly out the door, and headed to the parking lot, not bothering to look back as she hurried down the steps from his apartment. Mild fear gripped her as she hurried to her car.

Greg called out desperately to her. "Jane! Wait, let's talk, please," he pleaded.

"Later, Greg. I'll call you," she said with a breathless sigh, starting the motor. Greg was near the car, moving closer and calling out to her as she pulled from the parking lot and onto the street. She realized that Greg Jones too volatile and she had to break up with him. Thank God she had seen the real Gregory Jones in time. He definitely wasn't the man he pretended to be, and she thanked God for Lamont. She would have to think twice before she dealt with Greg again.

Chapter Fifteen–
Brother Love

"Gotta run baby, please," Lamont said while trying to dress swiftly and keep Jane from undressing him at the same time. She was still on fire from the previous night, even though they had made love at her place until dawn.

"Lamont baby it was so nice to feel you all hard and throbbing deep inside me while the birds chirped outside the window this morning," Jane said, while moving to unbuttoned his shirt as fast as he could button it.

Lamont couldn't remember ever seeing her so excited after such an incredible night of sex. He hadn't done anything different, except finally tell her the story about his relationship to Jake Cooper, and how he had rescued JJ with a kidney transplant.

She had seemed surprised and impressed and secretly Lamont was glad that he had impressed her. She had gone a little overboard with her praises about his noble actions, and her comments made him feel warm inside. Still, she treated him like a hero because he had done the right thing, but he could take the good with the bad. Breaking the news to her seemed to stimulate her sexual appetite and she couldn't get enough of him. "Come on baby, let me go to work," he said trying to dodge her barrage of kisses.

"Oh yes, that's what I say too," she said, moving back a few inches and placing her hands on her hips. "Come on babee, and go to work on me," Jane uttered in a throaty groan. She gyrates her hips in a sensuous belly dance. "Want some?"

"You want me to get fired from my new job? If I stay here I'd need the whole day off."

"Oh ain't nobody gonna fire you, honey, you're family. You such a *tweet man, jes shu* are," her voice was seductive and breathy and she altered her speech to make sexy baby talk.

"I wouldn't count on that. Business is business. And you better cut that out." He looked playfully at her and pointed his finger as if he were warning her.

"Oh Just give mommy a quickie baby, you don't have to even do anything, just let me sit on..."

"Jane. No. I'm leaving. I'll see you when I get back." He kissed her quickly, keeping his crotch away from her, while grabbing his briefcase then dashing to the door. He glanced back and saw her standing there like a pouting sex doll, wearing his shirt over her shoulders, and nothing else underneath.

"Okay then. If you gotta go, you gotta go." She dropped the shirt from her shoulders and spun around slowly, to give him a full overall view of her curves as well as her neatly cropped patch of womanhood. "It'll be here waiting for you when you get back. Think about that today at the office."

"Uh uh uh," was all he managed to say, capturing the sight of her perfect silhouette in the doorway. As he headed to his car, the sight of Jane's perfect body lingered inside his head. He couldn't deny that she made his life less boring, and his excitement grew at the thought of her. He was sat in the car, adjusted his crotch and the steering wheel, and then started the engine. He found it hard to stop thinking about Jane and that body on the drive up to Richmond, but there were other problems that he needed to tackle today, so his thoughts shifted.

He had setup a business meeting between Cheryl, Jake and himself for this morning, but it wasn't just about business, it was also about family. Admittedly, he wanted to make a good impression and a difference by solving family problems. He still felt a need to prove that an illegitimate offspring had principles and good judgment.

If he was successful in helping Cheryl, it could be the solid beginning that he needed in his attempt to win them over. On the other hand, even if he didn't win them over, he felt obligated to help because he was the strongest sibling. He liked being the strong one because strength was something that the others lacked. Lamont secretly felt as if he needed to watch over his helpless siblings, but that was ridiculous. They were all grown ups and if Jake hadn't monitored them, then he certainly wasn't qualified. Perhaps Lamont wanted to think that they were all helpless. Then he would be validated as a stable big brother, something that suddenly longed to be. Logically it should work out because, being needed was as addictive to him as being needy was to them.

They were pitiful helpless victims enslaved and oblivious to logic and addicted to money. It was mostly Jakes fault, and he did own up to it. Yet, he continued to coddle them as if they were his pets, Lamont thought. Lamont didn't understand that kind of family relationship.

In spite of his recent acquired respect for Jake, Lamont knew that Jake had made them all soft, dependant, and ungrateful. Jake improved the quality of his children's lives, but he never spent enough quality time with them. He compensated by giving them extra spending money upon demand. Money thus became a token and a symbol of love and set the stage for a different family dynamic. Maybe he would never know the meaning of true family chemistry as the Coopers knew it. He could see how that had led to such shaky bonds between them.

Of course as an only child he had never experienced the complications of family chemistry. He felt some envy because they all failed to realize how fortunate they were. He, on the other hand, was Jake's only offspring who had ever tackled the world without a golden parachute, and his landing had not been so smooth: so maybe he was jealous. Maybe his pursuit to bond was a passion to live their life style and gain Jake's unconditional love as well. He wanted to be a part of that complicated chemical equation that was family, even though it was far from perfect. So yes, perhaps he envied his siblings.

Hopefully the meeting this morning might be the start of some type of family dynamic. He was here playing moderator between Cheryl and Jake. Cheryl had sounded nervous when he spoke with her earlier about the meeting in Jake's office at nine. Lamont didn't give her the details on the phone, but he assured her that he had worked out a deal with Jake.

Cheryl arrived five minutes early and approached Pam. "Hi Pam I'm here to see."

"Yes Ms. Cooper, they're waiting for you," Pam said and cast Cheryl a toothy smile.

"Thanks Pam," Cheryl said and strutted down the short corridor into Jake's office.

Jake halted his conversation with Lamont when Cheryl entered the office. "Hi, sweetheart, come on in."

Cheryl's brief tension eased up when she noticed Jake's light mood. "Hi, Daddy, Hi, Lamont." She sat next to Lamont in the empty chair facing the desk. She tried to read Lamont's face to get a sign of what was going on, but he stared at Jake now.

"Lamont told me about your problem and the unfortunate fire at your friends place," Jake said gazing at her straight on. "Sorry about my skepticism earlier. I'm delighted that you're willing to help a friend."

Cheryl made a little face and shrugged her shoulders. "Well…Uh.. you know." She was overwhelmed and seemed shy, which was shocking.

Jake paused briefly, giving them both a quick scan. "Lamont made a suggestion, which I have agreed to, but under certain conditions."

Cheryl fought back the urge to hurry him along, she had little patience, and waiting made her crazy. "Okay, go on. I'm listening, Daddy."

"Okay here's the deal, Cheryl. I'll loan your friend the money, but only if you guarantee repayment. From what Lamont tells me, that shouldn't be a problem."

"Oh that's no problem, Daddy. She's gonna be so happy."

"Wait, don't go making phone calls just yet," Jake cautioned. "I have some conditions to consider." He looked to Lamont. "Lamont thinks we should treat this as a business loan and I agree. We'll have your friend sign a special loan contract, with suitable and liberal terms. Lamont even agreed to CO-sign on the loan."

She looked at Lamont. "Lamont that's thoughtful of you, but I don't think you should…."

"Neither do I. That's why I came up with an alternate solution." Jake picked up the form and held it up. "That's why the loan will be in your friends name with you as the CO signer instead."

"Cosign?"

"Yes. Didn't you say that this friend promised to pay you back when her insurance kicked in?"

"Yes and I know she will, but you're making everything so."

"So business-like? Well guess what sweetheart, *it is business.*"

There was a brief awkward silence at first. "Cheryl, repayment doesn't even start until she collects the insurance money." Lamont broke the silence in the room. "Then she has the option of either, paying in full, making monthly payments, or paying off any part of it. That's not a problem is it?"

"No, of course not," Cheryl suddenly blurted out. "The contract isn't a problem. I'll take it over to her right away."

"Good, good. Now that's out of the way." Jake handed her a folder with the contract. The sooner you get this back to me the sooner she can get the money."

"So do you make out the check at that time or what?" Cheryl asked putting the folder inside her purse?"

"I make out the check after I get Lamont's report."

Cheryl looked betrayed as she looked from Lamont to Jake. "Lamont's Report? What report?"

"The report he's gonna make when he goes with you to meet this friend, and see pictures of the accessed damage."

"Daddy, you still don't trust me," Cheryl said with an impatient smirk.

"Don't be ridiculous, Cheryl, this isn't about you," Jake said with a no-nonsense wave of his hands. "This is business. If I'm gonna issue out funds I have to have a solid reason and paperwork. You would know that if you were in the business world."

Cheryl couldn't speak on this because she didn't know enough about business matters to comment either way, or even attempt an argument. She had no choice but to accept Jake's solution. "Okay, I'll call her and set up the meeting," she said, looking towards Lamont. "What's a good time for you Lamont?"

"Lunch time is always good," Lamont said. "I have to see if Peter can run the place without me," Lamont joked.

In spite of her earlier doubts, Cheryl left Jake's office feeling positive about finally being able to help Rasheena. This sensation was new, confusing, and different from her bad girl image. She couldn't remember ever having such a feeling and strangely it felt good. Maybe she never had this feeling because she never really helped anybody before. It surprised her that helping a friend could feel so good.

It was noon when Lamont entered the small Italian restaurant near the Cooper Building. He spotted Cheryl sitting alone, and hoped that she was telling the truth about her friend. There was no reason to suspect that she wasn't. Lamont wanted to trust her, but Jake had expressed some doubts when they spoke earlier. Jake still didn't trust her completely because she had burned him repeatedly. "I love her, Lamont, but she was born for trouble," Jake had blurted out.

Now Lamont went confidently to the table where Cheryl sat proudly with her chin held high in the air. "Hi Cheryl," he said as he sat glancing about. "Your friend's running late huh?"

"Hi, and she called me earlier, she had a flat, but she's on the way. Let's order," Cheryl said, absently. She wondered if this would be the right time to tell Lamont the whole story. What difference would it make anyway? Rasheena would pay the money back and that's all that should really matter. Still the facts would eventually come out once they started discussing details. That's when the location and the nature of Rasheena's club would have to be revealed. "Lamont I have to tell you something," Cheryl said, wringing her hands beneath the table.

Lamont cringed, anticipating from the tone of her voice that bad news was forthcoming. Was she about to tell him that it was all a lie and no one was coming to sign the papers? Will she confess that she wanted the money for her own personal use, mainly a shopping spree? "From the look on your face it's not good is it?" Lamont tried to lighten the mood while studying her face. Before Cheryl could speak, he saw her eyes suddenly divert to the entrance. Now his eyes followed her gaze and focused on the two gorgeous female figures coming towards them.

"We'll discuss this later, that's Rasheena in the pink dress."

"So is the one in green her lawyer?" Lamont joked, but he wasn't laughing. He had a strange feeling about this meeting and Cheryl's two supermodel types.

"She's a good friend, Regina, I think," Cheryl said, not wanting to seem familiar. This was because Regina was an exotic dancer who performs at Rasheena's club. She had attended the club that catered to gay clientele but at the time she had her own reasons. She definitely wasn't gay herself. However, she wasn't about to run down details from her past. She only hoped that the nature of Rasheena's clientele wouldn't affect this deal. She would know once Lamont noticed the location of the club, but she couldn't think about that now.

"Well we're about to find out," Lamont said, watching the two women's runway strides. They looked delicate and ladylike, and at the same time, bizarre and off beat. He noticed now that Cheryl seemed like a scared little girl, and she wasn't the timid type. He shrugged off his feeling of discomfort, and assured himself that Cheryl wouldn't be a party to anything shady.

Yet, his instincts said that some mutual secret existed between the three of them. Was Cheryl telling him everything? He took a deep breath and greeted the two ladies with a smile. They were poised and graceful, but he sensed something peculiar, and his interest was aroused.

Chapter Sixteen-
Summit

Rasheena and her companion, Regina arrived at the large table stylishly dressed and smiling radiantly. After a brief greeting the two ladies took a seat at the table. Lamont felt as if he were sitting with high fashion models because the two women were wearing expensive clothes and jewelry.

Rasheena was dressed in a smart short, tasteful pink dress, four inch matching heels and a short black leather blazer. Her red hair was tied back in a huge pony tail, exposing ceramic pink ear rings. Regina wore a short green dress and black four inch pumps that gave her legs an exquisite shapely look. Around her neck was a gold necklace that matched her gold earrings. Her Ash blonde hair was short, hanging evenly around her neck, framing her face and giving her green eyes a three dimensional effect. The touch of a subtle side bang accented her face, and gave her sculpted shape chin dramatic flair.

"Cheryl, good to see you, girl," Rasheena declared. "You look great," Rasheena said, focusing her eyes on Lamont, and smiling warmly from across the table.

"Thanks, honey, you too. This is my brother Lamont. He's here to oversee the agreement that I told you about. Sorry about all the business stuff..."

"Girl, there's nothing to apologize about. It makes sense and I'm thankful that you can help me out." After a pause, Rasheena made introductions. "This is my good friend and business associate Regina Drake. Regina, Cheryl Arm...Oops sorry. Cooper now I guess?"

"Yes," Cheryl said.

Rasheena continued. "Cheryl Cooper and," she said pausing, and then asked, "Lamont Cooper?"

"No. Actually it's Savage," Lamont said without emotion.

"Sorry. I'll just stay away from last names then." She joked.

"Don't worry about it." Lamont smiled cordially.

"Regina is going to be my witness. That's all right isn't it?

"Yes that's fine." Lamont nodded. I have no problem with you having your witness here. In fact it shows sound business sense."

"Regina was thinking about opening up her own place and she's trying to get the hang of it," Rasheena added.

"Okay then let me show you the contract," Lamont said, getting back to business, anxious to end this meeting. "We ordered already, would you like something," Lamont said, smiling cordially still.

"No we ate earlier and we have another stop to make so we won't be here long," Rasheena said.

Lamont notice that Regina seemed to fidget when he spoke and he wondered if she was high on something. "Okay then," Lamont began. "I guess we can get this business out of the way. I just wanted to ask you a few questions."

"Sure go ahead, Honey," Rasheena said, then caught herself. "Sorry, I meant Mr. Savage." She smiled nervously, biting gently on her lower lip.

"No problem," he said with a smile. "Did you bring those pictures of the damage, and the contractor's estimates," Lamont said.

"Right here," she said, and took papers and pictures from her large bag."

Cheryl listened but she wasn't paying much attention to what was being said. She suddenly felt trapped because of her own dishonesty. Now that he knew the location of the club and had seen Rasheena and Regina close up, she wondered if he had guessed that the two women were really Transsexual. She dreaded telling him that Rasheena's club was the Joy House, a popular gay and transgender bar, because it might kill the deal.

These two gorgeous and convincing transsexuals easily passed for women, even in broad daylight, so maybe he wouldn't notice, she thought. Neither of them had a hint of chin hair or an Adam's apple. Still, as convincing as they are, she had to tell Lamont the truth, because he had trusted her. Besides he was very observant and from what she could see, he already seemed suspicious.

Presently, Lamont sensed Regina's eyes slyly watching him through her dark glasses, and he felt uncomfortable. A strange gnawing sensation grew stronger, and he believed that an invisible mishap was in the making here. These ladies were too flawless, almost like two actresses, playing a part.

He realized now that they might be on their best behavior to impress him or to get something from him. They saw him as an executive and had become obliging sycophants. They didn't have to put on a dog and pony show for him, just to prove that they were upstanding citizens. All Rasheena had to do was answer his questions honestly and tone down that show girl look. As a real executive, he would likely see much more of such behavior, and the thought of people kissing his ass made him uncomfortable. Now he could imagined how Jake felt

Lamont handed Rasheena a pen and refocused on the business at hand. "If you'll just sign right there on the lines underneath Cheryl's name and write in your bank account number, you can get Regina to witness it and we have a deal."

Rasheena briefly scanned over the document and quickly complied. She looked to Lamont. "How soon will the money be coming Mr. Savage.?"

"I'll give the info and pictures to Jake and he'll transfer the funds to the bank account number you listed here. More than likely you can start writing checks today, no later than tomorrow for sure, but don't do anything until you hear from Cheryl or me."

She stood, smiling brilliantly, obviously very pleased. "Okay then I'm gonna talk to my contractor first thing in the morning." She directed a warm smile to Lamont. "Thank you so much for everything Mr. Savage. You saved my life, you and Cheryl."

"Hey, no problem," Lamont said to Rasheena. Now as the two walked away, he caught the quick look Regina shot him. There was no mistake that she was sending him signals. Regina and Rasheena were attractive, yet strangely he continued to feel a mysterious anxiety.

Cheryl stared at the exit after the two left and now she and Lamont were alone at the table now. "Lamont, I was being a coward before," Cheryl started. "I'm sorry, but I got to tell you something about Rasheena."

"Okay," Lamont said and shot her a curious expression.

"Well she's not what you think she is. Actually neither one of them is."

"They're not business women?"

"Yeah, they're business but," she started.

"She's a stripper, right," Lamont interrupted. "Of course, that club is a strip club."

"No. Let me finish a sentence without an interruption please."

"Okay, you got my attention. So speak," he said staring at her now.

"Damn, you're gonna be pissed, but there's something you should know." She sighed deeply then spoke fast. "Rasheena and Regina are not females, they're transsexuals."

"Rasheena is a," Lamont couldn't finish the sentence. "I knew something was strange, I just couldn't figure it out," he said. "That explains that glamour girl makeup."

"Don't be mean, Lamont," Cheryl said. She felt bad enough thinking that she had to chose between betraying her friend, or her family. However since her father was putting up the money, he needed all the facts. "Rasheena was born a man, or at least with male parts. She says she never felt like a man and you can guess the rest." Cheryl gave Lamont a hard scrutinizing stare. "What are you going to do?" She couldn't read anything from Lamont's facial expression. "Is this going to change anything?"

Lamont sighed deeply. "I don't know," he said, looking directly into her eyes. "What else do I need to know?"

"What do you mean?"

"Is there really a club?"

"Yes of course there is. Everything I told you is true; it's just that I didn't tell you everything from the beginning. It's one of the few gay clubs in the area with good decent clientele.

"So it is a gay club?

"Yes couldn't you tell from the location?"

"Not really, I'm not that familiar with the city just yet." He caught her eyes and looked directly into them. "You've been there haven't you, Cheryl?"

"Yes, I've been there." Cheryl seemed angry. "But that doesn't mean I'm gay. Lots of people hang out there, not just gays."

"I'm not saying you're gay. Of course you're not gay. But that bar does cater to the gay community, right?"

"Well. Yes but..."

"Then the answer to your question is yes, this will change things, Cheryl."

"What? I can't believe this is coming from you Lamont. You're acting more like daddy everyday. I shouldn't have told you. I thought you would be fair."

"I am. That's not what I'm saying, Cheryl." He looked into her eyes. "Answer this for me, Cheryl. That fire. It was arson wasn't it?"

"Yeah, how did you kno....."

"I just assumed," he said interrupting her. "See, the fact that the club was deliberately burned down is an issue, and that's what changes things. No matter how Jake or I feel about gays personally, the fact remains that many people are offended enough to commit violence, such as gay bashing and arson."

"So what are you saying? She shouldn't get the money because of gay bashers?"

"You're missing the point Cheryl."

"Oh excuse me mister big business man, just what is it that ole thick head Shopping-Spree-Cheryl is failing to grasp?" Her voice reflected more pain than anger.

"Calm down will you? Don't go getting bent outta shape. I am on your side. But what I'm saying is that the risks are greater now. What if there are delays in construction because of harassment or injuries caused by gay bashers? What if the same arsonist repeats his performance once the club is up? There are a lot of variables to consider now."

Cheryl's anger cooled somewhat and she listened to what he was saying. She actually hadn't considered the points he was making.

"Right now the loan is scheduled to start one of three repayment plans when the club re-opens. What if the re-opening is delayed or if it never happens? Should Jake then be obligated to continue financing in order to get his money back? Should Jake call for repayment and harass her for the money, or just write it off as uncollectible? In which case everybody loses."

As much as she hated to admit it, Lamont made a good argument. "Oh Lamont she helped me out of a jam and I want to do this. What are you going to tell daddy?"

Cheryl's eyes were sad and Lamont felt terrible. He wanted to help his sister, but these developments were about to derail his good intentions. How could he not tell Jake? It would be unsound to ignore the facts and hope that things turned out for the best. "I can't see telling him anything less than the truth Cheryl. What do you suggest?"

"Couldn't we just loan her the money? I know she'll pay it back and it's possible that the arsonist has moved on."

"And what if he hasn't?"

"God, Lamont there's got to be some way to help her. She's making an honest living in the only way that she can, and some scumbag wants to deny her that. Are we going to deny her that too?"

Lamont knew that Cheryl meant well and frankly he was surprised at her compassion. He thought that maybe all of those unpleasant things that he had heard about her were just rumors. Still, he didn't have the authority to make the call. He didn't see any reason not to tell Jake. "I'm sorry, Cheryl."

"Lamont, please. I know you don't owe me anything and I shouldn't expect anything, but I promised her and now if we back out, she's gonna think I'm just a flake. She's certain that she will be getting the insurance money once this investigation is over."

"I tell you what Cheryl, let me sleep on it. I won't talk to Jake today, maybe we could come up with something. I don't know, maybe you're right and nothing would happen during the construction, but I have to look out for Jake's interest and do the logical thing. But, again, I will sleep on it."

Cheryl wasn't happy with this but she had to accept it. She couldn't come up with a solution and she sensed that Lamont wasn't anxious to help Rasheena, now that he knew the truth. "Okay then. Sleep on it," she said with little enthusiasm, feeling sure that he wouldn't make an honest effort.

She felt a bit disappointed in him now she expected more from him, because he was so strong and different. She had learn to respect and care about him, not because she felt any obligations to him, but because of his personality and strength.

Still, even the good guys sometimes fell short, and she couldn't blame him for being human. It was silly of her to look for a hero these days because there weren't any left. Yet she had seen something of a hero's quality in him. Of course she never expected him to epitomized good spirit and fairness, and certain expectations were unreasonable and idealistic. "Okay then, I guess we're done here." She said, with slightly teary eyes.

Lamont stood and reached for his brief case. "Don't worry, Sis, I won't abandon you. I'll do what I can, and don't think that I won't try just because of who and what they are. I admit I'm not comfortable with them, but no one has the right to judge them or prescribe punishment strictly because of what they are.

"I see this as your problem, not theirs. And since this is your problem, than it's my problem too. Believe me I will do what's necessary to find a solution." He looked deeply into her eyes. "Do you believe me Cheryl?"

She returned his intense look now and saw something in his demeanor that renewed her confidence. She smiled in spite of the pressure and distress she felt. "Yes Lamont. Strangely, I believe that you will honestly try to come up with something. I don't know why I believe it or how you can do it, but I do believe you."

Good." He said, and then kissed her quickly on the forehead. I'm gonna cancel my order and get back, I'll have something later." He stood and headed for the exit. "Hope you got your umbrella. Looks like rain"

Later that day Lamont gave Cheryl a call on her cell phone. "Okay, Cheryl, everything is set so tell your friend that the money is in the account and she can write checks to the contractors," Lamont said into the telephone receiver.

On the other end Cheryl was filled with glee as she replied. "Oh thanks Lamont, what did you do? How did you talk daddy into it? Oh never mind all that tell me later. Thanks again Lamont, I'm going to call Rasheena and tell her the good news. And believe me you won't be sorry."

"I hope not. I'm kinda sticking my neck out, but I trust you."

"Nothing is going to go wrong. Thanks Lamont, you're the best. I haven't told you this before, but I'm kinda glad to have a big brother. Especially when he is such a genius. Thanks again and bye. Love ya." The phone went dead.

After hanging up, Lamont believed that he had made a break-through with Cheryl. He was sure that she meant what she said, and he liked the sound of *big brother*. The only flaw in his plan was that he had just crossed a line to be a big brother. Had he gone above and beyond reason for the sake of bonding? Probably, but it didn't matter because his sense of obligation to his siblings somehow trumped all boundaries.

He had made the decision not to tell Jake that Cheryl's friend Rasheena was a Trannie freak, even though, technically she was male, according to Cheryl. He wasn't about to ponder about how she even knew for sure, but he believed that Cheryl knew all the details. More importantly Cheryl had been so sincere about helping Rasheena that he believed everything would work out.

He thought about Rasheena and realized that she had seemed honest and would fulfill her obligations. Still it didn't change the fact that he had hid the truth from Jake. Now his main salvation would be that Rasheena was as reliable as Cheryl thought. He prayed that no unforeseen misfortunes occurred, like some gay basher burning down the place again.

Lamont left the office that evening with doubts aside as he walked to his car. He felt elated that he was resourceful enough to help Cheryl, who seemed to be a perpetual damsel in distress. He had the feeling that this wouldn't be the last time that Cheryl would need to be rescued. He didn't mind helping her but he wasn't about to be on constant standby for her random calls of distress.

Chapter Seventeen-
All aboard

Jane sat on the bed, listening to the running shower, touching herself and wondering what had come over Lamont. She liked whatever it was that brought out his extra horny hunger. He had just about torn off her clothes last night before he ravished her. He had been extra good, she thought. Maybe this new apartment was enchanted and had changed him into a new man. If so, that would make it easy to get him to do some of the freaky things that Greg did.

Greg had called her just yesterday and apologized, and sent a nice bouquet of flowers to her at the station. She had told him that she would think about getting with him again, but Lamont was so attentive that she had second thoughts about cheating on him. If Lamont continued to be so horny, she would say goodbye to that loser, Greg.

She needed to slow things down with him anyway, especially after that scene the other night. He was a loose cannon and she no longer trusted him. She hoped that he wouldn't make trouble for her. Greg had his uses, but even though she was a glutton for sex, there was still that issue of trust between them. She would have to make a decision about him soon.

She would certainly have to play house and be faithful for a while once she and Lamont were married. Once she became a part of the Cooper clan, no one could interfere with her becoming an heiress. God, she loved the way that sounded. She told herself that she was marrying a millionaire, even though she knew that wasn't the case. It didn't matter though because Lamont was a potential Millionaire as long as he was connected to the Coopers. Lamont would eventually become a multimillionaire because he was Jake Cooper's son, and sooner or later Jake Cooper would die.

The idea of being married to a millionaire fascinated her and she equated it to being royalty, which meant saying good bye to her career. A millionaire's wife wouldn't need a personal career because of all the many social obligations. There would be pressing charity events, dinner parties, and even political rallies to attend or host. Perhaps Lamont could run for president some day, since Senator Obama has opened the door and just become the first black president. The image of it made her heart skip. "That would make me the first lady," she murmured loudly.

Lamont had stepped out the shower and had entered the bedroom. "Talking to yourself again," Lamont said, pulling his underwear from the bureau drawer.

"Of course, I wanted to talk to some one intelligent," she teased and moved to kiss him.

"You trying to start something again," He said, covering her with baby kisses.

"Maybe."

Lamont reveled in the taste of her and considered himself a lucky man. The past few weeks, Jane had spent a great deal more time with him; she even drove to Richmond two times a week to be with him. He was sure that she cared about him, and it never crossed his mind that she could be a very shrewd and clever gold digger. His doubts about marriage were fading fast and he was convinced that Jane would be a great wife. Her overall comportment was tailor made to fit with his new family.

He would know for sure if she fit in soon, because Jake had invited the whole family to a dinner party next weekend. Jane had even rearranged her scheduled and promised to attend. He was anxious for her to meet the family and he was certain that she would make him proud. She wasn't just pretty, she had style and class, and he would be spending his future with her.

Later that day Jane had gone shopping for the perfect dress to wear. She felt excited and eager to impress the Coopers. Lamont told her that she didn't have to buy any new clothes for the occasion, but that was a waste of breath. Jane had already made plans to buy a special dress just for the occasion. Frankly he wanted her to look extra special, and he wanted every one to see his soul mate sparkle.

While Jane shopped, Lamont went to visit his mother and to run some job related errands. His new job and his time spent with Jane prevented him from visiting as often as he liked. He planned to remedy that situation and he wasn't going to let anything prevent that from happening in the future.

Myra always complained that he was neglecting her, but he did call her twice a week. Myra was just nosey and wanted to be kept in the information loop. She constantly asked a million questions about everything from Jane to Jake. Mainly she was concerned with Lamont setting a date for the wedding.

Myra had met Jane for the first time six months ago, when Lamont had taken them both to dinner. Myra's reception to Jane was cool and civilized, and she told Lamont frankly that she saw Jane as very pretty, but phony. "I can live with your decision, son," she had said upon meeting Jane. "At least she's black and you won't have the kind of trouble you had with that Felicia girl."

Lamont followed through and had a long visit with his mother. They never talked much about his childhood because Myra had told so many lies about his father. The biggest lie had been that his father was dead. He had been more than upset with her when he discovered that she had lied.

Still he had gotten over it. She was human and he forgave her, but it would be a while before he would trust her one hundred percent again.

Their visit was cordial and friendly, and they talk about his job and her church briefly. She fixed him a bowl of her left over home made soup even though he said he wasn't hungry. Lamont almost mentioned the upcoming dinner party at Jake's, but realized that would be a mistake. Myra would want to be included in Cooper clan's activities because she was his mother. More than likely she would want him to try to make that happen. Lamont had no control of Jake's dinner guest list and he planned to keep it that way. Lamont did wonder where she would fit in if he bonded with the Coopers. Surely she would have to be invited from time to time.

She constantly inquired about the family, and had suggested that Lamont find her a job at the company. "I know you could find some work for your momma, Son. I could be an assistant, I know," She had insisted.

"I'm just an employee there Mom, I can't hire or fire anybody," Lamont lied. Coincidentally, he convinced Jake that allowing him to have extra help would further avert suspicions about his real purpose. No culprit would even consider a pampered brat as a threat. That's why Jake had authorized him to hire two personal assistants. He decided on Marcia and Hal, which was the other reason that he had come to Norfolk today.

Even if he was authorized to open another position, Lamont knew that it wasn't a good idea to hire Myra. The last thing he needed to further complicate matters was to have his unskilled mother working for him.

He understood that she was bored and wanted to work, but she didn't need money. Thanks to Jake, Myra was in a better financial situation than she had ever been. Jake had set her up with a profitable stock portfolio, which had grown exponentially in a short time. Even with the stock mess that's going on right now, she never had to work again because of Jake's astute knowledge of investments. That didn't matter because the life of leisure was not for Myra Burns. In spite of her new found modest wealth and free time, Myra was bored with church and shopping.

He hated lying to her, but Lamont wasn't going to be persuaded to help her get a position in Cooper industry. He didn't want to get into a long winded debated with her, so he lied. "I'll try, Mom," He said, feeling like a hypocrite, but it was for the best.

Soon after leaving his mother, Lamont, met with Hal at Eddies where they shot a few games of pool, and Lamont offered him the job as personal assistant. Hal agreed right away. "Hell, yeah. I appreciate you looking out for me. Sign me up, Man. I can quit this damn security gig rat now," Hal said enthusiastically.

Lamont shot a few games of pool, but left Hal a short time later, to contact Marcia. It had been weeks since he started working at Cooper Industries, and he failed to follow through on his promise to have lunch with her once a week.

He dialed his cell phone and listens. Marcia picked up on the second ring. "Hi Marcia, it's me, Lamont," he said feeling awkward and apologetic

She was silent briefly. "Lamont," Marcia said, revealing her excitement. "Well hello stranger. I thought you had forgotten about us poor folks," she said elated. "Thought you had gotten all uppity on me."

"No, Marsh. That ain't' me and you know it. I ain't never gon be uppity. And I'd never get so uppity that I could forget you. I know I owe you a lunch or two, and I didn't forget."

"Well you better not. And it's thirty lunches and counting."

"I know and I'm sorry. It's just that you wouldn't believe how fast time can fly by when you're buried in work."

"Tell me about it. I'm still trying to get around to sending out my resumes."

"Perfect, then you *are* looking for another job," he said with a sigh. "Marsh I know this is short notice but would you like to go for an early dinner? I'd like to discuss something with you. Are you hungry?"

Marcia wanted to play hard to get, and tell him that he couldn't just call her randomly and expect her to be available. Instead her pride faded and she felt anxious to spend time with him. "Sure, I could eat." Lamont said that he'd be there in twenty minutes.

She showered quickly, combed and brushed her hair until she was satisfied, then applied a little make up. She wiggled into the plain black dress. "Can't go wrong with black, "she mumbled excitedly to herself. She slid her feet into on a pair of three inch heels, and added pearl ear rings and a necklace. She stood before the mirror smiling with pleasure at her figure in the short dress, which exposed her shapely legs.

She looked okay, but she knew that she had to buy some new clothes. Her social life was a dull routine that she didn't think about shopping these days. Her whole existence boiled down to work, prime time television, and playing a weekly card game with her neighbors.

She wondered why Lamont wasn't with Jane tonight. Had he found out about her? That would be too good to be true. Jane was too slick and she had a strong hold on him. If he didn't discover her cheating, they would be married soon.

The doorbell chimed and Marcia suddenly felt nervous. She hadn't seen Lamont in weeks. She opened the door and her eyes met his warm smile, and her spirits soared. "Hi Lamont." Did she sound too cheery? Was that good? Maybe she should tone down her excitement. She had to stop second guessing herself.

"Hey, Marsh." He looked her up and down and gave a wolf whistle and two thumbs up. "Looking good. And smelling so sweet. Yummy." He teased.

"Shut up. I just put something together at the last minute. So stop it." She felt uncomfortable, and blushed slightly.

"Look at you, acting all shy," Lamont said, and smiled with amusement at her reactions. He saw something different about her and he stared boldly. She looked so fresh and different and he realized that he missed her more than he thought he would.

"Oh stop teasing," she said, scanning him quickly and admiring his casual look. He was dressed in pressed khaki pants and dress shirt. "Would you like to come in and have a drink?"

"Would you mind if we hold off on the drink until we got to the restaurant?"

"Yeah, okay, "she said with a pause then added, "I'm sure Jane will be expecting you."

"No, not tonight. It's just that I want to run something by you. We can always come back here later and chat some more if you're not too tired. I know you're doing all the work and running the Center even though Greg is in charge."

"You know it," she said."

"I know lot of things."

She wanted to say something about Jane now, but her response would be untimely and unpleasant. Lamont helped her into her jacket and his closeness unsettled her. "I hope Jane doesn't get mad at me for taking you away from her tonight," she said, fishing for information.

"We've been spending lots of time together so she won't mind."

"Oh, so I'm just your standby."

"No, of course not. I wanted to ask you about a business matter and I did promise to keep in touch when I left, so I decided to..."

"To kill two birds with one stone." She finished his sentence. "Gee that's flattering. How large is that stone," she said sarcastically.

"Sorry." He shrugged his shoulders. "I didn't mean to be insensitive."

"Oh Lamont I'm teasing, don't be so serious. I know the deal with you and Jane," she said aloud. Unfortunately you don't know the whole deal with Jane, she thought to herself.

Thirty minutes later they arrived at the Steak House restaurant and ordered. They had a cocktail while they waited for their order to come. They joked about the center, Lamont's job, and what the future might hold. Lamont realized that he felt light hearted for the first time in weeks. He was enjoying Marcia's company so much that he almost forgot to make the job offer. Finally, he got around to asking her to come to work for him at Cooper Industries.

When she heard the words she couldn't contain her emotions, or pretend that it didn't matter. "Really? Are you really offering me a job at?" She paused and took a breath. "Can you do that?" She gave him an inquisitive look. "You can hire people?" She asked him with a wild skeptical look. "But you just started and.."

"Marsh, I wouldn't lie about something like this. Trust me I can do this. Why else would I be making you an offer?"

"I know," she said with a nod. "It's just that." She failed to finish a sentence and Lamont smiled. She seemed very pleased right now and strangely, he was pleased even more.

"In fact it's already been Okayed. I just needed to see if you were interested."

"Of course I'm interested you silly man."

"Good. Welcome aboard."

"You're sure that I'm gonna be on the payroll," she said, still unsure if this was real.

Lamont sighed. "Marsh, you don't trust me?"

Of course I trust you, I trust you more than I trust anybody." She cursed herself silently. What was she ten years old?

Lamont trusted her too, and he wanted to tell her that Jake Cooper was his father, and had granted him privileges. Now that he thought about it, he had been wrong to think that Jake wasn't treating him special. He decided not to tell her anything about his relationship to Jake. She would find out about eventually anyway. He didn't see the harm in the slight omission of that information.

Secretly he didn't want her to think that he had changed, or that he was accepting favors from daddy. He would rather that she thought that he got the job because of his skills, although ironically, the job he was hire to do require no executive skills. It was a complicated mess and he wasn't about to confuse her with all the details.

"Okay then, Lamont, I'm your girl. For the job I mean," she amended

Her voice was soothing and he absorbed her radiant energy with a perpetual smile. "Marcia that's great. We're gonna give you a raise of five grand to start, that's more than the peanuts you're making now. From there it's gonna get better, I promise."

She hadn't even bothered to ask about the salary because she didn't care about the money. What mattered was that she would be working with him again. She scolded herself silently for clinging to this school girl like crush. She was a grown-up attractive and well educated woman, and her crush on Lamont was non progressive. Still she would welcome it if he tried to take advantage of her. Why didn't he try to take advantage of her? Maybe then she could take him off that pedestal and end her fatal crush on him.

Lamont laughed, joked and enjoyed Marcia's company tonight, and now he could plainly see that they had many things in common. Her presence at Cooper Industries was going to be a win-win situation for them both. However he felt some guilt about his actions, because he was playing his own little dangerous game. He hadn't meant to, but he wanted Marcia working with him. He had a vague internal compulsion to keep her near. She was a comfort zone and he needed her constant presence.

Still, it wasn't fair to her because he was taking advantage of her feelings for him. He knew that she was interested in being more than friends, and perhaps he had led her on. On the other hand should she be denied a better job, a better salary and better working conditions? After all it's just a harmless crush, not a fatal attraction.

He cast aside his reproach and concentrated on Marcia's refreshing attitude. She was constant fun, and in her company he felt various levels of contentment. Marcia cornered the market when it came to bubbly and sweetness, and he flirted in spite of himself. She was just too cute not to flirt with. Still he felt completely at ease in her presence. In contrast, Jane was serious most of the time, and her fun seemed to begin and end with sex.

In spite of her crush on Lamont, Marcia had never belittled or bad mouthed Jane in any way. Marcia was one of a kind and he recognized and respected her as a class act. She wasn't like those catty females, who resorted to tricks and lies to undermine relationships for their own selfish reasons. Thank God Marcia would never stoop that low.

Marcia's smile was contagious and rarely faded, and he had gotten used to seeing that fresh smile daily. Now that she would be working at CI, she would have even more reason to smile. He was sure that her emotions wouldn't disrupt any harmony between him and Jane. They had worked smoothly together before and he was sure that they could again. He was sure that Marcia hadn't changed.

However Marcia had changed because now she had first hand knowledge that could disrupt Lamont's relationship with Jane. It's true that she had never bad mouth Jane, but she had cursed Jane many times under her breath. Now she had the power to stop her ruthless cheating.

Normally, Marcia didn't like schemes or schemers, but sometimes necessities transformed motivation and changed personalities. She wasn't mean, vicious or diabolical, but she despised Jane, and ached to expose her. She couldn't expose Jane openly like she first wanted to do, because Lamont would question her motives. He would probably see her as a jealous scorned woman.

No, that wasn't the way to go. Instead, she would set the bitch up so that Lamont could discover everything for himself. That's the only way he would believe it. Jane had him blinded and lost with her phony actress bull. He couldn't discover the truth on his own, so she had to come to his rescue. She didn't know how she would do it, but she would make sure that Lamont found out about Jane before the wedding. It would hurt, and she hated that, but sometimes pain must come with truth.

Chapter Eighteen-
Family Affair

Lamont beamed with pride, while focusing on Jane's luscious curves and studying her arresting appearance. He smiles proudly, and quickly takes inventory of his luscious lady standing before the mirror. Jane was 5'7" with gorgeous long legs and caramel colored skin. Her dark green eyes set off her perfect arrow head nose and pouty lips. Her elongated face was fully surrounded by shoulder length strands of dark brown curly hair. He felt so fortunate because her intelligence, grooming, and confidence made her the perfect mate.

"You look awesome in that dress," Lamont said looking her up and down. "That green dress and those sexy shoes make my day, baby."

"Why thank you kind sir, you're sweet," Jane said playfully, smiling proudly. "I'm so excited and I want to make a good impression. I want you to be so proud of me," she said, still looking into the mirror checking herself out.

"I'm already proud of you, baby."

Shortly, they were on the road to the dinner party at Jake's place, and Jane snuggled up to him. "You smell so good and did I tell you that I love that suit? Burgundy and grey brings out your dreamy dark eyes, and your luscious lips makes you look like the worlds's greatest stud." She scanned him with a mischievous stare. "Looking at you right now turns me on. As a matter of fact, honey," she paused and ran her tongue across her lips.

Lamont recognized that expression. "Be serious, Baby, I'm driving. And what about your make up, and our clothes?"

She shook her head amused. "I'll be real careful. All you have to do is drive and let momma take care of you, Poppa. I need to taste you right now." She reached down and touched his crotch. "Just keep driving and let me do all the work, Baby."

Lamont felt her hands aggressively tugging at his zipper, as her head came towards his fly. "Jane, that's crazy. You'll ruin your make up."

"You said that already. I said I'd be careful," She said, continuing to grope at his penis.

"You're gonna make me have an accident. Besides we're almost there."

"I know, but I just want to feel you inside my mouth. Come on, sugar. Let your baby have a little taste. I'm salivating."

"No, Jane, that's too crazy, baby and like I said, we're almost there now. Let's not start something we can't finish." He reached down and forcefully removed her hand from his crotch and pushed it away. "Come on, Baby, I got to concentrate on driving. Stop being unreasonable and acting all crazy."

Her head popped upright and she wore an expression of indignation. "You're refusing me, Lamont?" She asked in an annoyed voice, two octaves higher than her normal low pitch sexual utterances.

"That's not refusing you baby, I'm just saying this is not the time or place. We'll be at Jake's place in fifteen minutes. I'll make it up to you later." He smiled cheerfully, thinking that his sound logic would diffuse her aggressive sexual appetite.

"Oh, I see," she said with icy anger. "So we can only do it when you want to." Her tone was uneven and irate. "Men are so damn selfish," she said almost under her breath but, loud enough to be heard. She slid across the seat to the other side, turned towards the window, and now rode in silence.

Lamont was puzzled as to why his gentle refusal had irritated her so much. "So now you're pissed at me? You think I'm being selfish?" Lamont was surprised that she chose to remain silent, and not respond, but frankly he had been more surprised by her bold insistence.

On the other hand perhaps he should have expected it since her sexual urges had become more energetic lately. She had even begun throwing hints about doing kinky stuff like tying her up and playing roles. It seemed that each day brought a new revelation to light, and now his old doubts were starting to resurface. Perhaps those doubts hadn't really been buried in the first place.

However, Lamont was relieved that Jane snapped out of her foul mood by the time they arrived at the Cooper estate. He wanted her to make a good impression and she certainly couldn't do that with an attitude. Now he wondered how this would go down and he was slightly nervous now.

The butler directed them into the huge parlor where Jake and the rest of the guest would be gathering. Jane seemed awed by the Cooper mansion, especially the huge bubble sky light in the foyer of the main entrance. Her gaze was almost trancelike as she scanned the highly polished floors, decorative interior, and original African art. There was a wide collection of various paintings, tribal African masks and various size sculptured pieces.

A quick tour of the Mansion revealed a variety of live exotic plants, a large heated pool, and a gigantic game and entertainment room. Jane observed the largest aquarium she had ever seen, with at least a thousand fish in the huge tank. Lamont notice how Jane was suddenly excited by all these material things and he pushed back the dark thoughts that persisted inside his head. Lamont wondered now if Jane had become star struck at the sight of Jake's abundance, and now wanted all these things herself. Would she insist that they too lived like this once they were married?

Lamont was humble and had no burning desire to live like this. Perhaps he just didn't know how to live like the rich. He sensed that Jane would try to push him to live like the Coopers. Her attitude was already similar to the Cooper women, and she probably wouldn't mind enjoying money that she hadn't earned. He had no problem enjoying whatever he had coming, but he wasn't going to start spending money on nonsense, just because it was there.

He saw Jake motion him over to where he stood talking to his guest. Now, Lamont and Jane joined the small gathering of people surrounding Jake. "Lamont," Jake said as he eyed Jane, shook hands with Lamont and gave him a quick hug. "You must be Jane? Welcome. Please to meet you." He smiled widely then added, "Lamont never told me he was dating a beauty queen. I hope that doesn't embarrass you," Jake said observing her expression.

Jane smiled. She liked him right away. "Thank you, Mister Cooper. I'm not embarrassed at all. And I'm pleased to meet you too." She offered her hand and he, shook it lightly, and then kissed her quickly on the cheek.

Jake turned to look over the small gathering surrounding him.

"Meet the rest of the clan. "Everybody!" Jake stood between Lamont and Jane waiting to get every one's attention. Now all eyes rested on him. "For those who don't know, this is my son, Lamont and his beautiful fiancée, Jane." Mostly it was family present, and Lamont had met every one except Preston's wife, and JJ's girlfriend. No one here had ever met Jane. The whole family had showed up tonight, but only Cheryl and Ruth showed up alone. Ann was escorted by her husband and JJ had a new girl tonight.

JJ approached and gave Lamont a brief hug, and Lamont got a close look at the young girl on his arm. The girl giggled at something JJ said, and Lamont wondered if the girl was still in grade school. "What's up, Bro?" JJ asked, with vigor, obviously he was high and so was the girl.

"Not much, Man," Lamont said reaching to hug his brother. They made introductions and now, Lamont noticed Candace, slowly gliding towards them wearing a large smile and a sexy strapless lavender gown. Her skin looked soft and edible and she was no doubt the star of this mansion. She came towards Lamont as swift and graceful as a top fashion model strutted down a runway. Candace kissed Lamont on the cheek before he realized that she had closed the gap between them.

"Hi, Lamont. Glad you were able to make it," she said in a jovial tone.

"Thanks. Glad I could too," Lamont said, awkwardly and quickly turned to Jane. "Candace, this is Jane, my fiancée."

Candace looked to Jane for the first time. "Hi Jane, so nice to meet you;" she said, flashing a radiant smile.

"Yeah you too," Jane said, through a thin phony smile, inching closer to Lamont.

Candice looked to Lamont. "Oh Lamont, she's a doll." She looked Jane in the eyes. "Lamont treating you right?" She slurred, giving Jane a wink, revealing long curly eyelashes.

Jane still wore her phony smile as she replied. "If he wasn't, he would be history," Jane said as she smiled tightly.

"Wow, now that's what I call confidence, girlfriend." Candace replied as she looked around with a searching motion. There was an awkward silence before she spoke again. "Well enjoy yourselves, I got to mingle and make sure every one is having fun," she said and glided away to fulfill her role as hostess.

Lamont watched Candace work the room with a radiant look and wearing that sexy form fitting gown. Briefly their eyes met from across the room, and vague unfulfilled hunger emerged within him. He still couldn't forget the night he met Candace, long before he knew about Jake or that she was his step mother. Guiltily he turned his attention and gaze to Jane and the guests in close proximity. He listened to their conversation, but didn't join in.

"She's pretty," Jane said mechanically, still eying Candace. "She's the same age as his daughters isn't she?"

"Yeah, I guess," Lamont said reluctantly. "I know what you're thinking," he said with an impatient sigh. "Let it go and just enjoy the party. We're not here to judge."

"I'm not; I'm just stating a fact, that's all. And from what I can see it's possible that she's with your father just for…"

"Jane please, will you skip it?" Lamont spoke through clenched teeth, suddenly annoyed with her.

"Why are you so defensive?" Jane asked, eying him suspiciously.

Lamont kept his composure. "I'm not. She's my dad's wife, and we're guests here. I'm gonna try and respect their hospitality and get along." Jane said nothing, but he felt her suspicious eyes on him. "Raymond," Lamont called out and signaled the butler over. He needed a strong drink right now even though he wasn't a drinker. The grey temple tall butler straightened his bow tie and moved towards them with a tray of drinks.

Now Jane sipped on her apple martini. "This is good. Just what I needed." She downed half of it. "And I got a feeling that I'm gonna need more," she whispered subtly.

Lamont tried to concentrate on Jane in an attempt to forget Candace Cooper. Jane was gorgeous and angelic at times, and she matched Candace's sexiness. "You know I think I need another drink too," he said, facing her with a warm smile.

She returned his smile and their earlier disagreement had passed. "Good." She quickly gulped down the rest of her drink and made a hand motion towards the butler. "Excuse me, Raymond!" The stiff butler turned with a nod and came to them instantly.

Jane felt tipsy and naughty after her third drink. "We're gonna have some fun when I get you alone later, big boy. I'm wet already just thinking about ways I'm gonna ravish you," she whispered with a naughty gesture of her tongue.

"You're nasty and I can't wait to get you alone and wrap you up," Lamont joked, feeling tipsy after having his third drink as well. He squeezed her buttocks. "Nice soft ass," he said with a goofy smile.

"So what's up, Bro," JJ's voice interrupted Lamont's lewd thoughts. He stood before Lamont and Jane leaning on his date with one arm wrapped around her. "You look good in that suit man." He looked at his date and stood tall in his own suit. "Don't we brothers know how to pick a suit, Daisy?" JJ asked.

The girl nodded and smiled giving Lamont a slow scan through glazed eyes. "Oh yes, he sure does." She stared boldly at Lamont, ignoring JJ.

"Hey, don't look at him so hard," JJ joked.

"I didn't mean to stare it's just that," She paused. "Are you guys twins?"

"Yeah, we're twins, JJ said joking, "but you're lucky because you got the handsome brother.

Jane inched in close to Lamont. "I wouldn't say that, and they're not twins, honey," she said giving the girl a piteous look."

JJ flashed Jane a crooked smile and a slow gaze. "And I might add that he really know how to pick more than suits, wow." JJ slurred again, looking flirtatiously at Jane's buttocks. Daisy poked him in the side and he yelled playfully. "Oow, don't hate, baby. Just being sociable."

"Just don't get too sociable," Daisy said in a squeaky voice.

Jane smiled, with confidence now that she was sure that she had enchanted all the Cooper men. Briefly, she imagined what it would be like to have all three Cooper men at once. A Cooper man in her every orifice, what a wicked image she thought as it played inside her head. They were all handsome replicas of each other, and if they were as good as Lamont, she would be insane with delight.

"How's work coming, JJ?" Lamont asked, changing the subject.

"Okay, so far," JJ said dismissively, sounding annoyed.

"You like your position with the company? You plan on ..?"

"Hey bro, don't mean to cut you off, but this is a party. I ain't here to talk shop; I'm here to hip hop. Let's have some fun."

"Okay, I feel you," Lamont said, but JJ's reluctance to discuss work showed that work wasn't important to JJ. Money was automatic for him, and work had never been part of his life style as a Cooper heir. Lamont hadn't got used to the idea of being an heir and work was a part of his own life style.

Shortly the two brothers and their dates mingled with the other guests and as expected, everyone was pleasant except Ruth. Ruth's behavior was even more abusive now than it had been in the past. She made inaudible comments and rolled her eyes at Jane, and scowled at Lamont. In spite of her past hostilities, Lamont had expected things to be different tonight. Nothing had changed, and she was just as hostile tonight as she had always been. Later Jane had asked: "What's wrong with that little bitch?" Lamont had felt offended at the use of the B word about his sister, but he couldn't defend Ruth's behavior.

"I really don't know. I can't remember ever doing or saying anything to offend her. Maybe I just rub her the wrong way."

"I can guess what her problem is," Jane said eying Ruth with obvious contempt. "She think her cut of your dad's money is gonna be smaller now that you're here."

"Naw, I'm sure she couldn't be that petty. Besides I'm not concerned about what's in Jake's will."

"Well you should be. From what I can see you deserve just as much as these spoiled brats. If anything you deserve it more than they do. At least you can appreciate it."

Lamont felt mixed emotions about Jane's statements. He could do without her harsh criticism, but she wasn't saying anything he didn't know already. "They're not all like Ruth, Jane."

"Maybe, maybe not, but they all depend on Daddy for everything."

"Jane, let's drop it okay? I don't want to do an analysis of the Coopers right now. Like JJ said it's a party. And Ruth's logic is not worth fretting about. She'll come around sooner or later."

"And if she doesn't?"

"It doesn't matter because I'm not planning on going anywhere."

"Yeah you're right, baby" Jane agreed. "It doesn't matter."

Even though Lamont had gotten Jane to drop the conversation about his siblings, Ruth's behavior still haunted and troubled him. He would make it a point to avoid her.

Chapter Nineteen- War

Finally dinner was served and Ruth was as obnoxious and disagreeable as ever. She commented harshly about Jake being like a military general. "Daddy assigned specific seats and got cute little place mats and everything." Ruth commented in an irritating squeaky voice. Every one directed mild irritated glances of intolerance her way, but said nothing. Lamont observed Cheryl restraining herself to remain silent, but he sensed that her silence wouldn't last.

Lamont was right and Cheryl's patience ran out when Ruth continued vocalize her random silly comments. "Ruthie, why don't you sober up and chill out for once? I don't know about any one else but I've had enough."

"You've had enough?" Ruth asked indignantly. "Who the hell are you," Ruth said with obvious contempt and on the verge of profanity.

"Ruth, Cheryl," Jake said sternly, glaring sternly at them both. "I'm not having this tonight," Jake said, through clenched jaws. "And Ruth you're already on probation with me." Jake's tone was low, but his glare left little doubt about his disappointed mood.

Ruth calmed down for a short while, but after dessert and two glass of wine, she was out of control again. "So Cheryl is it true that you been turning tricks?" She smirked at Cheryl as she spoke. "I heard that you been hanging out at that wild club where all the prostitutes work," Ruth said, giggling.

"You shut your filthy mouth you little bitch." Cheryl exploded. "Why don't you just drop dead?" She turned to Jake. "Daddy, why do you even invite her? All she does is start trouble."

"Why does he invite you? Slut," Ruth shot back with a wet slur.

"Cheryl! Ruth!" Jake said, wearing an embarrassed shocked expression. Now he stared them down, letting his expression communicate his thoughts while looking from Cheryl to Ruth, who sat facing each other. "Ruth, I warned you. If you utter one more word tonight, I'm throwing you out so fast you'll think this night was an illusion. You got that?" Ruth remained silent. "I asked you a question," he said with even more anger.

"You said not to say another word," Ruth said, pouting.

"Don't try me," he said with a no nonsense growl.

"Okay, daddy, I'll be cool."

"Cool? Humph. Try walking on water. That would be easier," Cheryl said, rolling her eyes at Ruth. "Disgusting pig," Cheryl said.

"Daddy," Ruth said, looking to Jake with a pleading expression.

"Cheryl, I want you to be quiet as well, Jake said sternly.

Suddenly, Ann uttered a surprising outburst. "This is so wrong. Every time you two are in the same room it's a damn war. The bible says that sisters are supposed to love one another," Ann said, shakily. "Why do you fight all the time about everything?" Ann was suddenly the center of attention because an outburst from her was rare. "All you two care about is your stupid feud. Why don't you rise above your petty bickering and show forgiveness and love?"

Lamont felt embarrassment and dread that Jane was here to see this tragic family drama unfold. It was a pity that such behavior was being displayed among a family that had been blessed so generously. Lamont's sympathies were drawn to Ann, and he wanted to comfort her.

"We're never gonna be a family, never," Ann cried. Fighting is all you care about, and you make every one dread being around you," Ann said as she stood and ran from the room sobbing.

Doug's towering frame rose before any one could react. "I better go to her," he said, then left the room as well.

"You two happy now," Jake said looking from one girl to the other. "You like getting everybody wired and screwed up. You've upset your sister. You know she's timid." Jake halted his words with a sighed and shook his head, while looking towards Candace. She returned his gaze from the other end of the table with sympathetic eyes.

"You're right daddy. I'm sorry," Cheryl said. "I acted like an idiot." She looked towards Ruth and smiled smugly. "Daddy's right, Ruth, we both acted stupid, and I'm willing to bury the hatchet. We shouldn't be carrying on like this. You're my sister and I should love you. I'm sorry."

Lamont observed that in spite of Cheryl's apology, Ruth seemed angry still. She shot Cheryl an obvious look of contempt, but now she had no choice but to accept Cheryl's apology.

Ruth looked to Cheryl strangely. "No, I get crazy sometimes when I drink," Ruth said, "I didn't mean to say those nasty things to you, and I should be the one apologizing." Lamont saw through Ruth's obvious insincerity, and he wondered if this was some game between the two sisters. They had both apologized, but he would bet that neither of them meant a word of it. Did any one else make the same observations or if it was just his own imagination. In any case it was a pity that they were formidable foes instead of powerful allies.

They didn't hold family with the same high regard as he did, and maybe it was because they took family for granted. Lamont's battling sisters were text book examples of hostile sibling rivalry at its peak. Now it was clear that family bonding would be much harder than he had first thought. He had not factored in sibling rivalry as an obstacle. Now he realized just how much of an obstacle it was. How could he bond with a family who couldn't even bond with each other? It was scary that Cheryl and Ruth loathed each other so much. Tonight they had been forced to call a truce, but it was only a pause and the vicious battle would resume tomorrow.

Chapter Twenty-
Heart to heart

Later Lamont, Preston and Jake slipped away to Jake's home office and discussed business. Jake informed Lamont that he was expanding his role in the business, and giving him more responsibilities as an executive. Preston knew nothing about Lamont's dual role. He only knew that Jake had hired Lucas Shepherd to investigate suspicious behavior from executives. Preston went along with whatever Jake suggested, but Lamont wondered why Jake hadn't told Preston about his dual role. Did Jake think that Preston would disagree? Surely Jake wouldn't avoid a confrontation.

Shortly they concluded their meeting and headed back downstairs to re-join the others. They were greeted by Candace in the upstairs landing. "There you are. Have you been hiding in there talking business," Candace scolded Jake playfully and quickly grabbed his arm.

"What can I say? I'm busted." Jake threw up his hands. "I guess you gonna have to punish me. Do with me what you want." He took her hand and headed down stairs.

Lamont and Preston were headed downstairs, until Lamont spotted Ruth near one of the bathrooms, checking her hair and makeup in the mirror. He stopped to talk to her. "Hello Ruth," he said cautiously. It was just the two of them in the foyer.

"Oh, Lamont," she said acknowledging him with an annoyed scowl, and then tried to ignore and go past him.

"Listen, Ruth, can I talk to you?"

"About what, Lamont," she hissed impatiently, stopping in her tracks.

"Well for one thing, about why you're so angry at Cheryl?"

"That's between me and Cheryl and it's none of your damn business," she said making an obvious annoyed smirk.

"Okay." He paused then asked. "Why are you so angry at me? What did I ever do to you?"

"I ain't mad at you," she said with an obvious tolerant sigh. "You can't help it cause you a bastard. But that's all right cause in case you didn't know it already, you're in daddy's will now and you gon' be a rich bastard," she said without emotion. She attempted to move forward, but he stepped in front of her. She looked up at him through stretched angry eyes and put one hand defiantly on one hip. "Nigger, you better get outta my space," she said, raising her voice aggressively, working her head in defiance, and shooting him a quick snobbish glare.

"I just wanted to talk to you for two minutes, that's all. Please.."

She scanned him quickly looking into his eyes, sighing impatiently. "Two minutes, Lamont, that's all. I ain't got time to stand here listening to no speeches or hosting no pity party for you."

He noticed that in spite of Ruth's tough talk, she calmed down. "Look I can understand that you guys don't want to accept me, that's natural. But what do you hope to accomplish by looking down your nose at me? Will that boost your self esteem?" He asked, realizing from her expression that he had pushed the wrong button with her.

"Low self esteem," her voice shot up an octave. Ruth glared at him with indignation. "Boy you're crazy as Hell," she said. "How you figure I have low self esteem? I got money, looks, and most of all the, Cooper name," she snorted smugly.

"Self esteem is not about money, looks or a name, Ruth," Lamont said patiently.

"Well you tell me what it's about, college boy."

"It's about independence, sobriety and concern for other people's feelings. It's about growing up and being a responsible mature adult instead of an immature child." She was about to speak but he cut her off. "I don't know the story between you and Cheryl but my guess is that it's about egos. Is it because you think she's prettier than you? Both of you are pretty, but the real measure is what's inside."

"Look, Nigger, don't preach to me about no damn inner beauty. You don't know what the hell you're talking about. You ain't been in the family two damn minutes, and now you got all the answers. Don't try to bullshit me because you went to some jive ass college. That don't mean you know me, or Cheryl, or this family. You'll always be just a stray to me. You're just a weed in a flower garden, Lamont."

"And the Coopers are the flowers I guess," Lamont said patiently, eying her with mixed feelings. Her words hurt because it shows the huge gap between them. On one hand he wanted to lash out at her, but on the other hand he felt sorry for her. She was unfocused and angry at the world, and feeding her anger would only leave her more befuddled. "Okay, Ruth, I get it," He said resignedly, "If your goal is to hurt me, then congratulations, you've succeeded." He paused and looked deep into her eyes. "How do you feel right now, knowing that you can hurt my feelings? Do you feel joy, triumph or, hilarity?"

"Wha..what?" She seemed confused and her face twisted as if she couldn't remember where she was right now.

"You gotta feel something good or you wouldn't waste time doing it so much. I certainly feel something. I feel pain, anger, and rejection, but mainly I feel regret because you chose to be a loser when you could easily be a winner."

Her scowl vanished and she looked at him blankly. "What are you talking about Lamont?" Her expression was neutral and softer even though she eyed him suspiciously.

"I'm talking about the things you got going for yourself."

"Yeah? Things like what?" She asked with a curious expression.

He turned to the mirror "Look at you, Ruth. You're are pretty, you got a dynamite figure and a good speaking voice. And it's easy to see that you're sharp, but you're putting your wit to waste cutting Cheryl down," he said, half smiling.

She was silent and seemed to consider what he just said. "You know Cheryl thinks she's hot shit and brags about having such a killer ass." "I guess everybody think Cheryl looks like a model with those long ass legs and big perky boobs." She searched for words. "I mean you know models are usually kinda tall like Cheryl." She unconsciously smoothed her dress, pressing it over her hips. I've got a good figure too," she said, sounding unsure.

"Of course you do and with curves galore." Lamont said light hearted.

She glowers at him suspiciously. "Have you been checking me out? Are you a pervert or something, Lamont? You're my brother, remember?"

"Ruth," Lamont said, giving her a scolding look, "please." His voice went deep and he cast Ruth a critical impatient scowl. "Cheryl's got a nice figure and so does Ann, but I know this because I'm observant, and not because I'm watching their asses."

"Sorry," she apologized without realizing it, "I don't think you're like that and." Ruth stopped in mid sentence and went silent. Now the look of contempt returned and she reverted to her critical scowl. "Oh no. Hell no." She paused. "I see what you're doing. You're asking me all these damn questions trying to get into my head. You're acting like a damn con man. That's what you are, but you ain't gon' change my mind."

"I'm not trying to con you, Ruth; I want to get to know you. I want to know all of you."

"Well I don't want to get to know your ass. I know all the people I need to know. You need to stop working your game so hard, Lamont. You're in the will so just slow down your sales pitch, college boy." She brushed past him and headed down stairs

"Sales pitch?" Lamont stood there frozen and stunned at Ruth's sudden turn around and he was more puzzled than ever. He thought he was making a breakthrough with her. What had he said, and why had her mood changed so suddenly? Maybe it wasn't his choice of words, but her volatile nature that was the blame. Suddenly he was fed up with trying to say the right thing and please people. Right now he didn't know or care why she turned on him. He was ready to go find Jane right now and get the hell out of here.

On the drive back to Jane's apartment Lamont remembered Ruth's attitude and continuously replayed her harsh words in his head. Something was wrong with that girl, besides being an alcoholic. She had some deep seated personal problems and would never seek help, because of her denial. Regrettably, he didn't have any answers. It was clear that he had to choose his battles and expect to lose any he waged with Ruth.

Chapter Twenty One- Beginnings

Jane felt Lamont wrapped one hand around her and she cuddled against him, purring slightly. She had made a good impression in spite of all the conflict. She had shown herself to be quite classy, in spite of her stooping to petty gossip from time to time. Jane was secretly praising herself for making a great impression and winning over all the men tonight.

Jake had been charming, and JJ's eyes were glued on her ass. Even Ann's husband, Doug, hung on to her every word. She had spoke in her sexiest bedroom voice and purposely flirted with her eyes. She had enchanted them all with her great ass. Wait until they see me in my black bikini, she thought.

"Lamont, that was quite an experience tonight," Jane said cautiously pausing. "And Cheryl and Ruth didn't pull any punches. Do fight all the time?"

"I don't really want to talk about that, Jane, so let's change the subject."

"Sure, Baby." She sighed. "You, JJ and your dad look so much alike, but..."

"But?" He paused and waited.

"But you're the handsomest of the trio."

"You're such a wise lady and you know just what to say don't you?"

"Well babe, I am a journalist."

"Yeah, words are your tools."

They were silent and the sound of the rubber on the road filled the night. Jane's thoughts turned back to the women, who as expected were jealous of her. Candace was the exception, but why should she be jealous, she had the big fish and Jane couldn't hate her for that. Candace was proof that Jake obviously liked young women, and if she had met Jake Cooper first, there would be no Candace. Lucky Bitch. Candace wasn't her favorite person, but she had to give the girl her props.

At least Candace acted like a lady. She couldn't say the same for Cheryl and Ruth, who made a spectacle of themselves. They were rolling in money and didn't have the slightest touch of class. Thank goodness she had been there to show them how a classy lady carried herself. Jane considered her future sisters-in-law non-threatening airheads. She would dazzle all her future in-laws with patience and tolerant just as she had dazzled Lamont, and changed his reluctance about marriage.

Lamont yearned for his freedom like most men, but he was unsure about what he really wanted. She considered all men as dogs who had to be house broken, even men like Lamont. That's why a real woman was able to control her man with feminine magic and good sex. She knew the recipe and that's why she controlled Lamont and would continue to do so.

Now that he was an heir to a portion of the Cooper fortune, as his wife she would be entitled to half his assets. Even though these brats saw him as an outsider and probably wanted things to be different, it didn't matter because they had no authority to deny Lamont his inheritance. Lamont was anxious to be accepted by them, but to her it didn't matter if they rejected or accepted him.

If they're smart they'll work with him because they couldn't do much without him. JJ was a hopeless playboy, and those bratty Cooper females were useless. Cheryl and Ruth couldn't get past their petty sniping long enough to do anything constructive, like working together, and it was a miracle that Ann hasn't had a nervous breakdown. Lamont deserved everything that he had coming and as his future wife, so did she. No one was going to thwart her dreams.

They arrived at Jane's place and as they walked to the path leading to Jane's apartment Lamont notice Jane's smile

"What you smiling, about," Lamont said as they walked to her door.

"About all the things I want to do to you," she said, switching her thoughts back to him.

"That's good," he said, smiling and holding her hand tighter.

"You got your key handy," she said. "Mine is buried in my purse."

Lamont used his duplicated key to her apartment and opened the door.

Shortly, their passion dominated their actions for a greater portion of what remained of this night. Jane felt empowered by Lamont's zealous lust, which attested to her manipulative skills. Poor boy was pussy whipped and she planned to keep him that way. Everything was going her way and she had every reason to believe that she could have it all.

In spite of these beliefs, she felt a craving for the kinky and bizarre lust that Lamont refused to provide. Being around so many lusty men tonight had gotten her stirred up even more. She pushed aside those random cravings and concentrated on Lamont. Still, at some point she would have to introduce Lamont to the wild side. She would wait until they were married, because once she got those papers, she could pretty much be herself whether Lamont liked it or not.

Chapter Twenty Two-
Booty Call

Meanwhile Cheryl decided to stay over night, and was settled in her old suite at the Cooper estate. She felt drained from arguing with Ruth, and wanted to sleep, but her eyes were wide open. She gazed at the wide screen TV and flipped through the channels, trying to shake the effects if her recent dispute with Ruth. She was startled by the knock on the door.

"Sis you up," JJs voice came through the door.

"Yes JJ, come in."

JJ entered the room and sat in the recliner next to Cheryl. "You okay?"

"Yeah, I'm good," she said cautiously. "Where's you date?"

"She's waiting downstairs. We're going to my place in a few minutes. I just wanted to holler at you and see if you're alright. You and Ruth raised hell earlier."

"Well she started it."

"I know, but you know she's got that big mouth. You just got to ignore her. She'll calm down. She's already sleeping it off and snoring like an old sailor in her old suite."

"I try to ignore her JJ, but she makes me want to strangle her."

"Why? Everybody knows Ruth is hallucinating,"

"I know but," She pause, feeling uncomfortable because Ruth had been partially right about her. Cheryl had once tried to become a prostitute and the results had been disastrous, but JJ didn't know that. She changed the subject. "So what do you think about Jane?"

"She's fine," JJ said with a shake of his head. "But you don't like her do you," he said noticing that look in Cheryl's eyes.

"She's okay I guess. That's Lamont's choice."

"But," JJ said anticipating that Cheryl was about to say more.

"But she's kinda smug and I don't know, she's secretive and she watches everything and takes it all in," Cheryl finished with a sigh. "But she is a reporter isn't she. That little performance between Ruth and me seemed to really get her attention. And those nosey eyes of hers had a haunting glare."

"She was fine though. Did you see that ass," JJ said with a low whistle.

"JJ please, I know you didn't just go there."

"You're right; I shouldn't lust after my brother's girl." He paused and there was an awkward silence until he finally said. "Well I guess you didn't make a very good first impression with her."

"I don't care about her, I care that I embarrassed the family." She paused and a brief silence filled the room before she continued. "I sense something negative from her. I hope that Lamont knows what he's doing because he deserves a good woman."

"What about me? I don't deserve a good woman," JJ said mischievously.

"You're not ready yet. You're trying to get all the good women."

"Okay I'll let that slide," he said, rising to his feet. "I'm gonna take my sweetie of the week to my place." He kissed Cheryl's cheek and left.

Cheryl turned the television off and now her mind rambled as she recalled the recent events of the last few days. She remembered the meeting with Lamont, Rasheena, and herself and the way it all had unfolded. She also remembered running into Tony Martin right after she left the restaurant. He had prepositioned her and she told him to go to hell at the time.

Now she remembered Tony Martin's recent words to her. 'Baby when it comes to sex you put them all to shame.' Surely that wasn't the only thing she could do. It certainly wasn't something to be proud about.

Suddenly she felt restless and Two Martin's image along with the suggestion of a no strings attached sexual relationship stuck in her mind. "He got some nerve, and some ego," she said aloud. "Why would he think I would agree to something like that? Especially with him." She tried to push him from her head, but those blazing images of their sexual encounters two years earlier resurfaced in vivid details now. She recalled with some relish, the things that Tony 'Two' Martin had done to her and realized that he had been her most skilled lover.

Her nipples stood erect and she squirmed, imagining the touch of his artistic hands, squeezing her breast and toying with her crotch. "Damn, this ain't good," she said stirring restlessly. The barrier in her mind fell and she no longer blocked those surging erotic memories. She remembered all the things that he had done to fired her up, and his purposeful patience drove her to an earthshaking climax.

She suddenly brought herself back from her deep thoughts. "What the hell are you thinking," She said looking in the mirror at her disheveled hair and unmade face. "That's insanity. He's a loser."

In spite of her self admonishing, thirty minutes later she dialed his cell number. "It's me. Yeah I need to see you." Shortly after hanging up, Cheryl dressed and headed away from the Cooper estate for a Two AM rendezvous with Tony Martin, pimp, hustler loser, and lover.

It all seemed unreal but her yearning became stronger as she drove her Camaro down quiet deserted streets and drew closer. "Damn, girl where is your pride," she heard herself say in an absurd attempt to regain some semblance of sanity. It was already too late for sanity because she had gone too long without sex and her physical urges had overpowered and whipped sane logic into submission.

She met Tony a few short minutes later at the Ramada Inn, a place that she had insisted on because it was a neutral site. The last time he had chosen the place it had turned into a disaster and an attempted black mail scheme. Tony was a snake and this was crazy and yet she ignored logical reasoning. This was about pure animal lust and nothing else.

A short time later, they made their way into a large hotel room and now she was glad that she had come. Tony was everything she remembered him to be and now he whispered into her ear, and showed her joys that she had never known. Even though she disliked him, he was good. That only proved the theory that every body was good for something, even Tony.

She floated off into that dream world of multi-orgasms as she emitted sounds that were foreign even to her. Why was such a bad and vile man so good at this? Why did the bastard have to be so talented? She asked herself with some regret. Suddenly she didn't want to think anymore.

****

Later, Tony Martin slipped from the room leaving Cheryl asleep and contented. She wasn't as tough as she pretended to be, but she was as good as he remembered. He fought the temptation to wake her and do her again. Instead he pulled out his cell phone and hit the speed dial, then stepped inside the bathroom for privacy.

"Hello, it's Two Martin, Carvoni is expecting me. I'm on the way." He pushed the button and sighed aloud as he broke the connection. He dreaded being Carvoni's flunky, but he owed Carvoni big. He cursed Carvoni for insisting that he report to him immediately. He was following Carvoni's orders specifically because he didn't want the little bastard to have an excuse to reprimand him. Carvoni wasn't a trusting soul and Two had already gotten on his bad side.

Two arrived at the Italian Stallion club about Four A.M. He gained access to the plush club through the rear entrance, and Bennie, his mammoth cousin/henchman, led him to Carvoni's office. Bennie had just woke up, and his big dark baggy eyes glared with irritation as he brushed his jet black hair. Two observed Bennie's unsmiling face and thought, damn this man is ugly when he wakes up.

"Tony's waiting for you." Bennie's deep voice exploded with a growl in Two's ears. Two followed Bennie down the small corridor and marched like a soldier to Carvoni's office.

Facing Carvoni was as gruesome as facing a starving man eating Tiger. Carvoni was one of the few men who scared him, because Carvoni could shift into attack mode at any given moment. Two was a strong confident man most of the time, but Two feared Carvoni's fierce reputation. He believed those stories about brutal executions that Carvoni engineered on his enemies. That's why he obeyed the man blindly.

When two entered he saw Carvoni hogging down a plate of Lasagna. Tony's sister owns a restaurant and brought home cooked meals over quite often. It was Four AM and Carvoni was still eating. Two was sure that the fat little man never stopped eating. He never went home to his wife because his office was a home away from home. This was better than home because he had his pick of all the female employees. Two suspected that the wife was more than pleased with that arrangement.

Two heard moaning, and saw a porno movie playing on the wide screen TV upon entering the office. Carvoni's shooed the two girls from the office when Two entered. He then turned to face Two and picked up a napkin and wiped his mouth. He then picked up an old cigar and stuck it between his teeth. "Tony, my Namesake, tell me some good news. My guy told me he saw you take little miss rich bitch to the whip shack. So fill me in.

Two was slightly annoyed, but unfortunately he was in no position to express his personal feelings. This whole scenario was a nightmare, but he had no options. "Nothing to tell, we had sex."

"Now we're talking," Carvoni said, watching the TV screen and wearing a lecherous grin. "I know you did. I know that shit was good too. She walks like it's good."

Two felt a sudden rise of confused anger. "Yeah, but the mission still isn't completed yet. This is just..."

"I know this is just the beginning. But hey, it's a beginning. That's all we want for now. I'm patient about this and I've got other stuff going on. Patience can be a great ally. So give it time," he said with a crooked smile, "but not too much time."

Two glanced subtly about the large plush office, observing the huge sofas, and various tasteless artworks. The six inches of carpet were like soft layers of cotton, and he wondered if Carvoni was too fussy about his carpet to off any of his enemies here. No way would Tony Carvoni risk getting blood on his precious carpet.

Now, Two spoke cautiously. "So what's the plan?"

"That don't matter, just do as I tell you and we're good. I have it all worked out. Besides what do you care? You're getting that Nookie, and from what I've seen it's prize stuff." Carvoni gave another lecherous grin. "Tell me does she like freaky shit? She looks like the type who likes weird freaky shit."

Carvoni obviously was trying to get details, and Two felt an urge to tell the perverted bastard to go to hell. Only fear and knowledge of reprisals rendered him submissive. Still, he didn't want to give Carvoni too much sexual information about Cheryl so he lied. "She's not all that. In fact she ain't as good as she looks, definitely not the best I've had."

Carvoni seemed disappointed at Two's reply and his lecherous grin faded. "Well in any case you've laid the ground work and it gets better from here on."

Two Martin left Carvoni's office shortly after ending their conversation, overwhelmed by a lingering dirty feeling. He wasn't a saint, but on the other hand Carvoni was the worst kind of criminal. He regrets the day he struck a deal with that animal, but his own greed and ambition had forced him into this situation. Now he was in with Carvoni for the long haul with no way out.

Chapter Twenty Three-
The Call

A week after Jake's dinner party, Lamont had long put Ruth's rude disrespectful behavior and nasty words behind him. He was in Norfolk to spend the weekend with Jane, and hadn't thought about the Coopers once. However that changed when Jane asked, "Have you ever thought about legally changing your name to Cooper?"

"I hadn't thought about it or even considered it an option," he said with finality. It was a moot point for him because he was Lamont Savage and that was that. However, Jane's expression told him that it did matter to her and her words confirmed it.

"But baby, you can get it done with no problems since in fact you are a Cooper," she commented, excitedly. I could even keep my same courtesy tags, and Jane Cooper sounds more poetic than Jane Savage?"

Lamont realized that names and titles were important to Jane and he didn't like this shallow side of her. She obviously wanted the clout that went with the Cooper name. "Do you want the Cooper name or do you want me?" He asked jokingly.

"I want you silly, it was just a suggestion. You say you want to bond and I just thought that might be a way, but forget it," she said.

Although Jane shrugged it off with a nervous laugh, Lamont sensed that she wasn't ready to let it go. What was this thing with names, he wondered. Ruth had also commented about him not having the Cooper name, as if that made a difference in the quality of his character. Now Jane expressed similar sentiments. Maybe he just didn't get it.

Later they went out to dinner and a movie, and then headed back to her apartment. Jane turned the discussion to the Coopers again, but this time it was about Lamont bonding with his siblings. Like Lamont, Jane was also an only child, and she had been very supportive. Lamont thought that was because they both felt the same about family.

Tonight Jane was sweeter than usual, and more supportive about him bonding with his family, in spite of their attitudes. "Honey they need you more than they know," Jane insisted. "You're independent enough to handle your problems, while they always had daddy to solve theirs," She said smiling proudly. "I think they'll come around when they see how awesome you are. I'd sure be proud to have a big brother like you."

"Thanks, baby, that means a lot to me that you feel that way. And you know what; I'm not sweating it anymore."

"Easier said than done. Can you do that?" She asked skeptically.

"I can try," he said sounding doubtful.

"One thing does puzzle me though," Jane said. "I don't get how any one so dependant and needy could be so head strong and envious."

"Neither do I. I'm stumped." Lamont held up his hands. "Look this is our time. No more discussion about the Coopers tonight."

"That's fine with me," she said looking down at his crotch. "I got other plans for you anyway." Jane had been frisky in the movie and they were both turned on. She went to him and smothered him with kisses. Suddenly she rose from the couch. "Come back to the bedroom in two minutes," she said as she slipped away from his grasp.

As ordered, Lamont strode towards the bedroom after two minutes past. She sat on the bed modeling a sexy black nightie for him. She loved the awesome power of her sexy body in lingerie. She went into his arms and he took charge, and started some serious foreplay.

Lamont pulled the shirt up over his head and kicked off his shoes. As he unbuckled his belt his cell phone rang. "Damn it, he said."

"Don't answer it," Jane said and started kissing his face all over. "I need you."

Lamont pulled the phone from his pants pocket and was about to turn it off until he read *R. Cooper's* name on the caller ID. Now he was too curious not to answer. "Sorry baby, this might be important."

"Lamont!" Jane droned, stretching her eyes in anger.

Lamont ignored her; his curiosity was stronger than his anticipation of Jane's reprisal. He pushed the talk button and spoke, but only heard muffled sobbing. "Hello," he said again. The sobbing returned but this time with words.

"Oh, Lamont, it's Ruth. I need help. I Lamont, I think I killed somebody," Ruth said, sobbing and stuttering. "You gotta come over here and help me. I just. I think I killed her..."

"What? How?" Lamont asked, suspended in disbelief. He couldn't be sure if Ruth was playing games or not. How and when did she even get his cell number? "Are you serious Ruth?"

"Yes, Lamont." The voice answered in a hysterical annoyed sob.

He gave Jane an apologetic look. "I gotta take this, Baby," he said, ignoring Jane's comments and evil eyed glare, while dashing to the living room. Jane remained sitting on the bed in her sexy black nightie, openly annoyed and mumbling under her breath. Once in the living room, he spoke again. "Ruth, calm down and tell me what happened." She spoke hysterical words that he couldn't decipher. "Ruth, stop crying and tell me where you are now."

"I'm at my condo," Ruth's shaky breathless voice came through clear this time, and after a quick pause she spoke more coherently. "I hit a woman with my car earlier tonight, and I think I killed her. She just came from nowhere, Lamont. It wasn't my fault. I need help.

"Did you call Jake?"

"No way. I can't go to daddy." She paused then blurted, "And you can't tell him about this either."

"Okay, calm down and give me your address. I'll be there shortly," he said, starting to dress. He wrote down her number and slipped his shirt and shoes on. He observed Jane's expression of disbelief as he prepared to leave. "I'm sorry, this is an emergency," he said with a contrite expression.

"Lamont," Jane whined, and then stood with her eyes stretched. She held out her arms spread eagle. "Baby I know you ain't about to run outta here and leave this. Momma's horny and she got plans for you, Poppa." She posed; turning to and fro, making her breast shimmy and jiggle. "Don't you want some?"

"Sorry, baby. Like I said this is urgent." Lamont said, while frantically picking up his things from the nightstand without hesitation.

Jane's overconfidence faded and his words shocked her. She was angry and embarrassed now. "What," Jane snarled, "urgent my ass." Her voice rose in protest. "I'm the one who's in urgent need right now."

Lamont was mildly surprised at her attitude and briefly found her unrecognizable. "Jane please, I got to do this. Ruth's in trouble." Lamont was about to head out the door. "I'll explain when I get back."

"Did you say Ruth?" She asked, twisting her face in obvious distaste. "That evil skank got the nerve to call you after treating you like a piece of loaded shit paper? How can you go runnin' to her like a damn flunky after the way she treats you? Oh No Lamont Savage, I forbid you to leave here," she spoke raising her voice.

Lamont glared at her through slightly narrowing eyes, and his look reflected surprise and annoyance. "Excuse you," Lamont said, freezing and observing her with clenched jaws. "You *forbid* me." He gave her a stone cold glare, obviously annoyed. "You don't forbid me to do a damn thing," he said, shaking his head in astonishment. "Let's get one thing straight. This is my family, with all their dysfunction and screwy attitudes. I'd be a hypocrite if I didn't give them the decent treatment that I expect from them. I'm not going to judge them because of who they are. Who's to say how you or I would act if we were in their shoes? I know you're angry, and this is unfortunate, but you don't dictate my actions when it comes to my family, so don't try it."

"What about me? Is all your loyalty always going to family? They sure as hell don't think the same way about you. Now you're gong to leave me here, and run to help that spoiled ungrateful drunken bitch."

"Chill Jane, this attitude is childish. For the last time, don't criticize my family," he said with a scowl.

"Why can't she call your father or one of her other siblings? I don't see why you so worried about any of them, they sure wouldn't do the same thing for you."

"You know something Jane, I don't get you," Lamont said, giving Jane puzzled stare. "Did all that support and understanding suddenly collapse? Now you're bad mouthing them all. I thought you wanted me to bond with them, or at least that's what you claimed." He paused and waited for her to reply, but when she didn't he spoke again. "The point is moot because I'm going." He went to kiss her cheek, but she pulled away. "That's how you feel huh? Okay then, see you later, or not," he said moving to the door and out.

After the door shut behind Lamont, Jane stood there frozen, and puzzled. It was unbelievable that he had actually left, when she was here looking so luscious for him. No, that was crazy, she thought as she watched the door. She expected him to come to his senses and run back to her any second. He must know by now how foolish it had been to leave hot and bothered. When he returned and apologized, she would tease him, and then let him take her to bed and ravish her with hot make up sex.

She waited for thirty minutes before it dawned on her that Lamont wasn't going to return. Now she felt like a fool sitting here alone, staring at the door in her sexy lingerie, with no one to tempt. "Damn you Lamont Savage, and Damn that rich needy bunch of sibling shitheads!" Jane was pissed off, horny and all alone and thought about calling Greg. Then she realized that she couldn't do that because he was too needy, and he might get crazy like the last time.

She threw on a robe and watched television and drank double shots of gin and gave up on thinking that Lamont would return. After a few shots of whiskey she calmed down and realized that she must have looked like a jealous bitch to Lamont. She wanted to kick herself because her protests were silly, and she had briefly lost sight of the big picture. The goal was to help Lamont bond with his rich family. It was a good thing that all of the helpless brats needed Lamont, and she should encourage him.

She would back off, make amends and plan her prosperous and secure future. She would get him in bed, regain control, and repair any damages thus far. First she had to apologize for being such a bitch, and then she would be extra sweet and understanding. She must refrain from selfish behavior and concentrate. She had come too far to lose the big prize now.

It was vital now that she showed patience. Once she had those papers Lamont and his family of rich dysfunctional misfits could all go to hell, as long as Lamont left half of his money to her.

Chapter Twenty Four- Hit and Run

Lamont arrived at Ruth's building and now he took the steps to the third floor instead of waiting for the elevator. He knocked on the door of apartment 347, hoping that Ruth had given him the correct address.

He heard movement inside as the door flung open. He observed Ruth standing there holding a glass half full of whiskey. She wore a short tight pink dress and an apologetic worried scowl. She was bare foot, her panty hose were tattered, and her dark hair was frizzy. Her lipstick was smeared from her open mouth to her chin, and dark blue eye shadow formed a thin Lone Ranger's mask around her eyes. She avoided his eyes and her words came hard and slow. "Come in, Lamont," she said making a half gesture with her arm.

Lamont entered a spotlessly clean, well organized, and smartly decorated condo. Modern art decorated the walls and there were lots of shelves. It was obvious by the expensive ambiance that a great deal of money had been spent on this place. No doubt Jake's money.

Lamont walked behind her to the large bar, and sat next to her on the other bar stools. "Okay, Ruth, what happened? You say you hit a woman tonight?"

"Yes," she slurred, speaking as if dazed. "I hit a woman tonight." She turned the glass up and gulped down the drink, then poured another. She slipped from the bar stool and stepped to the picture window and looked out on the city.

Lamont shuddered to watch her down the whiskey so quickly. "Ruth, you need to lay off of that stuff. That's why you're in this mess."

"Look I." She stopped in mid sentence and glared at him in silence. She apparently had decided not to antagonize him. "I need a couple of hits to steady my nerves. Besides it wasn't my fault. It was an accident."

"Okay then," Lamont said doubtfully, "I'm listening," he said, scanning her up and down, and moving to sit on the couch. "Well then whose fault is it? You were the driver."

Ruth stared out at the city as she spoke now. "It was like she just appeared from out of nowhere. There was no way I could see her coming. She just jumped in front of the car and." She paused and seemed to remember something.

"And then what?" Lamont asked. "Were you watching the road? Were you alone in the car?"

"Yes, yes," she said impatiently. "But.."

"But what?"

"I was talking on my cell phone and I felt a suddenly bump and that's when I saw her."

"And then what?"

"And then nothing. I saw her stretched out on the pavement and I took off."

"You just took off and left her there? That wasn't too smart, Ruth. Now we gonna have to clean up this mess."

"Yeah that's what I was thinking," she said turning eagerly to him. "We can check the hospitals and find out if any hit and run accident victims came in," Ruth said hoarsely.

"Good then we're on the same wave length," Lamont said, thinking that Ruth was at least ready to make some amends, even though she had left the scene. At least that's what he thought until she spoke again.

"That's why I called you. You can talk to some body and find out if anybody saw me or recognized my car. When we find somebody, we can pay them off to keep their mouths shut," Ruth said slurring excitedly. "And in the meantime I need to get my ass outta Dodge while you take care of that... and ...and.." She stopped speaking when she saw his grim expression. "Why you looking at me like that? You don't want to help me? I didn't see the damn woman, Lamont."

"I believe you, Ruth, but you gotta go turn yourself in. You can't run someone down and run away. For God sake show some concern for the woman's condition. Did you even call 911?"

"No, I couldn't think."

"Damn, Ruth, do you even care about the woman's condition?" He was openly annoyed at her lack of concerned about putting a human life in danger. "What kind of person are you?"

"What do you want me to say, dammit? It was an accident, I told you that. Surrendering to the cops won't make any difference now. Suppose she's not even hurt? She'll just want to sue when she discovers who I am."

Lamont shook his head. "Just who are you, Ruth, cause I sure don't know. You're not acting like a person at all. The only thing you're worried about is not getting sued? Suppose she's dead? Would that even faze you in the least," he said with a scowl.

"Look, Lamont," she sighed, "please don't give me no damn lectures right now, okay? All that talk at Daddy's the other night made me think that you wanted to be part of this family. But now all I hear is this bullshit about turning me in." She went back to the bar, lit a cigarette and sat on the bar stool. "You're supposed to rescue the damsel, not put the damsel in distress. Shit, I didn't have to call you over here to tell me how to give up," she said belligerently.

Lamont was angry, and now regretted leaving Jane to come here. Was Jane right and Ruth was just an ungrateful lost brat? "Ruth, you need to grow up. I didn't say anything about helping you break the law. And I can't believe you're standing here shifting the blame when this is entirely your fault. You hit someone tonight, and you have to face the consequences."

"See, see, this is just the bullshit I'm talking about," she said through clenched teeth and continued to pour whiskey in her glass. She took one long sip and sat it on the bar giving Lamont a pitying look. She shook her head, muttering at first to herself, and then to him. "Why you such a damn goody-two-shoes anyway?" She asked, obviously forcing herself to remain calm through clenched teeth. "You just a damn poor ass thug from down the bottom, so don't play like you never made a mistake."

"Of course I've made mistakes, and still do, but this ain't my mistake it's yours, so forget about flipping the script and own up to it, Ruth."

She took a drink from her glass and rolled her eyes. "You know what? I made a bigger mistake when I called you." Her eyes focused on the view through her living room window as she sighed purposely.

"So I tell you what, you just get back on your little white horsey, and gallop on back over to Camelot and slay some dragons. Or have some hot cocoa at the round table with the other good Knights. Have a safe trip and don't let that extra tight halo give you a monster migraine." She turned the glass up, and drank half of it, scowling as the bourbon slid down her throat.

"I can't do that, Ruth. I gotta report what I know to the authorities." Lamont's voice was quiet and low, but his expression was grim and serious.

"What? Now look, you're taking this goody two-shoes shit too far. You gonna turn your own sister in? I call you to save me from the lynch mob and you show up to pick out the rope. You dirty snitching bastard."

Suddenly, she hurled the glass at him, but it just missed his head, and shattered on the wall behind him. He looked towards her and was about to speak, but he only had time to get out of the way of another glass that zoomed past his head. Lamont stepped in and grabbed her wrists before she could throw anything else. "Calm down, Ruth, Damn you."

"Let go of me you ...you."

"Bastard? Go ahead. Say it. You like the way it rolls off your tongue."

"Yes, I do. You'll never be a real Cooper."

"Maybe not, but Jake's still my father," Lamont said with frustration, "and now matter how much you deny it, Cooper blood runs through me just like it does you. If you want to get technical, I'm more of a Cooper than you because I'm the first born."

"First shit, and let me go, or I'll yell rape," she screeched as she broke loose from his grasp and stood facing him breathless now. "You think you fooling everybody with your little nice guy act. Look at me I'm Lamont, and I want to be everybody's friend," she said imitating him with a mocking voice and comical smirk. "Yeah right," she said with a scowl. "You just a two bit con artist, and all you really want is to get your hands on my daddy's money."

"Our Daddy, Ruth, he's *our* daddy and in spite of the way you act, I don't mind sharing him or our money with you. I don't have to con him or anybody else because, as you pointed out, I'm already in the will. You're the one who needs to start acting more like family," Lamont said with a flurry of sarcasm.

Ruth was so furious that she could only make incoherent noises instead of words. "Wh..Yo..Why."

"Don't blow a gasket. Why is your resentment of me so strong? I think you feel unworthy because you're so selfish and unproductive. You're just a dime a dozen rich spoil brat with no ambition, and who has never met a challenge or proved herself worthy. You're not angry at me, you're angry at yourself because you're a useless drunk. You can only ease your self contempt when you lash out at others."

"Oh you're just such a damn educated bastard ain't you?" She shrieked sarcastically. "You think you can figure everybody out. Well you're wrong cause I love me, and I can do lots of shit. And guys love me too, in fact they're crazy about me, and they'll do anything I ask."

"So why didn't you call one of them instead of me, if they're so nuts about you," Lamont said coolly and without diplomacy or remorse. "I would bet that it's Jake's money they're after and not you, because obviously your personality is in a state of permanent disrepair."

"Fuck you, Lamont. You're a hypocrite. Acting like family means so much to you, but you want to snitch on me. You're jealous of the Coopers, and pissed off that we been living the good life while your poor nothing ass struggled on the poor side of town. The ghetto is in you boy, and money won't change that. That's your problem."

"I'm not the least bit surprise, that a blind and clueless person such as you would mistakenly think that my address is the ghetto," he said with a sigh. "It's shallow to think that a person's address defines their qualities, but I guess shallowness is all any one can expect from you, Ruth. In spite of all you say and think about me, I wouldn't change who or what I am even if could.

I also can't change that fact that I have to turn you in right now if you refuse to do it yourself, and give the information to the authorities. Then we can consult with an attorney. It's the only thing to do, whether you believe that or not"

She glared towards him, with contempt and a burning desire to inflict bodily harm to him. In spite of her attitude and evil stare, Ruth knew that she couldn't win this argument. "And what if I don't go along with you?"

"Then you would leave me no choice but to report what I know to the police myself."

"Damn you, Lamont. Why are you doing this?" She asked exasperated and teary eyed.

"For your own good and whether you believe it or not, I care about you and this family. Jake sure doesn't need this right now."

"Yeah, sure. Lamont; you're just so full of shit," she hissed with obvious scorn.

Lamont wasn't so sure if Ruth was worth the effort. Her attitude was badly damaged and he wasn't so sure that fixing it was possible. Could he ever hope to see any visible progress from a mind so badly infected with negativity? With her attitude the only thing she could look forward to was trouble. "Ruth, I'm part of this family now and I refuse to act like an outsider to please your indelicate sensibility. I'll be here and as long as I'm around, I'm going to make sure that you don't destroy Jake after all he's done for you. So I don't give damn if you hate me because I chose to make a hard decision."

She clenched her teeth and rolled her eyes. "You don't know shit about this family, so stop pretending you care. You really want revenge on all of us cause Daddy didn't want anything to do with you before JJ needed that kidney. You hate all of us because daddy was there for us and not for you. That's why you made daddy give you all the money for your stinking little kidney.

"So just can cut your holier than thou bullshit act, 'cause I know that you got paid millions for your precious kidney. I don't know why daddy even put your slick ass in the will in the first place. You done already got paid so why you still hanging around talking all that love crap?" She gave him a strange knowing smug expression.

Lamont cleared his throat then spoke. "You are so clueless and it's pathetic. Apparently you don't keep up with what's going on in this family. You should know all the facts and never make accusations based on assumptions, Ruth. Believe what you want about me, but that's not important. What is important is getting you the legal help that you need." He paused and there was noticeable silence in the room. "So what's it gonna be?" He asked. "Do you tell the police, or do I?"

Ruth realized that she wasn't going to change his mind. She gave him an acid glare. "If you turn me in, that means they're gonna come and get me," she said with concern.

"Yeah, that's usually the procedure," Lamont said impatiently.

"They'll probably put handcuffs on me, just to humiliate me. That's what you want isn't it? You'll probably be on hand to snap a few pictures."

"I'm going pretend that I didn't hear you, because I'm certainly not going to debate with you about your idiotic thoughts. There are just too many. So think what you want, but I got to know what you're going to do."

"Ooh you bitch ass nigger you just piss me off. Why did I call you in the first place dammit? You're a useless bastard," she said with a weary sigh. She was drunk, sleepy, and defeated, so she reluctantly submitted. "Okay, then, I'll do it your way. Shit. Damn you."

"Yeah, I love you too, sis," he said sarcastically on his way out the door now.

"Go to hell, asshole," she mumbled and slumped down on the couch.

Lamont was out the door and out of ear shot, thinking that he might have to accept the fact that Ruth was a lost cause. He had come here to help her, thinking that things would improve between them. Instead the gap between them had grown wider and more hostile, and right now he dreaded the he would have to deal with his sister on any level.

Chapter Twenty Five-
Secrets

The next day Lamont called some lawyers to represent and to arrange for Ruth to turn herself in. He kept his actions secret from Jake, not for Ruth's sake, but for Jake's. Jake had enough on his plate, and didn't need to be burdened by his brat's senseless actions. It was ironic that he needed to protect Jake from his own daughter, who seemed to have little concern about Jake. Ruth was concerned only with herself and couldn't care less about their father's health or feelings. Lamont wondered if this family was even worth the effort. He had to believe that they were.

Lamont hit the intercom. "Marcia, come in here please." Within minutes she entered the office with a cup of coffee, and took a seat in the large chair facing his desk. She wore a perky smile and her face seemed to glow with satisfaction. Perhaps because she was happy with her new job. He was happy for her, because he liked having her around.

Marcia was a supportive and comfortable good friend, and an efficient worker on whom he could depend. The staff here was cooperative, but they were strangers. Marcia was like a comfortable cushion.

"Lamont this place is just...words can't describe it. And this office of yours, it's...I've never seen such luxury in the work place. If your office looks like this, I can only imagine how Mr. Cooper's office must look." She was up moving about as if on a tour.

Lamont sipped from the coffee cup and watched Marcia as she moved about commenting on furniture and various works of art. He felt good about impressing her, in spite of his modesty. "Yeah ole Jake's got an eye for expensive stuff," he managed to say.

"Yeah I guess, but it's not expensive to him. I mean he's the richest man I will ever see, I'm sure." She paused and gave him a look. "Is there a reason that you didn't tell me that he was your father, Lamont? I thought we were friends, but I had to hear this through the grapevine."

"It's not a secret; I just don't like talking about it. To tell the truth,

I'm uncomfortable talking about it." Lamont was surprised that Marcia took this so personal. She seemed upset and he needed to ease her troubled mind about this. "Marsh, are we okay?" He asked focusing on her now.

She sighed and looked directly at him, wrinkling her nose. "Yes I'm okay." She said in a small voice avoiding his eyes.

"Does it bother you that I didn't say anything about my relationship to Jake? I mean I was going to tell you and."

"I know, Lamont." She paused and sighed once more. "It's just that we are supposed to be friends and."

"We are friends." He interjected.

"Yes we are, but I thought we were really close, and yet you purposely kept this from me. Were you afraid to confide in me? You should know by now that I would never have betrayed your confidence."

"I know you wouldn't Marsh, but there was no confidence to betray because there was nothing confidential about it. The information is public knowledge."

"Okay," she said with a pause, "So maybe you thought I would change is that it?" She asked. "I know some people would. It's good to have money, but money isn't everything. So if you thought the news would change me or my attitude towards you, then you really don't know me, Lamont." She sighed and stood to leave.

Now he felt terrible and was suddenly overwhelmed by a sense of vague sadness at the thought of losing her friendship. "I see your point, Marsh and I'm sorry that I was so over protective of my little secret. Had I known it would offend you, I would never have kept you in the dark about it."

He stopped and studied her closer. She looked so hurt and he could feel her pain. "But you are right in a way. I did think that you might change, but it has nothing to do with my trust for you. It has to do with my fondness for the way you are. It's important to me that you of all people don't change."

"Lamont, you of all people should know better."

He focused on her eyes. "You're right, but this whole idea of money is new and confusing, Marsh. Frankly I don't know if I like the idea of being an heir. I never know for sure who is for real. I always counted on your friendship, and I was paranoid about that friendship changing. I apologize for clumping you in a category, but this new situation overwhelmed me." He paused, and their eyes met.

"Oh Lamont," she sighed with exasperation. "Don't you know that I'm never going to change on you?" She asked, looking long and deep into his eyes.

"Can you forgive me?" He asked beseeching.

"No," she said firmly,

"No?" he seemed to deflate all at once. "Okay I under."

She cut him off. "Because there's nothing to forgive. If there was something to forgive I would always forgive you without reservations because, you're one of the good guy. I'm sorry I made a big deal about it."

"How can I make it up to you?" Lamont asked.

"Let's see," she teased and pretended to ponder his question. "How about lunch?"

"That's it? Lunch?"

"What can I say," she shrugged her shoulders, "I'm easy."

"Okay, lunch it is, but in all fairness, you get to pick something else because I was going to do that anyway."

He felt much better now that the awkwardness and the secret between them were dissolved. Marcia was a buddy who shared his ups and downs, something he shared with no one else, including Jane. Showing an occasional weakness with Marcia was okay, because she soothed and encouraged him without judgment or criticism. With Jane he felt pressure to impress her and never expose his weaknesses. It was clear now just how important Marcia was to him, and he hoped that his connection to money didn't cause friction between them. It would be ironic beyond belief if his sudden access to money drove her away.

****

Marcia was jubilant as she sat with Lamont at the table in the Italian restaurant, but her mood changed the moment Lamont mentioned Jane. Marcia wasn't interested in Lamont's comments and obvious affections for the fake diva, and the mention of her name sent sharp chills of envy down her spine. He spoke about how classy and impressive she had been at a recent family dinner party. Marcia fought back a powerful urge to scream out the truth. *Lamont the Bitch is cheating on you!*

Marcia was reminded of an innocent lamb being led to slaughter as she observed the loving gleam in Lamont's eyes at the mention of Jane. She found it inconceivable that an intelligent man like Lamont could be bamboozled by an obvious slut like Jane. Yet, like most men he was blinded by nice boobs, nice ass and the promises of sweet hot hysterical pleasures between her thighs.

Not to brag but she had all that too. So why wasn't Lamont all over her instead of being so proper all the time? She wasn't an ugly duckling, and her assets were as prominent if not better than Jane's. Besides, her assets were all natural, and she suspected that Jane had breast implants.

Apparently Lamont either hadn't noticed her stacked curves, or he simply lacked any romantic feelings for her. It didn't matter because nothing was as important as him discovering the truth. Right now it looked as if she was Lamont's sole source of truth.

Still, she dreaded being the messenger of bad news, but time and options were running out. Of course he would probably want to kill the messenger and break all ties. He might even suspect that her reasons were personal and push her out of his life completely.

Bitches like Jane were wicked villains, who got away with doing evil deeds because no one saw through their disguise. But every now and then the bitches slip, and some one see's behind their masks. She had seen behind Jane's mask, and observed her leaving her lover's lair. That was the ugly truth that she didn't know how to break to Lamont. She only knew that she had to for Lamont, and for herself.

Chapter Twenty Six- Helping Out

Lamont had enjoyed lunch with Marcia, but now he was busy in his office checking tedious paperwork. He was starting to realize the complex nature of this company now. Shortly, he received a phone call and an apology from Jane about her actions the night before. "Lamont, Honey, I was awful to you," she whined. "I apologize for being such a bitch. I made a big deal over nothing. Of course you had to go and help Ruth, because that's the kind of man you are. That's why I love you. I hope that turned out okay."

"Yeah it's working out, nothing to worry about," Lamont said remaining neutral.

"Good. In fact you need to spend time with your family. Just because I don't have any siblings, that doesn't mean that you can't spend time with yours. It's natural that you want to bond with your family and I'm willing to share quality time."

Lamont could hardly believe that this was the same contrary Jane from last night. Now she was all about making promises of peace. The question is how long would she abide by her promises?

"Listen Hone," she said seductively, "why don't I treat you and your mom to dinner and cocktails at that new restaurant on Main Street? Their steaks melt in your mouth. We could pick your mom up and drop her off later." She paused briefly and then adds. "Then we can kiss and make up at my place."

"Lamont heard himself say, "Sounds like a plan to me."

"Great," she said excitedly. "I'll make reservations for eight and we'll pick up your mom at seven. That will give me a chance to make it up to you and to see Myra again."

That settled, they said goodbye and hung up. Lamont was puzzled as he folded his cell phone and pondered Jane's invitation. He couldn't figure her out. He was surprised that she had made the effort to include Myra, because she never had before. He had assumed that Jane preferred to spend time with him alone. Maybe she was making an honest effort, and he should be giving her the benefit of the doubt. He smiled now when he remembered how sweet their make up sex had been the last time they argued.

It was good that she wanted the three of them to hang out together, and he appreciated her thoughtful gesture, but Myra could be a handful after a couple of drinks. Still he would feel selfish if he left her out just so he could be alone with Jane. He just hoped that Myra would keep her embarrassing comments and notorious flirting in check.

****

After hanging up, Jane smiled wickedly and sat back in the large lounge chair, sipping her coffee. "That was productive," she said to herself, looking to make sure that she was alone in the television station lounge. "The trap is set and the prey is on the move," she said with a low laugh.

Jane had met Myra once, and it was no surprise that there were no close ties or warmth between them. Jane regarded Myra as an aging bimbo with no class or etiquette, and more ego than she was entitled to have. She talked too much and openly displayed amorous behavior to any attractive male in the vicinity. She would never understand how a man like Jake could have ever slept with such a loser.

Jane sensed that Myra didn't like her and it was mutual, but she was Lamont's mom, and she would have to stomach her for tonight, and until she got what she wanted. She just hoped the oversexed old bag didn't start that nonsense about grand children, or about helping to plan the wedding. She didn't want Myra to have any hand in her wedding. She didn't mind making sacrifices to reclaim her hold on Lamont, but she hoped that she wouldn't have to make too many where Myra was concerned.

Later Lamont picked up Jane, and now he parked in front of the small house where he had grown up. "You wait here Jane, I'll just be a minute," Lamont said as he got out and headed towards the front door. Actually Lamont wanted to talk to Myra alone.

"Okay, baby," Jane spoke in her seductive voice, consciously on her best behavior.

Lamont knocked first then used his key to enter. Myra was dressed and ready.

"You're on time," she said, smiling and still checking herself in the mirror.

"Yeah we have reservations," he said, kissing her cheek and observing the low cut blouse she wore with the short skirt. Lamont wished that she had dressed more conservative, and prayed that she would cover her over exposed boobs. "Mom I need a favor."

"What?"

"Don't be asking a lot of embarrassing questions tonight please," he said.

"Oh Lamont don't be so fussy. Do I embarrass you?"

"Sometimes you do."

"Shut up, boy," she said not taking him seriously. "Let's go. I'm starving.

He grabbed one of her sweaters from the closet as they left out. "Aren't you going to take this?"

"What for? She asked. "I can't catch nothing if I don't show something," she said with a sly smile.

Lamont believed that he was in for an interesting night and his beliefs were confirmed later at the restaurant. Myra's ill timed comments about men and their anatomy were frequent. He wished that she would act more like a mother, but he didn't expect her to change. She had always been rowdy and bold, and he was always embarrassed by her frank and sometimes off color comments, even as a child.

Shortly Jane excused herself and strutted to the rest room. Lamont breathed a short sigh, thinking that he would get some relief from his embarrassment. He had learned a lesson tonight and he wouldn't get these two together again any time soon.

"Are those her boobs or did she have some work done?" Myra asked as soon as Jane was out of sight. That girl is kinda slim to have such large boobs and all that ass. That's why you like her ain't it?"

"Come on, Ma. I'm not going to talk about stuff like that with you, so please don't start."

"What?" Myra gave her son a knowing smile and feigned an innocent expression, but secretly she enjoyed Lamont's discomfort. "You don't know if they real do you? I think she had some work done and I know how you can find out if they're fake."

"Ma, please," Lamont admonished loudly, then lowered his voice and continued. "I don't think anybody ask you. So just let it go."

There was a brief awkward silence and Myra was the first to speak. "Well at least she is black. That's a good thing. I sure hoped you learned your lesson about them white girls," she said with a thoughtful pause. "What was that girl's name, Felicia? Yeah that white trash almost got my baby killed." Myra drank the wine down and pours herself another glass from the bottle on the table. Now she changed the subject "I like this place Lamont."

Lamont remained silent, hoping that she would take the hint and do the same, but he doubted if he would be that lucky. She had consumed quite a bit of wine, and was slightly out of control.

"Here she comes now," Myra, said looking towards Jane. "She sure got a proud walk, and the way she wearing the tight black dress, and strutting tall in her high heels." Myra didn't finish her thought, but continued to watch Jane. A few men recognized Jane from the local TV station and greeted her with enthusiasm. She acknowledged and greeted them in return.

Myra observed and commented on this. "She's a real career girl ain't she? Look at how she's flirting with those guys. She sure likes all that attention." Myra shook her head.

"She's not flirting. She's just being friendly. What's she suppose to do when fans say hello? Turn her nose up?" He changed his tone now. "Well, I like her okay. I'm not with her for you. You're never going to like anybody I pick anyway so I'm not sweatin' that. Let's just drop it please. Just chill."

"What you talking bout, Lamont?" Myra asked hunching her shoulders. "I never said I didn't like her. What you getting so bent outta shape for? I'm just comment on my future daughter-in-law. You know me, I'm gon speak my mind. I don't mean to embarrass you, son," she said with an uneven voice. Now he felt bad.

A short time later, he took Myra home and said good night. Now he was alone with Jane in her apartment, anticipating a night of passion. They could finish what they had started last night. She was looking extra luscious and seemed extra sweet tonight, which made him horny.

However, Lamont received a phone call in the midst of his foreplay. He hadn't planned to answer and was about to cut it off, until he noted that it was from JJ. He was torn now because he didn't want to let Jane down again. On the other hand it might not be urgent. But what if it was? He couldn't ignore it. "Sorry baby, I'm just gonna see what he wants."

"Lamont no, Please," Jane said trying to hold back her anger.

"I'll just be a minute I promise," he said hitting the talk button on his cell. "Hello!"

JJ's voice exploded into his ear. "Oh thank God. Lamont, I need your help man. I fucked up, man. I've been arrested behind some bullshit. Please Lamont, help me. I can't spend the night in jail. I can't," he said with pleading desperation.

"Calm down and give me the details," Lamont said reaching for the pen and pad on the coffee table. "Okay shoot." He wrote down the information and hung up. He looked at a disappointed and angry Jane, who was stripped down to her bra and panties now. He wanted to kick JJ for whatever he had done to land in jail. Still he had no choice but to help him. "Baby, you're gonna be angry, but I .."

"What?" Jane asked with a panic expression. "Lamont don't."

"I'm sorry, baby, but JJ's been locked up and he needs me. He's in jail on some trumped up charge, and I know just what he's going through because I've been there and."

"Wha..What? I don't believe this shit," Jane said shaking her head from side to side. "This is some horrible twilight zone Déjà Vu bullshit," she said. "Now it's JJ's turn, who's next? Dammit, Lamont, these needy brats are hindering our sex life. You might not mind, but it's pissing me off." Her rage was so overwhelming that she forgot her promise to be more tolerant.

She took a deep breath and regained her composure, but she was visible angry, which was obvious from her flaring nostrils and pouting lips. She wanted to protest but she had said too much already. She was trying, but this one sided family loyalty was outrageous. She had been loyal to Lamont these past weeks, and now she was primed, horny and eager. Apparently his loyalties lied with his family and not with her, so why should she remain faithful to him?

She hadn't slept with Greg for three weeks, and she wanted to remain exclusive, but she craved sex right now. Maybe Lamont didn't mind abstinence, but she hadn't agreed to any vow of celibacy. She refused to remain untouched and ignored while Lamont was off playing family hero.

Now she realized that Lamont and the rich brats were a package deal, and would be in her life constantly if she was going to be him. The reality was finally hitting home and she could only take so much. She couldn't wait for the day that she could take her share of the money and get out of his life. Then he would be free to bond with his bratty siblings. She wasn't cut out to put up with the things that Lamont and the Coopers were putting her through.

Now Lamont ignored Jane's anger and kissed her quickly on the cheeks before she could refuse. "Don't forget your red cape," she said coldly. He ignored the remark and headed out the door.

An hour later he arrived at the Richmond jail, inquired at the desk and was led to the visitor's cell. JJ was almost unrecognizable with his scraggly unkempt beard, rumpled clothing and scared haggard look. Lamont was surprised to see his brother looking so sloppy. The brothers shared a proud fashion sense as well as DNA.

"What's the charge, JJ?" Lamont asked eagerly. "Those rednecks wouldn't tell me anything at the desk," Lamont said.

JJ looked sheepishly at Lamont, lost for words. Then he shrugged his shoulders and spoke in a grunt. "They've charged me with rape of a minor," he said, shaking his head with a puzzled smirk. "Lamont, I didn't know that little trashy white slut was underage. It's still hard to believe."

Lamont could relate more than JJ realized because his past troubles resulted because of a white girl. "Tell me everything JJ."

"You gonna get me out of here?"

"I already made a call to the bondsman, and he's already on the way. Who is this girl anyway and what happened?"

JJ sighed and sat back in the chair facing Lamont. "She hangs out at all the adult clubs and got ID and everything, but it must be phony. She knows about dad's money, she threatened to make trouble, and bragged about getting a big payoff. I thought she was just bluffing, but she sent the cops to my house.

"So you did have sex with her?"

"Yeah I nailed her, but so did a lot of other guys. She didn't send the cops after any of them. I was set up Lamont, and if she's under age, she sure as hell ain't innocent. She was doing guys and drugs from what I heard. Now she's trying to black mail me." JJ's voice rose with fear and broke.

"Okay calm down, Bro," Lamont said soothingly. He wasn't surprised that JJ's active libido had landed him in trouble with a young girl. "What's her name?" Lamont asked. He hoped that this was a wakeup call and that after tonight, JJ would be discreet about dating young girls.

"Her name is Roxanne Perilli; she's a gorgeous little Italian girl who was supposed to be Daisy's friend. You remember Daisy from dad's dinner party Saturday night. Anyway this girl sneaked around behind Daisy's back to sleep with me.

I hate myself for not resisting, but man that girl is sexy as hell. She's one of those exotic brown Italian girls with perfect hips and pretty legs. Lamont if you see her." He stopped as if he was too overwhelmed to say any more. "And she got these unbelievable perky boobs and a soul sister's ass," he paused and shook his head with a deep sigh.

JJ paused briefly and shot Lamont an expression that was a combination of confusion and anger, before continuing his story. "I still can't believe the little bitch is underage. Any way she got possessive and controlling, and I don't go for that. She told me if I didn't date her exclusively she would make trouble for me. That's when I broke it off. That was last week, and today I get arrested for statutory rape. Ha! That's a joke. Shit that bitch damn near raped me."

She didn't believe that I was serious at first, but once she knew that it was over she decided to get revenge." He shrugged his shoulders and gave Lamont a sad quizzical stare. "What are we going to do, Lamont?"

Lamont gave JJ a brief once over, and tried not to be judgmental about his reckless life style. Right now, it would be so easy to point fingers and say I told you so, but that would only waste time and change nothing. "Okay, okay. The damage has been done. We've got to initiate damage control."

"Lamont, let's not bring dad in on this, please." JJ's eyes pleaded. "He's been worried about a lot of shit lately and this would really bring him down."

"Don't worry; there's no reason that Jake has to know anything about this if it's handled right."Lamont believed that it was best to shelter Jake from the burden of these family crises in light of his recent worries.

"Thanks, Bro." A smile appeared on JJ's haggard face. "So you think that bondsman is here yet?" JJ asked hopefully.

"He should be," Lamont said rising from the chair. "I'm going out to check. I'm sure you'll get to sleep in your own bed instead of on a jail cot tonight. The only problem I see is this girl and these charges. Jake might find out if she pursues it," he said staring hard and long at JJ. "But hopefully we can come up with something."

Lamont pause and gave JJ a long hard gaze. "Have you told me the whole story, JJ? There aren't going to be any surprises are there?"

"Lamont I swear to you I'm telling you the truth."

"Okay, just want to know." Lamont said thoughtfully.

JJ sighed deeply, shaking his head and looking out into space. "I still can't believe that she is only sixteen with that incredible body, and so much knowledge about sex. But I'm definitely through with her. I've learned my lesson."

Lamont observed JJ's glazed eyes when he spoke of this girl, and it was obvious that just the thought of her put his brother in a sexual stupor. "Okay, right now I'm going to talk to the bondsman and get you out of here tonight. I'll call a lawyer in the morning."

JJ looked at Lamont. "Thanks again bro, you really are the best. I'm sorry to be such a pain in your ass. I got to be more careful."

Lamont wanted to say: *yes you should be*. Instead he said. "For what? You made a mistake and used bad judgment. It happens."

"Yeah but..."

"But nothing, learn from it and don't let it happen again. Meanwhile just chill until I get back."

"Okay, Lamont, thank you." His voice shook with relief. "You saved my ass, man."

Lamont moved to the exit and went to check on that bail bondsman. He moved down the main corridor, thinking that JJ and Ruth were mischievous brats with no regarded for the consequences of their actions. It was obvious that neither of them wanted Jake to know, but not because of concern for Jake's feelings. They were simply afraid that he might cut off their generous allowances.

It was all about the money with his siblings, a fact which he disliked about them, in spite of his love for them. He couldn't change that about them and they both would probably continue to get into trouble.

Ironically he realized that he was bonding with them, but thus far all the effort had been totally one side, just as Jane had said. He was always coming to their rescue but they never reciprocated. Of course that was academic because he hadn't needed to be rescued. He wondered how they would react if he ever did.

Two hours later, JJ was released from jail and headed to his luxury condo across town. Lamont was too tired to head back to Jane's apartment since it was so late. Jane would probably be asleep when he got back anyway. So instead, he decided to remain in Richmond and crash at his own apartment a few blocks from JJ's building.

Once he arrived at his place, he made himself comfortable and called Jane to apologize for leaving her again. "Hey babe," he said when she picked up. "Sorry how the night turned out."

"That's okay," Jane cooed over the phone. "You on your way back now?"

"Well I was going to crash here tonight, but I'll make it up to you."

"What," Jane's soothing tone turned to a furious roar. "I can't believe you're doing this shit to me again, Lamont." Jane lost control of all patience. "I'm tired of being left hanging while you're out saving those sorry ass bratty siblings. Lamont, this is getting to be a bad habit and you're not thinking about me at all."

"Jane, try to understand. I couldn't leave my brother in that jail cell. And after I took care of all the details I just got here. It's late and I'm beat."

"Oh I do understand alright," her voice broke. "I don't mean shit to you, Lamont. If it ain't one of those brats, it's another and I'm getting fed up."

"Come on Jane, stop being over dramatic. I'll make it up to you. You know this has nothing to do with my feelings for you." In spite of his apology, Lamont fought back rising anger. "All your talk about understanding, was that just a lot of bull?"

"No, but understanding has limits."

"How could you be understanding one minute and so unreasonable the next? My brother was in trouble, and there was no way for me to ignore that. If you can't understand that I don't know what to say. I'm not going to apologize for helping my brother out of a jam."

"I see, that's fine, Lamont. You do what you have to do. You be there for JJ and both of you just go to hell." There was a loud click on the other end and his cell phone went dead.

Lamont felt strangely aloof from reality and he stood there with the phone in his hand. What was wrong with her, he thought. He had to help his brother. He wanted to be with her but this was a family emergency, and he had to make himself available. Who else could JJ have called and taken into his confidence? Most of JJ's friends were either young females or party boys, who couldn't or wouldn't make sacrifices.

He had seen a dramatic change in Jane over the past few days. She was so disagreeable about this, and he never expected that, especially after their talk a few days earlier. She had seemed sensible and clear headed, and had agreed that they wanted the same things. This dramatic turnaround mystified him. This was yet another puzzle to him about her, and he had to ask himself if he really knew his fiancée.

Meanwhile, Jane was still shaking after she hung up the telephone. She asked herself if showing such anger was wise right now. Yes, she had the right to be angry at him in spite of her own cautions. She wasn't going to be stepped on like some doormat no matter how much money was involved.

She looked around the bedroom feeling foolish as she observed the lit candles. She had decided to forgive him and expected him to return even if it was later. She was wearing Victoria Secrets' lingerie, aching with passion and anticipating his return, only to be stood up again.

"Well I don't have to take this crap," she said as she impulsively picked up the telephone and dialed. "The Hell, with you, Lamont. You don't have to touch me, because I can get laid. One monkey don't stop the show."

Suddenly a husky voice flowed in her ear from the other end. The penetrating husky voice heightened her urges and spread warmth to her sensitive areas, like a magic elixir. She felt dirty and hot all at once. She felt even hotter now than she had earlier. "Hi, Greg. Wha cha you doing, Babee," She whispered like a sexy Siren.

Greg felt an involuntary adrenaline surge and got an erection at the sound of her voice. He was instantly excited, thinking that this phone call could be his reprieve. He could finally make up for his shameful display three weeks earlier. Jane was a highly sexual animal who had neither patience nor faithfulness, and she would always need more than one man. He had expected to hear from her eventually, but not this soon.

She had Lamont, but she also needed him to affirm her sexiness, and he needed her to explore the avenues and excitement that they conjured up together. He had learned his lesson and would never push for more than she was willing to give him. He would do it her way and relish what he could get. He could live with having Jane part time if he had to, because, she was hot and gave one hundred percent sexually. Part time sex with her was better than full time sex with any one else.

He purposely paused for a minute before speaking into the phone again. "Sorry, couldn't talk before. He wanted her bad, but he had to make her fret a little.

"You're whispering. Have you got somebody there with you?" Jane asked uneasily.

"Uh, yeah," he said whispering into the phone. "She's in the bathroom right now," he lied. "She's kinda reminds me of you and she's good." He paused and changed the direction of the conversation. "So how have you been and why you calling me so late? I almost didn't answer and I shouldn't have. I was becoming obsessed with you and I want to thank you for guiding me in the right direction," he said. He hoped to piqué her interest with this line of conversation.

"Look Greg, I want us to keep what we got, you know we got a good thing right?"

"No, I don't. The last time I saw you, you said," he didn't finish because she interrupted.

"Forget what I said the last time. Listen to me now. I want you tonight."

"It's morning," he taunted. "And I don't know if I..."

"Well I want you this morning," she cut him off again. "So get rid of whoever you're with because I'm on my way over."

Greg wanted her too, but he couldn't resist making her squirm. "I don't know if I can even rise to the occasion. Mary here just took a hunk of spunk out my funk, baby."

"Bullshit! I'm not worried. I know you and I got a few tricks and some stored up energy just ready to explode."

"Really? Do you guarantee that?"

"Bet your ass on it."

"You're right because I got a boner just talking to you. Get your hot Tush over here and get you some of this."

"I'm on my way."

"Okay, I'll get this girl out of here."

"You better." Jane felt no guilt, because she convinced herself that Lamont was to blame for leaving her in the first place. She had made it obvious what she wanted, but he had to go play big brother instead of playing with her. She was tired of being second to all the damn Coopers. She wasn't going to stand for neglect from any man.

She was dressed in ten minutes and her eyes caught her reflection in the mirror as she flitted about, checking herself. She scrutinized her figure with a wide satisfied smile. "Girl you look too good, and got too much going to be mistreated and neglected by any man." She then strutted out the door with but one thought in her head right now.

Lamont's guilty thoughts of Jane made sleep impossible, so he hopped up from the bed and began dressing. He decided to go back to Norfolk after all. It's late and he would have to drive for at least an hour, but he was wide awake and he needed to do this.

He felt like he wasn't meeting her halfway, and he had to try a little harder. Maybe he was wimping out, he didn't know, but he did know that he hadn't been completely fair to her, and that wasn't right.

An hour later he was just a few blocks away from Jane's apartment, feeling anxious because she hadn't answered her telephone. He had called her several times after she hung up on him. The line had been busy at first, but after that he just didn't get a response. He assumed everything was alright and maybe she had just turned the phone off. Still he was eager about the situation and now wanted to be here for her.

He owed her that much, since she had juggled her schedule to be here for him. She could also be hurting her career and her chance of a promotion by spending so much time with him. He could see why she had been so angry at him and his needy family earlier tonight. This family came with a life time supply of problems and conflicts and could be a burden for anyone.

It was unfortunate that Ruth and JJ had back-to-back trouble, but he had his priorities straight now, and he planned to make it up to Jane by showering her with the attention that she deserves. More than ever he was eager to apologize and make it all right. As he slipped his own key into the lock of Jane's apartment, and let himself in, he decided to start making amends this morning.

He walked through the apartment looking for her. He was surprised to find the apartment empty this early. She couldn't have gone to work already. He had a strange funny feeling in the pit of his stomach, and fear that something has happened to her. He peered slowly out the large front window, and noticed that Jane's car was gone from the lot. "Well at less she wasn't dragged away," he said aloud, trying to calm down.

He slowed his breathing and relaxed, assuming that Jane was driving around to cool off. He guessed that she might be with her parents, since she had no other relatives and very few girl friends. He felt positive that she was alright and he felt anxious to make up with her so everything would be fine again.

He wanted things to work between Jane and himself, and he would have to stop whining about whether or not she's the right one. He no longer blamed her for being angry and directing her rage at him earlier, because it was partially his fault. She had been angry and honest about it and that was okay. Relationships needed honesty and freedom from dirty dark lies. Jane was doing her part and he needed to step up and do the same.

Chapter Twenty Seven- Busted

Greg slipped out of bed and looked in his underwear drawer. He was scheduled to go to work, but he was contemplating hopping back in bed on top of Jane's exposed nude body. Those pert nipples were so tempting and would suck on them real easy, without even disturbing her sleep. He gazed at one shapely leg hanging off the bed and the hard nipple of one exposed breast.

He couldn't resist hopping back into bed with her, and now he woke her, spread her legs, and eased his penis into her neatly shaved Vagina. He was all over her like a wild man, invading her deep, hearing her moaned, and feeling her scratch his back with aggressive intensity. "Oh Greg I'm so glad that you're like this," she cried out in the heat of her freaky insane passion.

"Oh baby, you satisfy my every fantasy," Greg puffed.

"Oh that's it, Greg. Stay right there in that spot. Yes baby."

"You know I will, sweetie. You like that huh." He measured his words and humped her with each syllable. "I'm gonna screw your freaky little brains out this morning," He cried out gleefully, shaking the bed with increased strokes.

Later Greg left Jane relaxing on the bed and made a pot of coffee and toasted some bagels. Now Jane smelled the coffee and started to stir. She stretched and yawned, then called out. "Greg honey, where are you?"

Greg went and peered into the bedroom from the doorway and observed Jane kneeling on the bed completely nude. "You better stop doing that," he said grabbing his crotch. "Want some more of this or you want some coffee?"

"I'll have some coffee right now, but I'm definitely gonna get me some more of that later." She licked her lips. "You were fierce. Are you taking Viagra or something? Cause you were uuuh," she made an animal noise and twisted her face. "I'm definitely coming back for thirds, maybe more. I'm a greedy girl."

"Sounds like a plan." He touched himself.

She looked around. "Where the hell are my clothes, and cell phone and stuff?" She asked throwing up her hands.

"Your stuff?" He asked lewdly licking his lips.

"Not that stuff," she said, playfully. "My other stuff.

"It's all over, just look, it's here somewhere," Greg said then went to pour the coffee. Now the phone rang, and he picked it up. "Hello."

"Hello? Greg?" The voice on the other end asked, sounding puzzled.

Greg's stomach churned, because he recognized Lamont's voice. "Lamont?" Greg asked. Now his heart pounded inside his chest like a horde of rats wearing combat boots. He thought that he and Jane were busted, and that Lamont's next words would be: *'Put Jane on, I know she's there with you.'*

Greg swallowed hard and he forced his heartbeat to slow down. It was impossible for Lamont to know anything. He had to calm down and not raise suspicion. Still, Greg couldn't shake the nervous butterflies in the pit of his stomach or think straight. Lamont must suspect something to call like this. "How's the new job," Greg said, making awkward small talk.

"Not bad," Lamont spoke hesitantly. "Things going okay with you?" Lamont asked sounding dazed.

"Yeah the job is still the same, still got a lot of confusion and Bullshit. You know how it is with the powers that be. They still don't want to pay us nothing. But I'm leaving as soon as I get my shit together."

"Greg! Honey! I can't find my bra and bikini thong panties," Jane yelled out in a tone filled with jubilation and volume. As she moved towards the kitchen, she froze upon noticing Greg's frantic shushing and tight grip covering the telephone. Jane lowered her voice, and shot him a strange expression. "I can't find my panties," she whispered, facing him now as she moved to the counter and poured a cup of coffee.

Greg held the phone away and leaned into her. "It's Lamont on the phone," he whispered.

Suddenly her eyes stretched and she bit on her lower lip. "Lamont? Damn, does he know?" She asked, continuing to whisper with stretched eyes and open mouth.

Greg held up his hand to silence her while continuing to speak into the telephone. "Look man it was good hearing from you, but I was about to head out," he lied. He was anxious to end this awkward conversation, and yet he wondered why Lamont had called. "What's on your mind?"

There was a hesitation on the other end before Lamont spoke. "Nothing man," he chuckled. "You ain't gonna believe this but I accidently dialed your number. Any way, you have a good day, Greg. I ain't gonna hold you. Talk to you later."

Greg was silent after hanging up, but Jane had a multitude of questions at once. "That was Lamont? What did he say? What did he want? Why is he calling here this early? Did he mention me?"

"I don't have the answers to your questions, but I don't like what just happened. He said he dialed my number by accident," Greg said, with a strange expression. "He sounded kinda funny. Something ain't right. He didn't sound like the Lamont I know. His voice didn't have that confidence, and he seemed surprised when I answered. Is he on drugs or something?"

"Who, Lamont? You gotta be kidding me," Jane said with a dismissive chuckle. Then she shot him a look of horror. "Oh my god," she said holding her hand to her mouth.

"What, what, what," Greg said impatiently.

"I wonder if he heard me yell out to you. Why didn't you tell me you were on the phone and...?"

"Don't start playing the blame game," Greg said, instantly annoyed with her now. "How the hell did I know he was gonna call, and how did I know that you were gonna yell like a crazy loud mouth bitch?" He mimicked her; 'Greg you seen my draws?'

"You mocking me?" she asked, glaring at him. "Fuck you Greg. Bastard."

"Not now honey, I have a headache, and you're getting me confused with Lamont."

"Don't play with me you piece of shit," she said as she moves closer and attempts to pour hot coffee on him.

"What's the matter with you, you crazy bitch," he shouted, grabbing her hand.

"So now I'm a crazy bitch huh?" She asked breathlessly, while managing to spill some of the coffee on his shirt.

"Stop it Jane," he said slapping her across the face. Just chill out will ya?" The slap slowed her down and she stood there stunned, unable to speak at first.

"You hit me," she said as if she just realized it.

He ignored her words and mood. "Listen to me; we can't be attacking each other. We got to find out if Lamont knows about us, and what we're going to do about it."

This seemed to register and her dazed expression was replaced with fear. "You think he knows? How? I've never given him any reason to suspect. I've never let anything slip and he's so busy all the time. How?"

"I don't know. Maybe he doesn't know, but it was mighty strange that he called here this early. And he just happens to call on the very morning that you spent the night here. I don't like this. It's too much of a coincidence." Greg seemed deep in thought as he said, "something's not right and I'm not so sure that I ever g...."

"Shit, shit shit," Jane shouted suddenly. "If he knows that means the wedding is off." She paused. "He's gotta marry me now. He can't back out."

"If he knows, or even suspects you're cheating, there ain't gonna be no wedding," Greg said. "I'm starting to think now that there just might not be a wedding."

"Oh there's going to be a wedding, Greg, there's got to be."

"Really? Why Jane? Greg asked with an amused puzzle stare. "Why does it have to be? If he knows, about us, there is no way that he's gonna marry you. Even Lamont's not that dumb."

She looked towards some middle distance now completely unfocused. "I've already met his family and they like me. He's got to marry me."

Greg sighed, threw his hands up in the air, and gave her the Samuel Jackson glare. "Bitch, you really are crazy as hell ain't you?"

Meanwhile Lamont's was shaking so bad that he was afraid to stand up right now. His head swam as he reluctantly fitted the pieces together. He had hung up five minutes ago, but he was unable to take his eyes off the telephone. His logic told him one thing, but his heart formed its own conclusion.

A simple telephone call had just become the most bizarre and unreal experience that he had ever encountered. Now all he had was the hoped that the call had been a bad dream from which he was about to awake. Yet he was already awake, and trapped in continuous nightmarish repercussion of the telephone call he had just made. He replayed the conversation again and again, hoping to make sense of what he had heard in the background.

He had been mildly shocked when he heard Greg's voice on the other end, but his shock increased exponentially when he heard Jane's voice in the background. Now tightness gripped his chest because, there was no doubt that he had heard Jane's voice. It was impossible for him to be mistaken about the distinct sexy voice that had scolded him playfully, and whispered in his ear. It was the same raspy voice that moaned, flowed, and filled him with excitement and passion.

He seemed to sense an out of body experience due to the bizarre confrontation with harsh reality and truth. It was unbelievable, and yet he hadn't imagined the conversation with Greg, or the sound of Jane's voice. As much as he didn't want to face the truth, he had no choice. The realization and logic fit together with the overwhelming speed of light: *Jane and Greg were lovers.* Jane had successfully rendered him blind and trusting, and then duped him so soundly that he never saw it coming.

Jane was a clever illusion, and maybe this was payback for his treacherous treatment of Felicia Courtney. He had duped Felicia with lies then tried to justify his treacherous deeds, claiming that it was to spite Felicia's racist brother. Now payback has come full circle and Jane had been playing games with him. Payback had come in the form of a bitch name Jane. He wanted to erase the last ten minutes from his mind, but it was impossible. Now he recalled events that led to that bizarre telephone conversation.

He had been determined to find her and remembered that he had gotten a busy signal when he called back the first time. He assumed that she might have called her parents and had joined them. He didn't have her parents' phone number, so he hit the redial button, expecting to one of Jane's parents to answer. There was a 50-50 chance that the abrasive Dan Curtis would answer, but he would risk it. He just wanted to know that she was okay and to apologize.

He had been stunned when Greg answered, but he was shocked when Jane's voice came through the receiver crystal clear. Her words haunted him and echoed in his head. *'Greg, Honey, where are my panties?'* He saw images of the couple inside his head, and his stomach flipped. Heat enveloped him and crawled up and down his flesh. The raw truth hit harder than a cold turkey drug cure. He didn't want to believe that he had been such a prize sucker, or that Jane and Greg had likely gotten a lot of laughs at his expense

Lamont dashed from Jane's place and drove around a while. He ended up in front of Hal's mother's house, and just sat there at first. He had to talk about this to some one and Hal was the only good friend he had. Still he didn't know if he wanted to reveal his stupidity to any one. Maybe this was a bad idea, he thought. He was about to drive away when he saw Hal observing him from the door way. Now Hal walked sluggishly to the car.

"Lamont? I thought that was you," Hal said, holding a coffee cup and staring at Lamont, with an inquisitive scowl. "You alright bro? You look like shit, man. What's wrong?" He asked concerned.

Now that Hal was asking, Lamont felt the need to tell some one. He didn't just feel down, he felt as if he were being pounded into the ground right now. "Everything has all turned to shit."

"Is it the new job man? They giving you a hard time?"

"I wish that was the problem. That would be so simple."

"Hey man, why don't you come in, and have a cup of coffee and talk about it. I just made a fresh pot." Lamont dragged himself from the car and followed Hal up the walk, entering the house. The house was made up of an abundance of small rooms, but the kitchen and dining rooms were huge.

"Sit man," Hal urged, indicating the dining room table. Lamont flopped down in a chair at the big table, in the center of the dining room, and Hal poured a cup of coffee. He put it in front of Lamont along with creamer and sugar. "Everybody sleep right now so we can talk without being interrupted."

The coffee smelled good and Lamont realized that he craved it more than he had first thought. He poured in some creamer, stirred and took a few sips. "It's good Hal," he said scowling.

"Well I try," Hal said then waited patiently, not wanting to push. He had never seen Lamont so down and he was anxious to know what had happened. Lamont didn't make him wait for long. He started slow and filled Hal in on everything that had happened. Hal said nothing, mainly because he didn't know what to say. Secretly, he had always thought that Jane was too in love with herself, and wrong for Lamont. It was mind boggling that she would two time Lamont with Greg.

"And you want to know the kicker Hal," Lamont said sipping the coffee, "I wondered now if all those trips out of town were bogus. What if she had used that as an excuse to meet with Greg, or even other guys? There's no telling how long they have been sneaking around behind my back," he said with a pause. "Now that I think about it, Greg called in sick some of those times that Jane was on her road trips." He stopped and looked up at Hal

"I feel like a prize fool. All this time she had been cheating right under my nose. How did I miss it? Were there others besides Greg?"

"Man it ain't your fault," Hal said shaking his head. "Women are smarter than we are. They do shit right under our nose all the time because they have it down to a science. We go along with it because we're slaves to the Pussy Factor."

Lamont seemed annoyed with Hal. "What are you talking about, Hal? Pussy Factor? I'm not in the mood for another one of your theories," Lamont said, absently sipping his coffee.

"Naw, Mont. I am talking truth. Here's the thing, if a man is getting pussy, he's a man. And the more pussy he gettin' the more other men envy or respect him. If a man ain't getting' none, then he's called a lot of unmanly things, and other men disrespect him and want to kick his ass," Hal paused and smugly sipped from his large mug as if he had made a great point. "And women know this too, that's why they put us through so much hell. They know if they take away the pussy, we ain't shit. That's why they get away with doing shit in our face. They ogle other guys and flirt even when they with their main guy. They know we need to get that pussy to maintain our manliness. Let's face it, a man who is controlled, henpecked, and pussy whipped by his woman, still gets more respect than a man without a woman."

"Yeah right, Hal," Lamont said skeptically. "Why do I even listen to you?" Lamont finished his coffee as he spoke.

"Okay I know you don't believe me, but that's the truth man."

There was an awkward silence before Lamont began to assess his situation. "It's funny how I thought that my life was finally going so great. I was sure that I had a good woman and a bright future. I could see bonding with my new found family, and having some kids but now..," he paused unable to finish.

"I wouldn't worry about it too much man. I know it's hard and it feels like the bottom dropped out, but you're strong and tough, Lamont and I know you. Yeah you've been deceived, but you can't let deception break you down, man. See deception is a double threat, it's a deal breaker and a will breaker, but you got to hang in there buddy." Hal paused and waited for Lamont to speak but when he didn't, Hal continued. "You said you weren't sure about getting' married in the first place remember? I know you didn't want this to happen, but maybe it happened for a reason."

"But I thought I could trust her, Hal," Lamont's voice was distant. "Even though I had doubts about marriage I agreed, and I was going through with it because I trusted her.

"I know. It's confusing and sometimes it's hard to get a clue about how things might turn out," Hal sighed.

"I never gave her any reason to cheat. Was I just not man enough? What's the deal with that? Is it because I'm not an asshole like Greg? Is that what women want?"

"Don't beat yourself up man. It ain't about you; it's that bitch that did the dirt. And even if you had done something wrong, you didn't cheat. You deserved better. Jane cheated to satisfy her selfish lust."

"Well one thing is for sure, I don't want to ever see her again because I don't know what I would do to her," Lamont said with his eyes fixed on some far distance.

"Naw man, you don't want to get into any trouble. Is she worth it?"

"No, probably not," Lamont said with a deep sigh.

"What will you say when you do see her? You will have to see her sooner or later."

"I don't know Hal, I haven't thought about it. I just know that I can't see her right now."

"I hear you on that, Bro."

Lamont's cell phone rang and he jumped with a start, but then relaxed, when he saw Jane's number on caller ID. Hal noticed that he didn't answer. "Is that her?"

"Yeah. I'll let the voice mail pick up. I have nothing to say to that bitch right now. I just don't have the stomach to listen to her lies, and I'm not ready to face her without feeling the urge to crush her throat."

"Well in that case, you're better off avoiding her for a while then."

"No problem there. I got plenty to keep busy." Lamont notice that she had left a voice message and clicked on to hear it. *"Hi honey,"* the voice came through the tiny speaker, *"I wanted to apologize for losing my temper last night. I took something and went straight to bed. I'm getting ready for work now and I'll call you later. Miss you, maybe we can get together later. Love you, Bye honey."*

After listening to the message, Lamont broke the connection and turned off the phone. Now he looked at Hal, who was shaking his head in disbelief. "Can you believe her? She didn't even sleep in her bed last night. She's a natural liar and I never even suspected."

"Like I said man, it comes natural for some women," Hal said.

"Well, I don't click with liars," Lamont said. He was remembering his anger upon discovering that Myra had lied to him about Jake. "Maybe you're right. Maybe all women are natural liars." Lamont thought about Marcia and how he had trusted her as well. Was she in the same boat with Jane and Myra? She seemed honest but so had Jane. He was puzzled and couldn't help but wonder about all women. Still in the back of his mind he didn't want to believe that Marcia was anything like Jane or Myra.

It was ironic that a random phone call had exposed his unfaithful fiancée, and that one new piece of information about her has changed every perception he had of her just twenty four short hours earlier. Now he knows that she is a cheater, a liar, and a slut with no conscious about her brazen deceptions. She's just a cold hearted stranger to him now, and he questioned her integrity on everything she's ever said. What a difference a day makes.

Chapter Twenty Eight-
Distance

Lamont left Hal, went home and changed clothes, and then dragged himself into the office. In his determination to avoid all contact with Jane, he shifted his concentration to his work assignments. He avoided Jane's phone calls for the few days and became a work horse. Eventually he would talk to her, but only to break it off. Right now the less he saw of her the better he felt.

His cell phone buzzed and he checked the caller ID and saw Jane's number. He didn't pick up but he checked the message she left. *"Hi Baby, I miss you and I'm worried. Please call me."* He had no plans to respond, and found her strangely amusing playing the worried fiancée. She sounded like an actress playing a part. He would let her stew in her treachery, before he confronted her. It didn't matter that it gave her more time to be with Greg, because they deserved each other. The only thing that mattered now was that he kept busy with the job that he was hired to do.

Suddenly Lamont's telephone rang and his mind snapped from all thoughts of Jane as he picked up. Peter was on the other end. "Hello Peter, what's up?" Lamont asked.

"I need to talk to you," Peter said on the other end. "Just want to discuss your work so far. I can be there right after I leave accounting. I'll drop by your office in about thirty minutes."

"Okay then, I'll see you shortly." Lamont suspected that Peter might have some suspicions, and it was important that he quash those suspicions. He buzzed Marcia on the intercom and as always she answered immediately.

"Yeah, Lamont."

"Marsh I need you to locate and print some folders for me. Get me the year end stock reports and the annual sales projections for the past three years."

"Right away." Marcia located the folders shortly and took them to Lamont. She noticed that he was looking into space while taking the folders from her. "Pressure of this job getting to you?" She asked but he didn't respond. "Can I get you anything, Lamont?"

"What," he focused on her now. "No I'm good, just thinking, Marsh. I'm fine." He began looking through the reports and she took the hint and left.

Lamont had just read the first page of the folders when the intercom buzzed minutes later. "What is it, Marsh?"

"Hal Atkins here to see you. Something about some uniforms."

"Yeah right, I almost forgot. Send him in."

Hal stuck his head inside the office door before stepping inside. "Hey man, I mainly wanted to see how you're doing. You look better than you did the other day. You okay?"

"Yeah, Hal, I'm keeping busy."

"Good," Hal said pausing briefly, "this will all blow over before you know it. You'll see."

Lamont didn't want to talk about his problem with Jane so he changed the subject. "You want to see what the uniforms look like?"

"Yeah man."

Lamont open his desk drawer and took out a catalogue and handed it to Hal. "Look at these proto types and pick one, then go to Human Resources and get set up.

Hal looked through the catalogue and pointed to one of the uniforms. "Man this one is nice." They quickly concluded their business and Hal was leaving just as Peter Vel Haus was entering the office.

"Excuse me," Peter said, giving Hal a surprise look while stepping pass him.

"No prob'," Hal said extending a hand. "I'm Hal Atkins."

Peter gave Hal a quick limp handshake. "Peter Vel Haus."

Hal made an unconscious scowl when getting a whiff of Peter's sickening cologne. He was glad he didn't have to work anywhere near the guy. Poor Lamont, he thought to himself while making his way down the hall to the elevator.

Later Marcia buzzed Lamont, informing him that she was leaving for the day, and asked if he would be needing anything else. "Oh no Marcia, you go on, I'll see you in the morning," Marcia heard him say. He didn't seem to be in a hurry to leave she thought as she gazed at the intercom.

"Something serious is wrong," she mumbled, "Lamont just called me Marcia. That's strange, because he always calls me *Marsh*." She suspected that he was thinking about something other than this job. She hoped that whatever it was, it was only temporary. She would try not to worry about it because she was confident that Lamont could handle the problem.

Marcia was greeted at the elevator by Linda Lassiter, and two other co-workers. "Hi Marcia," Linda said with a cordial smile.

"I Ii Linda," Marcia said, a bit surprised. "What's up?"

"Well, we're gonna stop at the Wolf's Den for a couple of drinks," she said, looking towards the two girls engaged in conversation, beside her. "Why don't you hang with us?"

As the new girl in the office, Marcia hadn't been very sociable, and the others probably thought that she was stuck up. Her first impulse was to refuse, but then she decided that it wouldn't hurt to have one drink before heading home. "Sure why not?"

However, things didn't go according to plans, because one drink turned to more, and shortly she felt tipsy. She hadn't thought that she would connect with these girls and enjoy their company this much. Unfortunately, time slipped away, and now she had a long drive back to Norfolk. "Ladies I got to be leaving," she slurred.

"Oh so soon?" Linda asked with obvious disappointment. "Girl your timin' is lousy. All the hunks are starting arrive," Linda said, hunching Marcia, and nodding towards the tall athletic young black man, with short wavy hair. "See what I'm talking about girl," she said then tried to slap a high five with one of the other girls, and missed. "How bout some of that dark meat on a half shell, Eve," Linda said and winked at the pretty little blonde sitting across from her.

"I can only wish," Eve slurred. Shirley, the other friend sitting with them looked, and joined in giggling. Obviously they were all more than just a little tipsy.

Marcia smiled then stood up wobbling slightly. "Girls, this really was fun and we gonna have to do it another time, maybe on the weekend. But now I got a long drive to make and I need to clear my head."

Eve stuck out her full lips, pretending to pout. "Oh girl, why you want to be a buzz kill? You're not in any shape to drive."

"Yeah, girl, why don't you stay with…?"

"I'll be all right," Marcia cut Linda's words off, "with some fresh air and a short walk. And I'm not breaking up the set, it's just that I got a full day's work tomorrow, and I got a long drive tonight and…"

"That ain't no problem," Linda said. "Come stay with me. Hell, I'll loan you something to wear, we bout the same size." She looked Marcia up and down. "I'm a six; you're about a six, right?" Marcia nods and Linda continues. "Actually, I'm a five but I wear six in tight dresses, cause a five makes my ass look like a Shetland pony." She said the last with a stage whisper.

"Girl you need to stop trippin'," Shirley said, "your ass ain't that huge. Hell I'd do you horse ass and all."

"Pony ass," Linda said, pretending to be insulted. Now she ignored Shirley and continued. "Like I was saying, some clothes make me look like I got too much ass. That's okay because guys are freaks for a big ass." She bounced up and down slightly to emphasize her last words.

Marcia was having a good time, but she had to cut it short and clear her head. "This is nice and like I said we'll do it again sometime, but now I need to get home. Tomorrow is still a work day."

"Right," said Shirley, "and you probably got something special you want to wear for that dreamy boss of yours. Can't blame you girl. Those shoulders, that voice and oowee, those lips makes me wet just thinking about them. I'd sure be trying to impress him. Shit, yeah."

"Word, girl," Linda said, "And those large hands. He'd probably handle this Shetland pony with ease."

Now Marcia felt offended at their lewd remarks about Lamont. "Sorry I got to go," she stumbles twice as she moved quickly past Linda who sat on the outside of the booth.

"Easy girl," she heard Linda call out, as she distanced herself from them. "I'm fine," she said moving swiftly to the exit. She should have just said no and let them think she's a snob. They all lived close to the job and would have little problem getting home.

She had planned to relocate in four months when her lease expired. However, she lived in Norfolk and now she had to drive back tonight. She had used bad judgment and now she had to figure out how to get home safely. Perhaps she should consider spending the night and borrowing some clothes like Linda had suggested.

Her thoughts were jarred when she bumped into some one suddenly. "Sorry, I wasn't looking," she apologized and looked up. She found herself staring into Lamont's dark haunting eyes, and felt flushed instantly. "Lamont," she whispered hoarsely, then stood frozen and laboring for coherent words. "I uh… stopped to have a drink with the girls and."

"Marsh, you don't have to explain."

"Yeah I know that. I just wanted to tell you anyway. I didn't want the girls to think that I was a snob or anything and." She paused. "Forget it," she said dismissively waving her hand. They moved to a nearby table in the foyer outside the bar and sat. "You just left work?" She asked.

"Yeah, came down to get some of this great coffee from next door, and then I'm going home," he said holding up the cup in his hand. "I been keeping busy and things are finally making sense. I'm becoming more familiar with the system."

Marcia thought he seemed sad in spite of his efforts to be upbeat. She felt a need to console him. "I knew you'd figure it out like you always do. You got the brains and the skills to figure anything out." She suddenly felt sober in her expression of concerns about his dreariness. She wanted badly to cheer him up.

Lamont suddenly felt self conscious about all the praise that Marcia was laying on him "Marsh look I'm sorry, I don't mean to talk shop. You hear that all day long."

"I don't mind, Lamont. You're my friend, and I have bent your ear about my wicked sister, Eunice, a time or two," she said, making a face. Now she became serious. "You've been there for me, and I can't thank you enough for coming through with this job, I love it."

"You deserve it. You're a great friend, Marsh," he said forcing a smile. "Some day some lucky guy is gonna be so thrilled to scoop you up."

"Well, so far no one is coming with a scoop," she said sadly. She wished that he would make a move on her, but maybe she's just not his type. She knew from the beginning that working close to him again would be hard, but she never thought it would be torturous.

"Oh it'll happen," Lamont said and sipped his coffee. Now he seemed more concerned. "You okay, Marsh?"

"I'm fine," she said, with a pause then continued. "Yeah, I'll find the right guy or he'll find me."

"That's right. When you least expect it. With that gorgeous smile and great b." His voice dropped and he stopped in mid sentence.

"Is that how it happened with you?" She asked quietly.

"Excuse me?" He stared into her eyes.

"With you and Jane? Was it sudden, or did you get to know her before you fell for her?"

Lamont was stunned by Marcia's words at first, because he had put Jane from his mine. He paused and looked at Marcia, wondering if he should discuss the status of his relationship. He had said no more secrets between them, but this was different. It wasn't a good idea to mention anything about his relationship with Jane. "Hey, how did this conversation go there? You have a talent for changing the subject when it comes to you. Now why is that?" He asked, looking at her with an amused stare.

"I don't like to talk about myself. You know that."

"I know, and I won't pressure you," he said. "So you're not planning on making the drive back tonight are you?"

"Oh yeah." She stood up and held her purse close. "As a matter of fact, I better get going." She glanced at her watch. It's almost ten now and it'll be after eleven when I get home."

"Marsh, come on. I can't let you do that. Come stay at my place for tonight."

"Your place?" She asked timidly.

"Don't worry I'm not going to attack you in your sleep or anything like that."

"I'm sure of that, but I can't be asking you for favors. You're my boss, Lamont. I can't ask you to do special things for me.

First of all you didn't ask me. Second of all we're friends first. And if I can't help my friend, than I can't be a friend. So let me be a friend," he said emphatically.

There was no argument that she could conjure at this moment, so she accepted his offer. "Okay, but I want the couch. I insist."

"We'll negotiate," he said with amusement.

She followed him to his apartment, and entered. It was the first time she had ever been to his place. She never visited him in Norfolk because she had never been invited, because of Jane. His place was smartly decorated, but it could use a woman's touch.

Much to her dismay, Lamont was a perfect gentleman. He allowed her to sleep in his bed and he slept on the couch. The next morning he fixed a quick breakfast of frozen pancakes and sausage, and was about to dashed off when he heard her stirring about. "Good morning, Marsh."

"Hello Lamont," she called from the bath room. "Do you have an extra tooth brush?"

"Sure, in the cabinet beneath the sink," he said, while dressing hurriedly. "Sorry to run off and leave you but I want to get down to the office."

"Sure go ahead. I'll see you later."

"Hey don't worry about coming in today. You just take your time and go back to Norfolk. Do some shopping and get your head together."

"That's sweet Lamont, but I told you I don't want you doing me favors."

"Well you don't have any clothes to wear."

"I can get some clothes, but I'll have to report late for work. Is that okay?"

"Sounds like a plan to me. You can go shopping this morning and come in around noon. It's going to be hard without you, but I can survive for a few hours I'm sure."

"Lamont, I don't expect you to bail me out, and I won't put you in position to have to do that and."

"Hey, stop apologizing woman." He teased. "I'm the boss and I said don't show your face until noon. Is that clear?"

"Yes sir." She saluted him playfully. "Hey I'm gonna leave now too. Just let me finish here and get all my stuff." She moved quickly and shortly they both headed out. She brushed up against him on the way out and a spark of static electricity popped between them. "Oops, sorry." They both apologized simultaneously.

They remained silent until reaching the ground floor, and then

203

moved across the cobblestone pavement. "I'll walk you to your car." He said.

She looked about then pointed to a pole in the lot. "I'm over there near that crooked green telephone pole. As they walked silently to the parking lot, Marcia was curious about the sadness that she sensed in Lamont's mood. She wondered, and even hoped silently that Jane was the problem. It was wrong to think that way, but such thoughts gave her great relief and elation at the possibility.

Marcia longed to take personal satisfaction in seeing that slimy bitch exposed. She had the explosive information at her disposal, but she had a change of heart. She wasn't up to any underhanded tactics to expose Jane. That would be cowardice. She had to tell Lamont face to face, even if it meant that he might misread her motives and have nothing more to do with her afterwards. She hated Jane even more for putting her in this precarious predicament.

Chapter Twenty Nine-
Follow up

Lamont arrived at the office an hour later, settled in and made a phone call to J.B. Smith, the attorney he had hired to represent Ruth and JJ. His brief conversation revealed a shocking development.

"Ruth discharged me, Mr. Savage," Smith said. "She said that she made her own settlement and no longer need my services."

Lamont was suddenly furious with Ruth. "What? She made her own settlement?" He asked fuming now. "Why didn't you stop her or notify me?"

"This happen late yesterday and I was going to call you this morning," Smith said neutrally. "Anyway, I was helpless since she took action without consulting me. Besides, I can't anticipate when a client is going to take matters into their own hands."

"Did she say anything about the settlement?"

"No, not a clue. All I know is that Ms Cooper missed our meeting yesterday morning, and when I called her she told me that my services were no longer need. I insisted on seeing her, but she assured me that she had taken care of everything."

Lamont cringed to think of what that might mean. Had she paid them off, and if so how? They wouldn't settle for a skimpy payoff once they knew who they were dealing with. What solution had Ruth's twisted mind come up with, and how she could get her hands on that kind of money without Jake knowing?

Ruth was determined to keep this from Jake and Lamont ruled him out as a source immediately. Through Lamont's own past conversations with Jake, he knew that his siblings' personal accounts were all negligible. The Cooper heirs had little patience for savings and spent money like there was a time limit on keeping it.

That left but one conclusion, Ruth had settled this matter without money, and he pondered the possibilities of what she used instead. He was trying to put the pieces together, but he didn't like the scenarios floating in his head. A nasty feeling gnawed deep inside him, because he couldn't imagine what insane route Ruth had taken. "Why had Ruth rushed to settlement when we already had it under control?" Lamont asked.

"Beats me," Smith said. "I thought that we had a chance to reach a reasonable settlement. My associates talked to the victim, and we were prepared to offer them the deal that you proposed. I'm sure they would have taken it, but I never got the chance. It was foolish of your sister to take matters into her hands, and now there's nothing I can do. It's over."

"I know you did what you could Mr. Smith and I thank you for that. I should have stayed on top of this, but I never thought she would do something like this," he said with a sigh. "Okay Mr. Smith I appreciate your sound judgment."

"Sorry I wasn't more help." Smith was silent briefly. "As for JJ, I'm still working on that one."

"So have you talked to the girl's parents?" Lamont asked.

"Parent," Smith said, correcting Lamont. "We're dealing with a single parent, and frankly she's going to be a problem. She's a stubborn single mom, looking to hit the lottery. She's convinced that her worries are over, so she's not backing off. She laughed and turned her nose up at the fifty grand I offered. She said that was peanuts to Jake Cooper."

"That means trouble."

"And we probably need to tell Mr. Cooper tha...."

"No," Lamont said, cutting him off. "We can't do that right now."

"Look, Mr. Savage, I can't do anything if my hands are tied. Can you cover the ante if I raise it?"

"Probably not for the amount she has in mind. She's probably looking to be set for life. We're talking millions here."

"Okay so what do you suggest?"

"Let's follow up on her. She doesn't sound like a nice lady to me, and I can understand why her daughter is wild. According to JJ that girl is totally out of control. She's a party girl who dresses like a Hoochie, and keeps late hours. Apparently she gets very little supervision from her mother. Besides that, this girl has had multiple sex partners, so she's no innocent bystander. And her mother is too anxious to collect on her daughter's so called misfortune. Frankly it sounds like a set up. Let's investigate her further. I'll bet you that we can probably find something on her."

"Probably, I've been in this business long enough to know that everybody has something they want to hide." He paused. "You'll need a private investigator for that though. I can hire one or you can handle that on your end. In the meantime I can stall the mother if you'd like."

"Okay, that sounds good. I'll get Jake's investigator on the mother."

"Okay, I'll stay in touch." He hung up.

Lamont dialed JJ's office, but the secretary informed him that JJ had called in sick, so Lamont dialed JJ's home number. He heard loud music in the background when JJ answered. "Hello, JJ," said loudly into the receiver.

"Yo, what's up bro?" JJ yelled over the music, slurring his words slightly. Lamont checked his watch to see that it was only Nine AM. Surely JJ wasn't indulging this early. On the other hand he shouldn't be surprised, because recently he concluded that JJ was irresponsible in his personal life. How could he ever become a real executive and be taken seriously? "JJ, your secretary said you took off today, you alright?"

"Yeah man, I'm getting my head together. That office stuff is child's play and I'm on top of most of it."

Lamont hoped JJ wasn't taking anything for granted, and that he realized that he was still not cleared yet. JJ however didn't even seem concerned. Over the past few months JJ's subdued attitude had changed abruptly, and his once casual Marijuana use had become more frequent. Lamont suspected that he might be doing other drugs as well.

JJ didn't understand the implications of drug usage, and thought that smoking a little Marijuana caused less harm than alcohol. He did understand that if he damaged his other kidney there wouldn't be another operation to save him. Lamont was in the same situation, having donated one kidney, but Lamont has been very careful about his physical upkeep, while JJ has not. JJ needed to grow up fast or there would be physical disaster ahead. "JJ, I need to discuss the latest news on your case. You got a minute?"

"For you, always, man. What's up?

"Well, I just talked to Smith."

"So did he take care of everything?" JJ asked eagerly. "Am I off the hook?"

"No, we got some problems with the mother. She won't settle for what we offered"

"Greedy, bitch. Like mother like daughter, I guess. I thought she would be glad to get a large chunk of money to support that monster coke habit of hers."

"What?" Lamont asked anxiously. "The mother is doing drugs? Do you know this for sure?"

"Duh, the bitch is on that stuff so bad that she got permanent sniffles. Lamont, when the bitch answers the door, she got enough residue of white powder on her lips to make a little white Hitler mustache. Doing a line of coke is the first thing she does in the morning and the last thing at night. The bitch doesn't work, and she turns trick. That daughter got to be doing the same thing with all those titties and ass. Now that I think about it, that girl acts too much like a porn star to be innocent."

"JJ, why didn't you tell me this before?"

"I don't know. Didn't think about it."

"Never mind, I should have asked you about their background," Lamont said. "My head's been in the clouds, but I'm back now.

"So does this make a difference?" JJ asked hopefully.

"You bet your ass it does. For one thing, if the mother's doing illegal drugs we have some leverage. If she still refuses to drop the charges, then we'll just let her know that the Narcs could step in and force her to submit to drug testing. We can notify Child Protective Services to take some interest and investigate her fitness as a mother of an underage promiscuous daughter," Lamont paused now. "This might be the break we need."

"Yeah," JJ yelled excited. "Blackmail, that's the way to go," JJ said more elated. "I love it, man. You're brilliant bro. Why didn't I think of that?"

"Don't count your chickens yet, JJ. I have to get investigators on it, but I'm sure we'll get what we need."

"I think you're right. Blackmail is the answer. I'm getting excited just thinking about it man, you're a genius." JJ laughed loudly and squealed with relief. "Man this calls for a party. I'm gonna invite some people over later, why don't you and Jane come and help me celebrate."

"JJ, it's too early to celebrate this right now. Let me get the investigation going, and then I'll get back to you, so don't start making plans yet."

"You worry too much bro. I ain't worried, and I know that between you, me, and a hot shot investigator, we're going to come up with something. Besides, I can always think of something to celebrate, and I want to celebrate with my big brother. So you coming? Please."

"I don't know JJ."

"Please," JJ begged."

"Okay," Lamont gave in, "I'll drop by on my way home, but I can't stay long."

"We'll see. Once you and your foxy lady get here..."

"Jane won't be with me."

"Well that's even gooder," he laughed at his misuse of the word. "That means you're free to hunt foxes and d-e-a-r." He spelled out the word. "And believe me there are gonna be some helpless foxes, and willing dears on the scene, and you don't need a hunting license."

Lamont shook his head but made no reply to his brother's words. That kid didn't see anything as serious, and saw a party as the answer to everything. Having money meant that you never had to end the party or go to work. Rich people learned to live that way because they had enough money to buy labor and shun responsibility.

For the first time, he wondered what this family would do if Jake lost the company, or if the family lost Jake. How would they provide for themselves if that money tree was suddenly cut down? He shook off the premonition since he already had enough to fret about. He had a new job as double agent, wild siblings, and a cheating fiancée, whom he had avoided thus far.

He thought about his cheating fiancée after hanging up the phone, and shuffled the paperwork on his desk. No doubt Jane was unworthy and rotten, yet he was reluctant to face her and get her out of his life for good. He was a coward for not confronting her, and that was unlike him. He usually faced his demons head on regardless of the suspected outcome. Perhaps he feared that a confrontation of truth with Jane would some how cast doubt on his own manhood. Had he driven her to cheat by not submitting to the bizarre things that she suggested they do in the bedroom? Was she simply a freak who sought to find some one with common interests? Was that why she sought Greg, and did he do all that freaky stuff that she wanted?

He was puzzled as to why she even wanted to marry him because it didn't make sense. Why didn't she break it off? She definitely wouldn't have a problem getting men if that's what she so desired. More than likely they would jump through hoops to do what she wanted.

"Oh God," Lamont said aloud and slapped himself in the forehead. "Dammit she knew all along about my connection to Jake. How could I have been so stupid? Of course she knew. It was public record and she was a nosey reporter. She could have discovered it doing research or something." Now he felt worse.

He wasn't just a chump; he was prize blue ribbon chump. "Bitch, slick bitch," he said, realizing the gravity of her complex sinister deception. He had warned JJ about gold diggers, when he had been captured but the all time champ of gold diggers. There should have been lights going on in his head like neon signs.

Fortunately for him, Jane's Achilles heel had been her greed and unnatural lust, which lead to her exposure. Obviously, one man wasn't enough for Jane, because her ego needed intense and constant stroking. It was strange, but just like that; he now knew more about her than he ever had. Now that he knew her bad side, he understood clearly the kind of person that she was and why she acted the way she did.

He felt relieved now that he didn't feel the urge to wring Jane's pretty neck. He finally admitted to himself that their relationship had always been as dubious as an out of body experience. Now his logic and sanity were intact, and he was himself again. He knew exactly what he had to do and he had no more doubts. He had to get far away from her as soon as possible.

Chapter Thirty-

Independence

Lamont didn't have to force himself to forget about Jane any more, she was much easier to forget after his sudden recent epiphany. Presently he was anxious to speak with Ruth, and get the details about the settlement she made. He reluctantly left several voice messages, but he was sure that Ruth was purposely not answering her cell phone. He imagined that she had done something totally irresponsible, and hoped that her actions hadn't made a mess of everything.

Shortly, there was a knock on the door and before he could speak the door opened. At first he wondered why Marcia hadn't buzzed him, but then he remembered that he told her to report late.

"Hello Lamont," Ruth said as she entered the office, closing the door behind her.

He looked up and his expression twisted in surprise, at the pleasant expression Ruth was wearing. At least she was sober, he thought. "Ruth. Hi," he said with a surprised look as she came closer. "I tried to call you."

"Yeah, yeah," she said intolerantly. "I got your lil message, and I wanted to come over and see your face when I talk to you." She hesitated and sat in the chair opposite his desk. The expression on her face ranged between pleased and amused. "So this is your little office huh?" She asked, scanning the room with a smirk. "Sure is nice to be the boss' son ain't it?" She stood and moved around the office. "Look at this," she said as she moved around pointing at things, imitating the models on The Price is Right TV show. "This nice office is so plush. I bet you never had any shit like this, huh?"

"Look, Ruth, ragging on me is not going to distract me. I want to know what happen. Did you make a deal, and what kind of a deal did you make?"

Yeah, I made a deal and it ain't any of your business. You ain't involved no more. So get off my ass." She moved towards the door. "So everything is okay. I'm not getting sued, and I'm not being charged with anything." She made a deep pleased sigh and gave Lamont a smug haughty stare. "I did it my way, and it worked out.

"How did it all work out Ruth? What did you do?"

"I handled the problem." She raised her voice and glared into his eyes. "I'm not a complete Duffus because I didn't go to college." Her voice shook.

He backed off, knowing that it was useless as always with her. "Ruth, I don't feel up to arguing with you this morning, but you better not screw things up for Jake."

"I'm not here to argue either Mr. know-it-all, I'm just here to show you that all we Coopers aren't idiots, and some of us can handle our own problems without help from daddy," she paused then added, "or from the great Lamont Savage."

"I don't believe this," Lamont said shaking his head in disbelief.

"Well it's true. I handled my own problems."

"I wasn't talking about handling the problem. What I can't believe is that you're here gloating about doing something on your own, and it might not even be the right thing. Ruth, do you even know the consequences of your actions? Do you think you've done something miraculous, and now you're looking for praise?" Lamont hadn't meant to be so confrontational, but Ruth as always stirred his anger.

"Lamont, please." Ruth scoffed with a twisted smirk. "You think I don't know what's really bugging you. You're just pissed because I didn't need you to save my ass," she said as she stood and gave herself a dramatic slap on her buttocks. "See, poor ass niggers like you need to be the hero, dashing to the rescue, because that's your salvation. You like stepping up and pretending to be the knight in armor, or the caped crusader and shit. That makes you feel worthy. Now you're pissed because you can't take the glory for solving my problem yourself. You're pouting because mean old Ruth wouldn't let you earn your little Boy Scout badge."

Lamont was speechless. How could she look at this situation and come up with such a bizarre conclusion? No doubt he was dealing with the workings of a slightly twisted mind. "God help you," he said with a sigh, sadly shaking his head.

"Oh, so you're a preacher too? I guess you gonna free my soul next and save my evil spirit, huh? Well, no thanks reverend. I'm not sick and

I'll do my own praying." She fixed the small Bolero jacket and adjusted the matching hat. "Gotta run now. Got more important shit I can be doing." She cast him one last knowing look and strutted proudly out the door.

Lamont sat there for a moment after she left and wondered how two people who actually spoke the same language could interpret same words so differently. Did she have some and mean incurable inborn mental defect imbedded inside? Any hope of bonding with that one was evaporating along with all his noble intentions.

Lamont hadn't counted on confronting such open hostilities when he first planned to bond with the Coopers. It's obvious now that bonding will be much harder than he first believed. That was because he found it difficult to love Ruth, and would no longer make excuses for her rude behavior and insults. Nothing gave her the right to treat him with such lethal disrespect. A truly good soul breaks free from the prison of its evil essence. Perhaps Ruth's soul has been unable to do that because there is no basic good inside her. He didn't want to believe that, but so far Ruth hadn't given him any reason not to.

This made him sad because apparently deep pockets and millions of dollars hadn't solved the Cooper family's complicated personal dysfunctions. Perhaps deep bonds wouldn't solve anything either.

Chapter Thirty One– Party People

Lamont had just clicked off the computer and prepared to leave when JJ called to remind him about the party. He had completely forgotten, and now he was sorry that he had promised to attend. He felt weary now, but he couldn't back out of his promise to JJ. "Okay man I'm gonna show, but be aware that I can't stay for long. It's been a long day and tomorrow is gonna be the same. You might think about that yourself." JJ just laughed and said he could handle it.

Twenty minutes later he approached JJ's door, greeted by loud thumping music and gleeful voices coming from inside. Lamont was apprehensive about meeting so many strangers, especially now with so much on his mind. Besides that, all of JJ's friends were very young and immature, and he knew that he wouldn't fit in.

He knocked on the door several times before a scantily clad girl, whom he guessed to be about seventeen, finally answered. Lamont noticed her well endowed body and good looks. He thought that she looked like a younger version of Tyra Banks.

She smiled flirtatiously, showing sound white teeth. "Well hello there sweet face," she said, jutting out her chest, and scanning Lamont flirtatiously. "Where the hell have you been hiding, Sugar? And can I have your babies?"

Lamont smiled cordially, but ignored the girl's obvious drunken remarks. He had enough trouble already, and he sure didn't need this jail bait adding to the mix. "Hello. Is JJ around?" Lamont asked, feeling out of place, while observing all the underage youths present.

"Well excuse me," the girl said as she made a face, obviously offended by Lamont's lack of interest. She stepped aside allowing him entrance. "Don't have to be so antisocial," she said angrily, moving pass her.

"Don't mean to be Miss. I'm just having a bad day and I'm a little tired." He flashed a quick smile and her facial expression became more forgiving. "There's JJ, she said pointing in his direction, and then rejoined her friends. Lamont spotted JJ with his back to him, and moved to where he stood, talking to a shapely young girl. She smiled and focused on Lamont as he moved closer.

JJ turned to follow her gaze and spotted him. "Hey there he is," he said and moved to Lamont, giving him a hug. "What it be like bro?" JJ spread out his hands as if showing Lamont an exhibit. "This is how I party bro." He turned to the young girl. "And this is Maureen, the dream, ain't she smokin'?" He asked, openly looking Maureen up and down. "Does she look like a movie queen or what? Turn around girl and let my brother see them onions."

"Stop JJ you're embarrassing me." Maureen hit his arm playfully, but she wasn't embarrassed.

"Embarrassing you? Baby you should be flaunting all that, not be embarrassed. You're blessed with a whole lot of what other girls wish for."

Lamont gave a reluctant smile and changed the subject. "Yeah man you know how to throw a gig," he said looking around.

"And I got good reason to after all," JJ commented gleefully.

"Oh yeah?" Lamont asked inquisitively. "You know something that I don't?"

"Cause life is grand," JJ said, avoiding Lamont's question and his eyes. "Come on and have a drink," he cried, moving to the rotating bar in the living room. He reached beneath the bar and took out a small silver canister. "You want some of this killer weed from my private stash?"

"I'll take a light beer if you got it. I hope you're taking care of yourself, JJ."

JJ pretended that he didn't hear Lamont's warning. He was in denial about having one kidney and he still hadn't changed to a more cautious life style. "Come on loosen up man. Hit it once, you might like it," JJ said in a pleading whining drone.

"JJ, no," he said firmly when JJ wouldn't back off. "Tomorrow is a work day, and I can't stay, remember?"

"I thought you was jokin' about that. I figured once you got here and saw all this ass," JJ said holding out his arms as if to demonstrate. "That you might change your mind." He looked around the room. "Plus they eyeing you man. You can't be walking out on all these foxes. They have been asking about my big brother all night, and I been building you up. You can have your pick. Look at all that." He nodded towards the large patio where three very provocatively dressed young females stood near a huge rubber tree, sharing the latest gossip. Lamont observed that their skimpy garments wouldn't make a complete outfit if the material from all three outfits were combined. They were young, high, and proud of their exposed anatomies.

"JJ, I am looking, and you know what I see?" He didn't wait for an answer. "I see a room full of jail bait and trouble. I'm talking a whole lot of charges and prison time. You're serving alcohol and drugs to minors, and they're high and out of their minds. I assume that some of them are driving, and that's dangerous man. You already in a mess and you sure don't need the cops coming down on you with moral charges. Man you need to chill."

"Naw bro, you chill." JJ's expression changed to anger. "You need to loosen up cause you bout to blow my high being such a party pooper. I got everything cover, and anybody who can't drive can crash here. I got plenty of blankets and pillows. Hell, what you want me to do check ID up in here? People just having fun."

"Maybe you need to check ID, man and for a lot of reasons. Don't you know that these girls are slick, and they know what you're worth? That's why you got a statutory rape charge pending right now. Didn't you learn anything from that, JJ? "

JJ was annoyed with Lamont. "Not any more I don't," he said and his anger dissipated. "And yeah I did learn something.

"What?" Lamont asked, scanning JJ with an inquisitive scowl. "What do you mean?" Lamont sensed that he wasn't going to like the answer.

"I mean that I took care of that mess," he said with a proud vibrant smile. JJ paused as if waiting for praise. His eyes locked with Lamont's.

"So what are you saying JJ? Did you pay those people off on your own JJ?"

"You might say that yeah. Ain't that what you do to everybody? They all got a price."

"How? You don't have that kind of money. Did you talk to Jake?" Lamont asked.

JJ seemed uneasy now and changed the subject. "Lamont, would you lighten up? It's been taken care of, so let it go."

Lamont realized that JJ wasn't going to reveal anything else. "Okay, I will, but what are you going to do the next time?"

"I'll cross that bridge when I get to it. I ain't worried about it."

"So you're going to make a career of paying off gold diggers?"

"Look just drop it," JJ said impatiently. "Damn, Lamont, if Dad's got money and I'm not allowed to enjoy my good fortune, then what good is it? I sure ain't planning to be watching over my shoulder all the time, or getting uptight just because I might run into a gold digger now and then. So what if I do and they happen to get a few bucks? Daddy's got more damn money than God, and ain't none of these young gold digger smart enough to get it all. I'd rather just take my chances and have some fun getting laid in the process. So just let me have some fun will ya?"

Lamont had never seen this side of his brother, but he shouldn't have been that surprised. Maybe he wanted to think that JJ was different. He knew JJ was young, impetuous and spent lots of money, but he never suspected that he was so self serving and unwise. Lamont surmised that JJ might never change. Perhaps it wasn't JJ's fault. Jake's money had served only to make the Cooper siblings weak, dependant and imprudent in their expectations of the real world. In their case, having so much wealth was a crisis as well as a curse. "Sorry to hear you talk like that JJ. It doesn't make any difference what you think though. Money doesn't grow on trees and there will be a lot of girls in your life just like the Perilli girl. They're attracted to the scent of money."

"See, you're wrong man. Cause that chick didn't settle for any money."

Lamont was puzzled and gave JJ an inquisitive frown. "What do you mean she didn't settle for any money? Are you telling me that she agreed to some other kind of a settlement? What are we talking about here JJ? Are we by any chance talking about anything to put the company in danger?"

"Of course not, I don't have that kind of power."

He shrugged his shoulders and looked deep into JJ's eyes. "What kind of a deal did you make then?"

JJ changed the subject. "Look bro, why are we fighting about this?

Look around." He made a gesture of scanning the room quickly. "All this booty in here just for the asking, so why are we standing up here discussing something trivial?" He moved closer and hunched Lamont slyly. "Come on man relax. That honey in the blue dress, with all those titties hanging loose, that's Molly and she can't take her eyes off you, Bro. All you got to do is go get it."

Lamont was angry with his brother for the first time. He didn't like JJ's seedy lecherous and selfish side, or his assumption that he could distract him from important issues with the promise of promiscuous sex. JJ was very skilled at using his wealth as a panacea for everything. JJ was rich and based his actions on money. No matter how close he wanted to get to JJ, or how close they would become eventually, they would always be worlds apart because of their initial economic orientation. JJ saw things from a perspective of wealth and price tags, used money as a tool, and therefore had no sense of value. On the other hand, Lamont found value a better tool, because value was found in people as well as things.

It troubled him that he and his brother were destined to remain miles apart because they grew up in different worlds. Standing there in the midst of this youth fest of loud music, and sniffing the faint smell of Marijuana in the air; Lamont's one thought was to get away from here. "JJ, you haven't heard anything I've said."

"Lamont, please just stop with the lectures, I'm trying to have a party here."

"You're right, I'm a party pooper," Lamont said in a voice loaded with disappointment, "and I really do have something important to take care of," Lamont said and started towards the door.

"Oh come on man," JJ said throwing up his hands. "I know you ain't leaving. Don't tell me you're pissed at me now. Why? I just want to show you a good time, man. Come on bro. Look, Lamont, I'm sorry. Okay? Stay here and party with me," JJ said throwing his arm around Lamont's shoulder. "Everybody's watching man. You can't do me like this."

Lamont smelled the Marijuana on JJ's clothes, and slowly removed JJ's arm from his shoulder with a no nonsense glare. "Later man." He strides to the door, ignoring JJ's pleas and the probing eyes of his guest.

Once he was inside his car he paused briefly and tried to get his thoughts together. He shouldn't have walked out on JJ like that, and now he hated himself for allowing his temper to take control. He lost control because he didn't like the person that JJ had become. Perhaps he had been that way all along. In any case, he sensed that JJ wasn't dependable and that was sad.

He had dreamed of working as a team with Jake and JJ, but he didn't see that happening now. JJ's attitude was in party mode, and he was armed with unlimited cash and gunning for fun. Giving him control to money was like putting a kid in control of the cookie jar. With all modesty aside, Lamont realized that maybe Jake was actually being truthful when he said that he was the only person that he trusted.

Lamont put the Town car in gear with a deep sigh and sped away from the bizarre scene, disappointed and angry about JJ's lack of concerned and seriousness. JJ was juvenile and immature, which made him a constant prey of predators like Roxanne Perilli. His brother thought with the wrong head and Lamont wouldn't be surprised if he saw Roxanne again, in spite of the trouble she had caused. Sooner or later, JJ would get into serious trouble, unless he underwent a dramatic change.

He tried to forget the event that took place between JJ and himself, but he remembered JJ's claim that he had resolved the problem. How coincidental that JJ and Ruth claimed to have solved their own problems at approximately the same time, and unassisted. Was it just a coincidence, or could there be some connection? Neither of them had the savvy to deal with just simple everyday problems, so he seriously doubted if either of them had made a smart move.

He smelled something fishy, and hoped that their decisions wouldn't result in disaster. He was getting crazy thoughts about the family's shares of stock, and wanted to check it out. The problem was that he would have to get that information from Jake. He had to figure out a way to do that without telling Jake about Ruth's and JJ's trouble. Those two were experts at screwing things up, and even though he couldn't imagine how, they might help the enemy's cause.

Chapter Thirty Two–
Confrontation

Lamont drove around for an hour to clear his head and re-think her morbid thoughts. He felt exhausted when he arrived home and got out of the car. He walked towards his apartment entry way, unaware of the waiting, observant eyes scanning his movements. As he walked towards the entry door of his apartment, the steady clicking of high heel shoes echoed off the pavement. He became alerted to the steady even cadence of the pace that carried the essence of a woman's strut. The cool surrounding summer air reeked of rare perfume, and he knew the identity of his mysterious stalker, even before turning to confirm his assessment. How could he forget that haunting flowery fragrance?

He turned in time to see her fighting with the dress now caught in the wind. She laughed nervously, and her tall curvaceous form glided closer. Her hips gyrated with more vigor, and instinctively he knew that he now had control. He see's the effort she makes to impress him with the leg show, but it no longer affected him.

He decided not to speak before she reached him, so he froze in front of his apartment door, and waited for her to get closer. Before this moment, he had dreaded seeing her, but now he was relieved. It was time for confrontation and presentation of truth.

Jane smiled and bit on her lower lip seductively, showing bright perfect teeth as she reached him and stood. Lamont noticed that her smiled was forced, perhaps because she detected his grim expression. She must suspect that he knew about her and Greg, and dreaded this confrontation. She wasn't that clueless.

"Well you certainly are a hard man to catch lately." Her voice shook with false confidence. "I guess you don't answer your phone anymore, huh?" She asked with even less confidence now. The look in her eyes confirmed what he already knew: She *was* aware of his suspicions, and any uncertainty on his part was erased. There was no doubt that the voice he had heard over the phone belonged to her.

"Hello Jane. You're a long way from Norfolk," he said coolly, while turning to open his front door.

"Yeah I need to talk to you, and I needed a long drive to clear my head."

"Come on in." He entered, without kissing her cheek, or looking back at her. He didn't even hold the door for her as she expected, and she was thrown off guard. She caught the door and followed him inside.

He had avoided her since that phone call to Greg the other morning, and he was satisfied in his own mind about what was fact. No matter how much she denied it he had no plans of being swayed. She had lost all credibility with him and he was ready to end this bad movie.

Jane was intimidated, which showed that she did feel some guilt. Things had definitely changed and he was seeing the real Jane for the first time. "I'm having a drink. You want one?" He was already pouring the liquid into his glass.

"Sure, I'll have one." Her voice was low and shaky, and she seemed nervous. It was obvious that she had no idea what to say right now.

He watched, as she sat on the couch and hiked up the short light print dress, crossing her long legs nervously. She struck a pose that seemed intent on seducing him, but he scowled at such a juvenile gesture. He was past that stage, and completely immune to the charm that her body once held for him. Sex was no longer a factor, because cheating had cured him from pussy whiplash.

Lamont set one drink in front of her on the coffee table, and made a point of sitting on a wing chair a short distance away from her. "I'm glad you showed up here tonight."

"Oh really," Jane said with a smile, obviously misinterpreting his meaning. I hadn't heard from you. Hey I'm your fiancée, remember? Why are sitting over there?"

Lamont purposely didn't answer. "Jane, I need to talk to you, and frankly I've been putting it off. I knew that eventually I would have to."

"God, am I going to like what you got to say? You sound serious," she said and sipped nervously from the glass.

"I am serious Jane," he said with obvious impatience, "I'm not gonna beat around the bush, especially when I'm sure you already know that I know, so let's be clear," he paused and sighed deeply. "You're sleeping with Greg aren't you?"

"Greg? Lamont, be serious! How could you ask me such a thing?" She asked holding her hand over her heart, seeming stunned.

Had he not been so sure of what he heard, he might have believed her. Apparently she had vast talents for deception. "Oh you're good, but you're not that good. So don't give me that surprised look because I know you're lying."

"Lamont, I'm not lying. Me? And Greg? Please," she said with a look of distaste, and feigning shock. "Of course I'm not sleeping with Greg. I've only met him once. How could you accuse me of that? I thought you loved me," she asked, pouting visibly.

He gazed intently at her, obviously she wasn't going to admit it, but he didn't expect her to. He wasn't looking for a confession; he just wanted her to know why he was breaking up with her. "I thought you loved me too, until I called Greg's number the other morning."

"So? You called his number. What's that got to do with anything?" Jane asked, dropping her fake façade.

Lamont knew for sure that she was rattled, but apparently she was sticking to her story. It didn't matter, because denying it that way had only convinced him that she was a born liar. "Enough of the games, Jane. We both know that you're cheating on me with Greg." He paused and looked her directly in the eyes. "I heard you at his place when I called. I'm sure you remember your words. Were you getting even with me for neglecting you, or is cheating just your style?"

"Oh, Lamont, of course not. First of all I didn't cheat, and I wanted you to go help your brother," she said with a scowl and a head shake.

"Yeah, so you say, but I remember different. It's kinda hard to believe you any more, Jane."

"Why? What, are you saying Lamont?" Her voice went up an octave.

"You don't know what I'm saying? Are you hard of hearing? Do you no longer speak English? Do you think I'm really stupid?"

"Lamont, baby," she pleaded, "why are you talking all this trash to me, sugar? You know we belong together. Why are you saying these things? So you called Greg and he was with some bimbo. What makes you think it was me?" She asked, hunching her shoulders.

"I'm really disappointed in you, Jane," he said shaking his head and looking through her. "I can't believe I fell for your lies. I even let you con me into an engagement. Maybe I just closed my eyes because I wanted to believe you."

"Damn it Lamont, I'm not cheating on you and you can believe me. I was not at Greg's house. I don't even know where he lives." She raised her voice. Her indignation and pretense of innocence was an obvious act and Lamont was ready to end this conversation. "Jane, just cut this bullshit, okay? Maybe you don't understand what I'm saying, so let me say it again. I know that you're cheating on me with Greg. I know this, and I know what's next."

"Why won't you believe me? I told you I never been to Greg's house?" She paused and took a handkerchief from her purse and pretended to wipe tears.

Lamont scrutinized her thinking that she was pulling out all stops. He wasn't about to let her get away with anything. "So you never been to Greg's place?" He asked in a neutral tone.

"Of course not." She spoke with more equanimity and control now, and seemed to gain some confidence because of his sudden calmness. Apparently she thought that he was convinced. "Like a said, I don't know where he lives." She teared up and batted her eyes.

"Have you ever called him?"

"How would I? I don't know his number either. Lamont don't you understand? I am not having an affair, especially since I don't even know the man."

"Incredible," he said, "are you telling me that you never been to Greg's house and that you never called him?" His voice was lower now.

"Never, Baby, I swear." She said then remained silent, watching his reactions.

Lamont moved closer and touched her hair lightly, and traced his fingers over her freshly painted lips. He looked into her eyes. "You're really quite amazing you know that? So damn pretty and."

"Take me, back to your bed and let me show you something really amazing," she said, not allowing Lamont to finish.

Lamont pretended not to hear her. "Yeah you're the most amazing and prettiest cheating lying bitch I've ever been engaged to. You must get lots of practice."

"What?" She glared at him with a scowl. "How could you say that to me, Lamont?"

"Because it's true. You lied about having Greg's number, and you lied about being at his place."

"Lamont, please. Would you just listen?"

"No, Jane, you listen. You made a mistake. See that lie you just told makes everything you said bullshit," he said holding his hands up to shush her before she interrupted. "Don't make it worse," he said and continued. "See, Jane I know you know his number."

"What? I didn't. I don't." She insisted. "You can't prove I know his number, Lamont."

"I can to my satisfaction and that's what counts. See I called Greg from your house the other night by hitting the redial on your phone. Well you can imagine my surprise when my good old buddy, Greg answered the phone," Lamont said with exaggerated sarcasm.

"And you think I."

"I know that you called him," he said cutting her off.

"But Lamont, you used my phone too remember?" She asked, sounding stressed.

"But I called my mother to let her know that I was on the way, not Greg."

"Oh Lamont, you probably dialed him and forgot about it and."

"That makes no sense and it's not possible anyway, Jane." He cut her off again.

She gave him an annoyed angry scowl. "Why isn't it possible you can't make a mistake now? You perfect or something? I guess next you'll turn water into wine and feed the village with two loaves of bread," she finished sarcastically, dropping all pretenses.

"No Jane I'm not perfect and I make mistakes, but not this time."

"Why not? I don't see how you can be so sure with them Coopers always on your mind." She was becoming hysterical.

Lamont studied her with a calm patient glare that ranged between disgust and pity. "It's not possible, Jane, because *I don't know Greg's number*," he said as his voice shot up in volume.

"Wha..yo..." She was at a loss for words. "Bullshit, that's a lie. I..I

225

can't believe that. You guys worked together, you had to have his number.

"I did have his old number, but Greg changed his number a few months ago as you are probably aware. He was supposed to give it to me, but neither one of us followed up. It's not like we're buddies who keep in touch, and since we don't I just forgot about it. Apparently he remembered to give it to you."

"But, Lamont."

"Jane! Stop! The game is over so let it go. You cheated, and you got busted. So cut your flimsy lies because I know you were there. And I did hear your voice as clear as a bell. Do you think I don't know the voice that has whispered lies about love in my ears? Did you ever find those missing panties?"

She couldn't put her words together, and her mind rambled for some way to make it right. She had been foolish and was about to lose Lamont. He was going to be wealthy, and she had just blown her chance to become his wife. She couldn't let that happen. This was a critical time, and she couldn't get dumped now. She needed the status and the financial clout that her connection to Lamont and the Coopers would generate.

She felt desperation now. "Lamont honey, I don't know what came over me. I didn't want to, but I think Greg must of put something in my drink and."

"Jane, please. As smart as you are, all you can come up with is that third grade version of a lie? Please. I'm not dumb enough to think that this was a onetime one shot deal. Did he put something in your drink all the other times too? You even tried to avoid suspicion by pretending not to like the guy."

She had just made things worse. That's what desperation and lies did. Knowing this, she still persisted. "He kept hounding me and."

"And he wore you down right?"

"Right yes see he."

"So it's Greg's fault?"

"Well yes, but I'm not saying that I don't share some of the blame, Baby. Oh Lamont I'm not like that." She moved closer.

"Of course you are, Jane. You're exactly like that. How did I miss seeing it?" He sighed deeply and twisted his full lips. "You might be a beautiful lady to those with shallow minds and limited expectations. But I see standing here before me a monster with a grotesque Godless soul. Sure you got style and you know how to work it, but you're a no class slut Jane and style can't change that.

"You lie to me and cheat on me, and now you're lying on Greg. Do you think that I would consider anything you say to be the truth? I see you Jane. Can you understand that now? You've shown me just what you are, and frankly you deserve Greg." He gave a penetrating sideways glance and curled his lip in disgust.

"Lamont I know I messed up, honey, but I was weak. I'm sorry, Baby. I promise that if you'll forgive me, nothing like this will ever happen again. I promise you that for sure. Lamont, we got something good here, let's not blow it." She kneeled down on the floor beside him. Tears, of self-pity, ran down her cheeks. "Lamont, please, Baby. I'll make it up to you."

"You're not listening Jane. It's over. There will be no compromise or second chances." He got up from the chair and moved purposely to the door and opened it. "Get out." He stood there waiting, refusing to look at her. He waited patiently at the door holding the glass in one hand and the door knob with the other. He watched in his peripheral vision, as she rose from her knees and moved towards the door.

"G...Goodbye? What do you mean goodbye?" She stammered.

"Good-bye, adios, vamoose, so long, arrivederci, scram. I know you're smart so you must speak one of those."

She looked at him still unbelieving. It was as if she had just seen him for the first time. "Lamont I know you're angry, but I know you still care and we can fix this. I got stupid and I should never have done what I did, but everybody makes mistakes. I made a terrible mistake. You're the only man for me. You're the only man I love."

"But not the only one you're screwing. Yes, Jane you did make a mistake. So did I."

"Oh Lamont, why are you so hard? Why can't you forgive me?"

"You figure that one out. Just go."

"Okay Lamont, I'll give you some time to think about things and then I'll give you a call and we..."

"Jane! Don't you get it? Listen for a change."

"What?" Her face twisted in shock "What do you mean?"

Lamont sighed and twisted his mouth. "I see you can't take hints so let me break it down. I will never trust you again, Jane. You're a cheating, lying, horny slut. I trusted you, and all the time you were screwing some shiftless low life excuse for a man, and making a fool of me. That's how much you valued our relationship. It's an insult that you think, that I would be stupid enough to ever trust you again."

"I never knew you had such a mean streak in you," she said in a hushed whisper.

"It's not working, Jane, so don't try to flip the script," He said coldly, then stepped back and opened the door wider. "Now get your whoring ass out of here. The sight of you makes me want to puke."

She stood silently looking at him, and searching for the right words to win him back. "Lamont just let me make it up to you. Let's go into the bedroom now and we can fix this." She moved closer and, attempted to kiss him.

Lamont grabbed her arms, "Dammit are you hard of hearing? I said get out. Didn't you get the news? I don't want you Jane. Good-bye," he said and gently forced her outside the door and closed it quickly behind her.

Jane stood there on the other side of the door, stunned that she was outside before she even realized it. She had spent a lot of intimate moments with him, and she didn't deserve to be set out like a leaky trash bag.

She dried the tears from her eyes and walked to her car, thinking about what her overactive libido had cost her dearly. She had made some bad moves; mainly she had called Greg from her house phone. That was stupid. Then she had opened her big mouth when Lamont called Greg? She wanted to kick herself, but she needed to concentrate on damage control and not dwell on her mistake.

She promised herself that if she talked her way back into his life, she would do whatever it took to keep him. She had already dumped Greg again, and she wasn't going to give up or let him go. He had to take her back. She had charmed him once and she had the skills to do it again. She refused to be shut out of Lamont's life. If she played him right, she would still be Mrs. Lamont Savage. She had the looks, and the confidence and her mission was to wear him down once he got over his present anger. How could he resist her? After all he was just a man.

Chapter Thirty Three-
The Switch

Lamont felt liberated and positive now that Jane was out of the picture and he could move on. This morning he settled down and concentrated on the task at hand. He looked into some files, in hopes of finding some useful information. "Mr. Savage," Lamont heard as he looked up to see Peter's head inside his office door. "We have a group meeting in ten minutes. Are your reports ready?"

Lamont looked puzzled. "What reports? What meeting?"

"Have you forgotten about the meeting with the board members and department heads?" Peter asked, giving him a bewildered look as he stepped inside his office. "You got the memo didn't you?" He asked smugly.

"No, I don't recall getting a memo about any meeting." Lamont gave him a suspicious look. "You sure you sent me one?"

"Of course I'm sure." Peter almost snapped, but instead he added. "Well it's informal, not a big deal. I just need you to be in the eight floor conference room in ten minutes." He started for the door, then stopped and turned. "Oh and bring the marketing reports and the projections I ask you to work up for me." He paused then asked. "You do have them ready don't you?"

Lamont hadn't checked recently because he had been burdened with so many other things. He did remember completing those reports a few days earlier and putting them aside. Now he felt as if he needed to double check and update them. However, he was unable to take the time right now because of Peter's surprise meeting. "Yeah I have them ready," he said realizing that he had to go with the figures that he had. Still this abrupt notification made him nervous.

"Good, then I'll see you upstairs," Peter said with a smile and walked quickly out the door. Lamont didn't see Peter's smug expression as he left the office. He thought it was strange that Peter never asked to look over his work, which should be standard procedure for his supervisor.

He got a strange sensation in his stomach and for some reason dreaded this upcoming meeting.

He got Marcia to make copies of his reports, and ten minutes later, he joined the others in the conference room. He had to rush to make the meeting on time, and didn't look over his copies. Now he felt trapped in a hostile environment, with Peter's protégés. He felt conspicuous and odd among them, and anticipated that some of them even resented him. That didn't matter because his work would speak for itself.

However, when he opened the folder for the first time and studied the material closely, his reports were way off. He didn't recognize any of this information, and had to wonder what happened to his work.

"Lamont what have you been doing? Peter asked, before Lamont could figure out what was happing. Now Peter led the criticism, after briefly scanning his copy. "These figures aren't even close. This is sloppy work, real sloppy. I'm disappointed."

Lamont felt betrayed and stunned at Peter's acid tone and cutting words. He was still in shock, while continuing to study the unrecognizable work before his eyes. The projections and numbers were all wrong, and he was sure that this wasn't even his work. "What is this," Lamont said in disbelief.

"Yes, that's what we'd like to know," Peter said, casting smug glances about the room.

"I mean these aren't the reports that I prepared."

"Oh," Peter said smugly, while looking to make eye contact with the others. "Then who prepared them, and why did you bring them here? And why is your name on them?"

"Look I don't know what happen to my reports, but I certainly didn't do this work." Lamont wanted to kick himself for being so careless and not checking the reports before handing them out.

"Then can you explain what happened or where your reports are?" Peter could barely contain his pleasure at seeing Lamont squirm, and he savored the moment.

"I don't know what happened, but I guarantee you I will find out." Lamont's tone was louder than normal and his anger was obvious. "Somebody is playing games." Lamont was up from the chair, looking directly at Peter. "Excuse me gentlemen. I need to check on some things." Before he could hear any protest, he was out the door. God that was humiliating, he thought. He walked down the stairs to his office instead of taking the elevator. He needed to cool off and think.

There was immediate silence after Lamont left. Peter glanced around the room then spoke. "I wonder what happened to his reports." Peter seemed slightly amused. "I guess the dog ate them." Peter was especially pleased that Lawrence Preston had attended this meeting. Normally Preston didn't attend any of the power group meetings, but Peter had taken great effort to insure that Jake's personal flunky was present today. Peter already knew that the outcome would be disastrous, and he needed Preston here to witness Lamont's incompetence. "Sure is a hot head isn't he? If he wasn't Jake's son we all know he."

"But he is Jake's son," said Walter Holland, head of advertising, cut Peter off.

"Well son or not, somebody needs to tell Jake that this boy is a screw up," Peter said, glancing subtly to Preston.

Beatrice Manley's dark observant eyes scanned the room, and then gave Peter a hard penetrating stare. "That sounds like a good idea Peter. I trust that you will let the rest of us know the results of that conversation. After all he is your apprentice isn't he?"

Peter met Beatrice's cold grey eyes, which seemed to challenge him. He knew that Preston would report to and advise Jake as to what to do about his son. He knew all about the so called secret plan to expose him. That plan wasn't looking so good right now with the board on his side.

In the mean time he would remain a neutral party, standing by to witness Lamont's demise. The plan was perfect and he would avoid any blunders or suspicions by keeping his distance from Lamont's mess.

Still he had to play the game just in case. "I guess I can overlook this and work more closely with the lad." Peter put on his best performance, pretending to show concern and sympathy. "It's obvious that he's not as bright as I was initially led to believe, and he does have a lot to learn. I suggest that we forget about this major gaff for now, and I'll work harder with him and bring him up to speed."

Walter gave Peter a knowing smile that was neither friendly nor easy for him. "That's a solid and humane thing to do Peter."

"Okay, then I suggest that we get down to other business." Peter's voice was strong and confident. It was obvious that the blunders on the reports hadn't dampened his spirits. If anything, he seemed quite elated with the turn of events.

Meanwhile, Lamont sat in his office looking over the bogus reports on his hard drive. He concluded that so much foreign material was on his hard drive because someone had sabotaged it. Sure he was new to this operation, but this work was familiar to him. At the Center he had made out similar reports and done various accounting functions many times. Only a careless amateur would have committed the obvious mistakes that he had observed on those reports. He knew that his reports were tampered with, and instinctively suspected Peter.

That's why Peter had rushed him into that meeting, before he checked his information, and that's why Peter had been the main critic of his alleged mistakes. It was more apparent that Jake was right about Peter being the snake in the garden. Lamont still didn't remember any memo and neither did Marcia. He assumed that Peter lied.

The buzzer on the intercom interrupted his thoughts and he was aware of yelling coming from his intercom. He recognized Marcia's voice, and she frantically called out to someone. "Look, I already told you that you can't go in there." Marcia's voice raised an octave. Just as Lamont pressed the intercom to inquire about the commotion, Jane burst through the door. "Lamont, I need to talk to you," She said rigidly.

Lamont felt an adrenaline rush at the sight of her unattractive side. Perhaps he was seeing that side more often now. "Jane, this is a business office. You can't come charging in here to discuss personal business. I said everything to you last night and I'm done with you. Please leave."

"Sorry, Lamont. I told her she couldn't come in here," Marcia said, standing in the door behind Jane. She had gotten an earful and she felt elated to hear Lamont's words. She couldn't be sure that she had heard him right and she froze in her tracks. Did he say that he was through with Jane? Of course, that's why she's so angry.

"It's okay Marsh. I got it now," Lamont said and watched silently as she left, closing the door behind her.

Jane watched him intensely, never turning to acknowledge Marcia.

"Lamont you got to at least give me another chance. Everybody is entitled to a second chance."

"Not everyone, Jane." He sneered. "Leave on your own power so that I don't have to call security."

"Security?" She looked intently at him for a few brief seconds. "You're gonna kick me out just like that? After all we had together, and all we meant to each other, you're not even gonna make an effort to save what we have?"

He looked at her, as if she were a slow learning child. "Are you being this thick deliberately? There is nothing else between us, Jane. What we had was an illusion, and now that has vanished, so therefore we had nothing. Do the math. You were making wedding plans, but you were never a blushing bride because you were screwing some one else. I didn't cast you aside, Jane, I simply stepped aside because you're a lost cause. Now you go back out the way you came in. I'm not going to waste any more of my time on you."

"But you can waste your time on that stuck up bunch of spoiled brats, who can't stand you. They're never going to see you as their real brother." She wore a sneer and continued to lash out. "You're fooling yourself if you think you can blend in or bond with them. You're a fool Lamont and they know it, that's why they're gonna keep right on using your pathetic dreaming ass until they don't need you anymore."

"You're right, I am a fool. I actually thought I wanted to marry your sorry ass." Lamont hit the buzzer. "Marsh, I need to see you."

At that time Marcia entered the office. "You need me, Lamont," she said giving Jane a smug sneer.

"Yes, call security if Ms Curtis is not out of here in five, no make that two minutes"

Marcia gave him a nod. "Okay, Lamont, you got it. Anything else?" Marcia asked, purposely eying Jane and enjoying her discomfort.

"No. Thanks Marsh." He watched as Marcia walked out and shut the door. Lamont noticed that Jane wore a weird look and her eyes locked on his eyes.

"I just recognized that bitch. That's the skank secretary that worked for you before." Suddenly her mouth dropped. "Oh now I see. You're screwing that slutty bitch ain't you? You changed jobs and you brought her with you. I should have known. You're just like every other man. All of you would sell your souls for a set of nice tits and legs."

"Like I told you before, Jane, flipping the script is not going to work. You're the one who got busted for cheating, not me. You can believe what you want, because we're done and it makes no difference. So I'm gonna say this once more. I got too much work to do so get the hell outta my office, and don't pull this stunt again." He moved back to his desk and sat, staring towards the computer screen and ignored her now.

"Okay then, if that's the way you want it, then that's the way you got it buster." She was angry now and venting. "Hell I don't need you. I can get any man. Men fight to get next to me. Men crawl to me, not the other way around. Don't think I'm gonna crawl to you and don't think I can't get some one better. I got plenty of offers.

"Yes I'm sure you do. So I suggest you stop wasting time and go check out some of those offers before some one takes your corner."

"You bastard. You talk that shit but I sure wrapped your stupid horny ass around my fingers didn't I?"

"The conversation is over, and anything else you got to say put it in a memo." He never looked up from the computer, but her words did sting.

His attitude infuriates her so much that her speech flustered and stammered. "I'll show your ass," was all she managed to utter as she headed through the door."

There was silence after she left, and Lamont realized that in spite of the wrong that she had done, he still hated that things had ended with such negative energy. Their union had been sometimes filled with beautiful intoxication and wondrous euphoric contentment. However it was never love and he saw that clearly now. She had been a good sexual partner, but sex was merely a component of love. He felt that love should be about two worthy dedicated people, caring and trusting to one another. His passion for her had been deep and lingering, but passion wasn't love. In his heart he knew that love had to be more than what they shared and that's why he had so many un resolved doubts. It was hard to figure such an emotion as love, and he sometimes wondered if love really existed, or if it was some intangible essence based on pure faith. He had almost made a fatal mistake, but blind luck had stepped in and offered him a reprieve.

Everybody talked about love and everybody had their own definition of it. Perhaps he was so jaded that he wouldn't recognize love if it did exist. After this experience with Jane, he wasn't sure if he believed in anything so fickle anymore. He wasn't going to let Jane's actions douse his hopes of seeking the right woman. Even though Jane's actions were bad, he was partially responsible, because he had volunteered to be blinded by desire.

Hadn't he made excuses for her flaws, at every turn, just because she was fine? He had mistakenly thought that it was more important to have a worthy prize than a worthy partner. He opted for great physical assets instead of good character. Now the sudden shock of his victimization had a cleansing effect, and he felt a sense of rebirth and relief.

He anticipated focusing on his recovery, thinking positive, and moving on in spite of his misstep with Jane. There were other pitfalls and failures ahead of him, but it didn't matter because now, thanks to Jane, he saw everything from a realistic perspective. He would no longer wear rose colored glasses to buffer hard reality, because that would make him a perpetual victim. Instead, he would embrace the future by facing and analyzing that hard reality through microscopic lenses.

Chapter Thirty Four-
Plan B

Lamont fell back into his work once Jane had cleared the office, and was off the premises. He was able to rule out the possibilities of computer error once Marcia found a copy of his original work. His instincts had been right, and the best move he ever made was hiring Marcia. Even he had been unaware that she backed up all his work each day. The information on the saved disc was different from the work she had copied from the hard drive, and proof of his good work. That meant that someone really had tampered with his files, and Peter remained the number one suspect.

He had neither DNA nor fingerprints to place Peter on the scene, and that meant that he would have to tolerate the man, and constantly watch his back. He wondered what wicked schemes Peter had in store for the future. Surely he would tamper with more files, and do some things beyond Lamont's imagination. He couldn't accuse Peter of anything or throw him out without proof, so he had to figure out a way to discredit and expose him.

After finding his original work to be accurate, he thought briefly about showing the disc to the Board members, but decided against it. If he did that, would have to explain the untrusting working relationship between Peter and himself. They might not feel comfortable knowing that. It didn't matter about the report anymore, because he didn't care about impressing the Board and winning points. People believe what they want and what's convenient for their own purposes. The board might even conclude that he manufactured new reports in an attempt to exonerate his mistakes. After all he was the boss' son. He decided to let this all blow over, but he would definitely be watching his back with Peter from now on.

Lamont was about to buzz for Marcia, but he remembered that she went to lunch with some of the other office workers. He was about to head out for lunch when Hal stuck his head inside.

"Hey, Mont, look at what I got here." Hal held up an elongated carrying case. "Got a bargain on some Pool Cues man and I'm anxious to spank you on the pool table. Again!"

Lamont smiled and nodded. "You know what, Turkey, I'm gonna take you up on that," Lamont said jokingly, while stretching and suppressing a yawn. "Just because you beat me a couple of games the last time we played, you getting sassy. You know I was distracted, and it was just a fluke that you won. I got to teach you some r-e-s-p-e-c-t." He spelled out the word.

"Yeah, okay, fluke." Hal shook his head. "Man you gonna have to live with the fact that my game has surpassed yours."

"Talk, talk talk. Everybody knows that you can't buy a cup of coffee with talk. There's just one way to prove it."

"I hear that tune," Hal said, suddenly dancing on one leg and holding his stomach. "Oh hell."

"What you nervous already," Lamont joked.

"Naw, but I need to use your bathroom. That chocolate bar and black coffee running through me."

"Please Hal, I don't need details. Just go use the can and I'll be waiting for you downstairs. Light a match when you get through, and lock up when you leave." Lamont moved swiftly down the hall and got on the elevator.

Peter stood out of sight and watched Lamont get on the elevator. He felt smug about his recent sabotage of Lamont's work, but that wasn't enough. Lamont's presence here hadn't met with enough opposition to suit Peter. That's why he was going to make his sabotage an ongoing project. It was going to be fun discrediting him and making a fool of both him and Jake before they got kicked out on their asses.

Once Carvoni took charge, it would be a different situation, because he would be a part of Carvoni's team. Even though Carvoni was a seedy little creep, Peter wasn't worried because he figured that Carvoni needed his skills, and he assumed that would give him much more power.

He checked his watch one more time before proceeding to Lamont's office to do his dirty deed. He felt bold now because all the workers on this floor had gone downstairs to the cafeteria, and other surrounding restaurants. He proceeded to what he presumed was an empty office.

Hal smiled while scanning the inside of Lamont's spotless sanitary office bathroom. "You deserve this Mont," he murmured, picking up the soap and smelling it. "Expensive shit." He observed the size of the large hot tub and checked the contents of the medicine cabinet. He didn't see anything of interest on the scarce shelves, just a few bottles of aspirin, band aids and soap. He closed the cabinet and opened the door to leave, but he stopped in his tracks when he spotted some one at the computer.

Hal thought that Lamont had changed his mind about playing a pool game. Apparently he had doubled back to continue working. Hal chuckled to himself, thinking that his buddy had become a workaholic. Now he focused and recognized Peter's profile sitting at Lamont's computer. "What the hell is he up to?" Hal whispered under his breath, while peering through the slightly opened door.

He observed Peter working diligently at the computer. "Something is wrong here. Why isn't he using his own computer? Is it broken or something? If it is then why didn't he use one of the computers on his floor, instead of sneaking around in here?"

Hal's instinct alerted him that this guy was creepy from the first time he met him. Even worse, he was sure that this creep was out to get Lamont. "Not if I got something to say about it," he whispered under his breath.

Hal remained in the bathroom and watch silently, deciding that it would be better if Peter didn't know that he was here. If he were to say something to him, the nerdy bastard would probably come up with some logical explanation, and make everything seem okay. He might even try to have him fired just to cover his slimy little ass, Hal thought.

Peter finally sneaked out of the office, and soon afterwards Hal followed. Hal moved anxiously to the elevators and rode down. Hal stepped off the elevator and went to the Billiards Lounge to inform Lamont about what he had seen. He spotted Lamont. "Mont, I got to talk to you, Man.

"Hal, where you been man? You did all that talking, and then chickened out on me." Lamont shook his head in mock disappointment. "I was going to spank you good. Too bad lunch time is over."

Hal moved closer but didn't reply to Lamont's comments. "I got something to tell you and believe me, man you need to know this." Hal's eyes locked on Lamont.

"Okay, buddy, what's up?" Lamont asked, giving Hal his full attention now.

"That guy Peter, I just saw him in your office. He sneaked in there and did something on your computer. He was looking real sneaky, tipping around like a crack addict looking for something to sell," Hal said with a sigh and stretched his eyes. "Man I think he's out to get you. You gotta watch that asshole."

"Good looking out Hal," Lamont said. Hal's eye witness account only confirmed Lamont's suspicions about Peter, and after he left Hal and returned to his office, he checked his recent work on the computer. He discovers that figures on several financial reports had been changed. The dates that those files were last modified were at 12:15PM today, which was the approximate time that he was downstairs. Peter had been caught in the act, and he had an eye witness. The problem was that he still couldn't accuse him outright just yet. Hal might not be a credible witness because he was Lamont's personal assistant.

That didn't matter any way, because now that he was sure about Peter's underhanded methods, he would find a way to trap him. He couldn't make a move yet because he needed Jake's okay. However, Jake was presently out of town because of the sudden death of his mother-in-law. He was in San Antonio helping with the funeral arrangements because Candace was all to pieces. He would have to wait for Jake's return before he could act, but in the meanwhile he would watch Peter closer. He wished that he could kick him out, but he didn't have the authority or the solid proof. Still he had to do something, but what?

While Lamont pondered what to do about Peter, he got a visit from Lawrence Preston. He was in a foul mood and reluctant to talk at first. His conversation sounded suspicious and strained, and Lamont concluded that he was dying to talk about those infamous reports. Lamont was anxious to hear what Preston had to say. "Mr. Preston if you got something on your chest I think you should get it off. You want to talk about it?"

Preston gave him a sheepish look. "Yeah you're very perceptive." He paused and sighed deeply. "Lamont I'm getting migraines because I'm torn between my obligations to Jake, and my regards for his personal feelings."

"Meaning?"

"Meaning that I'm going to have to report to him what happened with the reports the minute he gets back. It's not so urgent that I need to distract him right now. I know Jake wants you to be a part of this company, and I know how much he trusts you, but I think he needs to know the truth."

"And you think that truth is what? I'm incompetent? Is that what you're going to tell Jake, Mr. Preston?"

"What choice do I have?"

Lamont threw his hands up and stood. "Do what you have to Mr. Preston," Lamont said, while moving from the desk, and pacing around the floor in small tight circles. "I know you're a smart man, Mr. Preston, or Jake wouldn't trust you so much. Do you think that I have any skills at all?"

Preston sighed deeply and blew out a quick breath. "Okay you want to know what I think. I think Jake let sentiment get the best of him. I think he felt guilty about neglecting you in the past, and he went overboard to make it up to you. He chose you based on his guilt and feelings of obligations, and apparently not for your skills. I know you're new, but still," he hesitates and shakes his head to gather his thoughts.

"Those reports you presented were." Preston paused and twisted his mouth with dramatic flair, at the mention of those reports. He took a deep breath, and then turned to face Lamont behind his desk now. "What I'm saying, Lamont is, there's just no excuse for sloppy work. It's just laziness."

"Mr. Preston, I know those reports made me look bad, but I'm really surprise that you have made your decision without hearing my side of the story. I always thought that you were a fair and objective man, but you've judged me and found me guilty, and I haven't even presented my case. Apparently you see me as another one of Jake's unskilled brats, and I resent that," he said looking Preston squarely in the eyes. "Am I not entitled to the benefit of a doubt?" Lamont asked.

"Of course you are," Preston said uneasy. "But I haven't heard a peep out of you since the meeting yesterday. What am I to expect? I thought that you were hiding out."

"Well I wasn't," He wondered if it would sound as if he were whining and making alibis, if he told Preston about Peter. It probably would, but none the less it was the truth. He knew that he couldn't just sit back and hope that everyone would accept him because he was Jake's son. He had to prove himself and earn that acceptance just like any one else. He sure didn't want to be considered an idiot. Even though he hated to admit it, Preston's opinion of him did matter.

"I can see why based on those reports you have doubts about my competence. That evidence was very damaging," Lamont said, moving around the desk to sit in the chair next to Preston. He looked Preston in the eyes. "What if I told you that someone tampered with my computer? That someone deliberately sabotaged my good work? That would sound far fetched and fantastic wouldn't it? Like some spy novel or some conspiracy theory."

"Is that what you're telling me?" Preston asked with a skeptical fixed gaze. "Who, Lamont? Who would do something that despicable and why?" Preston paused then seemed sparked by a new thought. "Was it who I think?"

"Probably," Lamont said, giving him the once over. Lamont knew that Preston knew that Jake suspected Peter, but Preston was unaware of Lamont's dual role with the company. Lamont realized that he could tell Preston what he suspected and what Hal had seen without revealing that role. "Okay Mr. Preston I'm gonna tell you what I know and what I believe.

"I'm all ears," Preston said as he sat back and focused on Lamont. "Shoot."

Chapter Thirty Five- The Talk

Marcia was startled from her thoughts when Lamont's voice sounded over the intercom. "Marsh, hold my calls and tell everyone I'm in a meeting for the next hour."

"Ten four, Boss," she replied absently. Marcia's thoughts were focused on her own private mission. She had felt so relieved after hearing Lamont say that it was over between him and Jane. Now she wanted to jump up and click her heels together. Now she felt an obligation to keep Jane out of Lamont's life, for good. Today, she would take matters into her own hands and take steps to make sure that Jane wouldn't return. She wasn't going to let that unworthy tramp put Lamont through one more day of deception.

It was obvious to her that Lamont had some how discovered that Jane was a cheating liar, and that was good. Today she would go on a special mission to make sure that Jane stayed the hell away from Lamont. If that meant that she had to kick the bitch's ass, then she would do what was necessary. Actually that's exactly what she needed, but Lamont was too much of a gentlemen to do it.

Later that day, Marcia sat patiently inside her car listening to the radio in the WRAY-TV television station parking lot. She spotted Jane strutting through the main door with two white co-workers. She was laughing loudly, and flirting shamelessly. "What a bitch," Marcia said to herself.

The two men continually glared with enchantment at Jane's tight fitting short dress. Marcia was close enough to hear their remarks, and see the lewd suggestive gestures they made. Jane gave a fake scream when the tall red head pretended to bite her on the neck. "I'd like to put you in the dying cockroach and raid your goodies," said the chubby one. Jane's ridiculous giggle made Marcia want to gag.

What a slut, Marcia thought, shaking her head in disgust. Jane was allowing these idiots to be so disrespectful, Marcia thought, as she continued to watch Jane perform. She had little doubts that Jane had provoked their action, because she thrived on attention. She also had very little doubt that Jane would probably sleep with both of them.

They were treating her like a piece of meat to be passed back and forth, between two hungry wolves. "No, let me," Marcia heard the short one say, as the two openly fought for the honor of carrying her large bags. They hovered around her like a couple of eager flies about to pounce on a full garbage can, as Jane played the role of diva. "Boy's, Jane said, "Don't fight."

"Cold phony bitch," Marcia whispered silently, "never gave a damn about Lamont."

Both men seemed under her spell and struggled to gain favor from the luscious beauty. They were reluctant to part company with her, even after she slid behind the driver's seat and said good-bye. The tall one got in her face to talk, and then the other nudged him out. Finally after what seemed like hours, Jane pulled out from the parking lot, and Marcia pulled out behind her.

Shortly Marcia watches Jane enter her apartment, and after waiting a few minutes, she gained access to the building and rang Jane's doorbell. The door flung open and Jane stood there looking at Marcia with a scowl "Who the hell?" Jane started to ask."

"Hello Jane, I'm Marcia Dawson. I want to talk to you," Marcia said before Jane could say any more.

"Marcia?" Jane twisted her face in a puzzle scowl. "I don't know any Marcia. How do you know me? From the station?"

"I'm Lamont's friend. I need to talk to you." Marcia had barely finished speaking when Jane cut her off with an angry scowl.

"You," Jane hissed, as she glared at Marcia, with eyes that reflected intensely. "You're his secretary."

Marcia made an effort to remain calm. "May I come in?"

"What would you possibly have to say to me?"

"It's about Lamont."

"Lamont?" Jane dropped some of her hostility and inched sideways, allowing Marcia access.

Marcia moved quickly past Jane and inside the apartment, with a brief nervous smile. "Nice place you have here."

"Look, Honey, cut the home decor chatter. I know you didn't come here to discuss accessories and drapes. What about Lamont?"

Marcia sensed Jane's expectations of good news, and relished seeing Jane's disappointment once she explained why she had come. Marcia looked Jane in the eyes. "Okay it's like this. I know you were cheating on Lamont and that's the reason you guys broke up. The fact is, Jane that Lamont is through with you and he doesn't want to see you anymore. So pulling stunts like you did the other day is not going to change his mind. If anything, you're just making it worse, and you're making a fool of yourself. Do yourself a favor and quit while you're ahead. The things people do in the dark always manage to come to light. You had to know that eventually this would happen."

Jane's face contorted into a horrible vicious scowling mask. "You Bitch! You got the nerve to come in here and smirk about my broken relationship. Preaching to me about right and wrong? You homely little slut." She stopped abruptly, seeming to change the direction of her focus. "I was right about you the first time. You *are* screwing him, aren't you? That's it. You screwing him and you scared that you gon' lose him because you ain't woman enough to keep him. Is that why you're here? To threaten the competition? You know he still loves me, and I can get him back whenever I want."

Suddenly Jane burst into loud harsh laughter. "You a pitiful little lovesick creature," she chuckled. "You're following him around like a sad, sniveling little puppy dog. Girl, have some self esteem, because he'll never respect you if you don't. He was probably thinking about me the whole time that he was screwing you. You can't compete on my level, honey. You're just a rebound chick, filling the void. He'll come back when he comes to his senses."

Marcia seemed amused, and her expression was pleasant. "Honey you just can't see the big picture can you? You don't know him as well as you think. Cheating on a man like Lamont is an unforgivable cardinal sin. Your ass and tits won't help you this time."

"We'll see about that. I'm the bomb baby and women like you bow down to me."

"I've never seen a woman so stuck on herself, with so little to offer." Marcia scanned her openly. "You don't have that much and you don't have anything that I don't have. You want to talk about pity. Lamont was doing your slutty ass a favor. You lucky he didn't find out that you were screwing Greg months ago, and kicked your whoring ass into unconsciousness. Greg would kick your ass if he were in Lamont's shoes, you dumb slut."

Jane looked her up and down with a suspicious glint. "He told you about me and Greg? Was I the subject of your pillow talk?"

"You're not worth discussing, and Lamont didn't tell me anything."

"He told you something."

"Why, because I know you were cheating on him? I knew about that because I saw you myself."

Jane opened her mouth, but no sound came out. Had she been that careless? Who else had seen her?

"That's right," Marcia continued, "and with Greg of all people." Marcia made a face like she had just taken the world's most horrible tasting medicine. "No class at all."

Now Jane became angry again. "This ain't over yet. I had him pussy whipped once and I can do it again. Then I'm going to marry him."

Marcia smile smugly and her insides danced with glee. "Marry him, ha," Marcia laughed, "you're funny. Apparently you don't know him, but that doesn't surprise me. You're such a selfish bimbo and he knows that now. I have no doubt that you are out of his life, so get a clue."

"You can't say that for sure. Lamont's a man and men think with their tools, if you know what I mean. When it comes to a piece of ass, all men fall into the same category. So just maybe."

"No maybe baby, your cheatin' ass is history."

"Well sweetheart, whether I'm gone or not, one thing is for sure, you'll never get him."

"Lamont and I are friends, Jane, nothing more. That's something you would never understand, because you're just a pair of tits. You think that every woman and man who associate, are having sex together. That's not so."

"Oh my God," Jane said suddenly, wearing a smug expression. "I don't believe this," Jane said astonished. "You've never even slept with him have you? Did I underestimate you or what?' She let out a smug chuckle. "I only thought you were pitiful before, but Honey you win the pity prize. You're quietly stalking him like some serial killer, but you're trying to get laid and he won't touch you," Jane continued to laugh now. "Why is that? You're more pathetic than I thought."

In spite of her apathy for Jane, her harsh words stung Marcia, because they held the haunting ring of truth. Suddenly, Marcia was on the defense and felt like a hypocrite, because Jane was right. She was preaching about being friends, when she longed to be his lover, just like Jane was saying. Damn her.

She felt as if Jane had just exposed her soul, because the truth made her see herself in a different light. However, there was no way she would admit anything, or expose her personal feelings and weaknesses to Jane Curtis. "You can say and think what you want Jane, but stay away from Lamont or you'll be humiliated beyond your wildest dreams."

"So *you* say. I think you're trying to eliminate the competition so you can have him all to yourself. But I doubt if that will ever happen. You don't have what it takes to get a man like Lamont, and if you got him you'd blow it. So just keep on dreaming, Miss Pitiful, and I'll do what I want. It will be a cold day in hell when I take advice from a pathetic loser." Once again Jane flashed Marcia a smug smile.

"Now would you please remove your hopeless carcass from my residence?" She added the last with a Jennifer Lewis dramatic air.

"I'm going, but I'm warning you, if you do anything to hurt Lamont, you'll see me again. Call me pathetic, pitiful, and anything else that pops into your confused backwards immoral brain, but I'm warning you." Marcia started for the door.

Jane was on Marcia's heels as she reached the door. "You skanky little Bitch, I ought to kick your ass, talking to me like that." Jane grabbed Marcia's shoulder, and spun her around as she opened the door. Marcia reacted impulsively, and gave Jane two quick hard slaps across the face that shook her up.

"You whoring back stabbing black bitch, don't you ever put your contaminated paws on me," Marcia said, looking into Jane's frightened eyes. "Come on slut, just touch me," Marcia pleaded. "Give me a reason."

Obviously, fighting was the last thing on Jane's mind, as she touched her stinging cheek, in a state of semi-shock. She looked at the hand she had just touched to her cheek, seeming to check for blood. "You hit me," Jane said timidly as her moist eyes focused on Marcia.

"Yes I did, and I'm not sorry about it." Marcia said, turning squarely to face Jane with a scowl, and tightly balled fists.

Jane was prissy and had never been in a physical fight in her life. All of her physical confrontations were sexual in nature. "Just get the hell out of here before I call the police. Get out of my house, thug bitch," Jane said, holding on to some of her anger.

Marcia gave Jane a pleased smirk, and purposely scanned her up and down with a slow deliberate movement of her head. She brought her eyes to Jane's and looked deep into them. "And you call *me* pitiful. You're just a pathetic pussy." Marcia turned slowly and strutted through the door, light headed, smiling, and filled with adrenaline.

Jane darted to the bathroom mirror and looked at her face, checking for damage. She breathed a sigh of relief to see that no swelling or welts were present. That bitch had struck her so hard that she had actually seen a light flash, and felt her taste buds rattle. Lamont was such a coward to send that lovesick skank to do his dirty work. Jane recalls Marcia's ready-for-combat-attitude, and there is no way that she was going to challenge or confront Marcia. There was nothing more dangerous than a jealous, horny, frustrated bitch.

She assumed that because Marcia couldn't have Lamont, she was ready to take out her frustration on her. Jane only did her fighting with words, not fist. There was no doubt that a woman like Marcia might go into a rage and beat her to a pulp.

Marcia's visit made Jane realize that she had to travel in more gentle circles. She couldn't have jealous women scarring her face now that she must pursue her career actively. She had destroyed her own American dream, and now she had no other choice. She wasn't going to be a rich society type after all.

Lamont was a good catch but he wasn't worth getting her ass kicked. She couldn't stand physical pain and cringed at just the thought of being hit in the face. Besides she wasn't about to fight over a man, so to hell with Lamont if that was the only way that she cold get him back. Men fought over her, and she had never had any trouble getting them to impress her by spending their money.

She studied her face. "Shit I hope my face doesn't swell. If it does that bitch is gonna be sorry, cause I'll get daddy to sue her ass. Bitch," she said in a voice barely audible as she stood before the mirror, turning her face from side to side.

Her mind raced as she put the bag of ice on her jaw. Tomorrow was another day, and her first day back in the hunt. She was single again, and she felt quiet excitement stirring inside her. "Forget you, Lamont; daddy wasn't that fond of you anyway. Take your psycho bitch and go to hell. I've got options."

Chapter Thirty Six-
Surveillance

Lamont dialed the number of Lucas Shepherd's private detective agency, as Preston had suggested after hearing his story. Apparently, Preston believed him and that's why he suggested this course of action. Preston was aware that Lucas was working with Jake to uncover the suspected spy.

Lucas himself answered on the other end, and Lamont introduced himself, and then made an appointment to see him. He was surprised when Lucas said that he would be right over. He thought that maybe it was that Cooper clout that brought such a swift response.

Lucas Shepherd arrived thirty minutes later, and was slightly disappointed when he was lead to Lamont's office instead of Jake's. He had hoped that it was Jake who wanted to see him, because he would feel more comfortable in the familiar surroundings of Jake's office. He also anticipated catching a glimpse of Candace Cooper's startling movie star quality, on the photo in Jake's office. He had even hoped that she might happen to stop by. That would be its own reward for him. However, since he was here to see Lamont, he put Candace from his mind.

Some of his disappointment faded when he spotted the pretty young female at her desk next to Lamont's office. His gaze locked on hers, while moving mechanically towards her desk. As he got closer, she looked up into his eyes and smiled, and his heart raced.

"Hi, I'm Marcia Dawson." She introduced herself. "Can I help you, Sir?"

"Yes I'm Lucas Sheppard and I'm..."

"Oh yes Mr. Sheppard, he's expecting you." She said pressing the intercom. "Lamont, Mr. Sheppard's here."

Strangely, Lucas' disappointment returned when he realized that he didn't have to wait. He wouldn't have minded waiting a few more minutes, because then he could drink in Marcia Dawson's stunning beauty at length. However duty called and he was a professional.

Lucas was surprised seeing Lamont up close for the first time. He knew all about Lamont from his past surveillance, and from the information he had gathered for Jake. Lamont looked up when Lucas entered.

"Mr. Shepherd," he smiled and came from behind his desk to greet the shabby private detective. "Pleased to meet you, I'm Lamont Savage."

Lucas gave a half smile. "Pleased to meet you too."

"I understand that you're working with Jake in trying to find out what's going on here. Jake is very pleased with the work you've done in the past, and you have quite a reputation."

"I hope I can live up to it." Lucas had seen Lamont, but had never met him up close. Jake had hired him to find Lamont three years ago, and he had studied Lamont from a distance. Up close, he was impressed by Lamont's show of respect and honest eyes. Lamont looked directly into his eyes when he spoke. Lucas read people's eyes accurately, and he attributed that talent to his success. The eyes reflected many things including respect, and Lucas treasured respect because it came so rarely to him, even from Jake.

People respected his work, but once he had served his purpose they wanted him gone. Being somewhat of a social outcast, he witnessed sinister things perpetrated on downtrodden and unattractive people like him. Yes they needed his skills, but need was not respect.

It hadn't seemed possible for him to earn Jake's respect, because of the many levels of complications. He didn't consider himself as Jake's equal, so therefore Jake probably didn't consider it either. Even though he knew Jake was a good man, he had seen the quiet arrogance that only critical observers such as he could detect. He accredited himself with 20-20 insight most of the time.

Perhaps he gave himself so much credit, because no one else did. He didn't have many talents and he wasn't a good looking man, but he knew that he was the city's best detective. In fact, he was probably the best in the state when it came to tracking leads, and meeting the challenges of his work. That was because he loved being a detective, and he was living his dream.

"I have no doubts that your reputation is well earned," Lamont said. "Please have a seat. Did you want Marcia to bring us some coffee or anything?"

"Black coffee please." Lucas said, thinking that now he would get a chance to see Marcia again. Lucas was right and Marcia brought them coffee and cinnamon rolls along with her sparkling personality. Lucas slipped into a brief fantasy at the sight of her curves, and great legs. He almost forgot why he was there, but once Marcia left he found his bearing.

"So Mr. Savage, what is it that you want exactly?"

"Well I'd like to be brought up to speed about what you got so far, and I need to extend the surveillance on Peter Vel Haus. I need to know his every move," Lamont said, looking Lucas in the eyes.

Lucas cleared his throat self consciously. "Excuse me a minute, Mr. Savage."

"Please, call me Lamont."

"Lamont, I don't mean no disrespect, so don't take this the wrong way, but I need to talk to Jake. You understand it's a matter of professional ethics. Since I normally report to him I'll need to get his approval to do otherwise," Lucas offered hunching his shoulders humbly.

"Yes, I am aware of that, Mr. Sheppard."

"Call me Lucas," he said with a crooked smile.

"Lucas, I understand and I respect your professionalism, however, Jake is out of town attending his mother in law's funeral. He'll be back in a day or two. In the mean time some pressing things have come up, and I need to see your surveillance report on Peter Val Haus, and as I said, to extend surveillance. I want a camera inside this office for starters.

I believe this action is necessary, because Peter's actions could jeopardize the security of the company." Lamont hesitated again and blew out a sigh. "Of course I can wait, but I really wish I didn't have to. I'm hoping that we can work something out between us. I assure you that Jake will approve of this one hundred per cent."

Lucas quickly scanned Lamont and sized him up. He wanted to trust him, and he did feel like he knew something about his character. After all, he had followed him for several months in order to get that information that Jake needed. He concluded that he was a good kid and all, but this was his reputation.

In spite of his instant lust for the young and luscious Marcia, he couldn't put his ass on the line. "I don't know if I can help you on that. Something goes wrong, or any dispute about the contract and..." He didn't finish, just shrugged his shoulders and gave Lamont a sorry-I-can't-help-you look.

"Look Mr. Sheppard, why don't we run this by Preston. He's the one who gave me all those glowing recommendations about your work. He speaks very highly of you. I assume the two of you have met. You gotta trust him. He's Jake's right hand." Lamont moved from the desk putting himself between Lucas and the door.

"Preston you say? Preston can vouch for you and okay this?"

"Yes," Lamont said without hesitation.

"Preston's a good man. I've worked with him and I trust him." Lucas seemed to contemplate some strategy.

"He's the best." Lamont said, not because he knew this, but because he thought it would sway Lucas' decision. "And he'll tell you everything you need to know. Believe me, Mr. Shepherd, neither one of us would do anything to hurt Jake in any way." Lamont spread out his hands palms up.

Lucas scanned Lamont briefly. "Yeah I believe that." He gave Lamont a nod. "Okay I'll do it based on what Preston tells me. If he can assure me that you're authorized, and put it in writing that I won't get sued, I'll turn over my reports, extend my investigation, and brief you on what's happening."

Lamont smiled. "Good, I feel better about that already."

"Thanks Mr. Shepherd."

"Lucas."

"Thanks Lucas," Lamont said, hesitating and giving Lucas a look. "How soon will it be before you get back to me?"

"That depends on what happens once I talk to Preston," he said, starting for the door. "But it will be sooner rather than later."

"Okay, I have no choice but to wait then," Lamont said, slightly disappointed that he couldn't get instant results.

The men shook hands and Lucas left Lamont's office, and walked slowly past Marcia Dawson's desk. She was such a pretty female, and he imagined that he could taste her essence in the air. She had the looks of an ebony fashion model, but his trained eyes saw something more to this girl than just great looks.

He observed the way her shoulder length brown hair framed her high apple cheek bones and sexy valentine full lips. The gold earrings dangled from her luscious lobes like sparkling pieces of lost treasure. He was instantly infatuated, and named her the 'Magnificent Marcia'.

He smiled at her, and to his surprise; their eyes met and she returned his smile. For a brief moment, his heart beat froze. He swore that she was flirting with him. This woman was as sweet as she was sexy.

She was nothing like, Pam, Jake's stuck up secretary. He might get to like working with Lamont after all. He stopped in front of Marcia's desk. "Excuse me. Marcia? Right?" Of course it was Marcia, he already knew that. He eased closer and let her perfume invade his nostrils and jolt his olfactory senses, as brief fantasies reigned inside his mind.

"Yes," she said looking up from her computer. "What can I do for you Mr. Sheppard?" She asked with a wide smile.

Several lewd punch lines ran rapidly through Lucas' mind as his eyes locked on hers, but he would never disrespect her by saying them aloud. "You can tell me how to find Lawrence Preston's office, if you don't mind." Lucas already knew that information, but he was compelled to say something to her.

"Yes, Mr. Preston's office is Fifth floor, five twenty four," she said after checking the directory on her desk.

"Thanks, Marcia. You've been a big help."

"No problem at all Mr. Sheppard," she said, still smiling.

Lucas was intoxicated by that warm smile, which revealed teeth that glowed like gleaming pearls. Her sweet voice echoed still in his ears, as he floated towards the elevator.

Inside the office, Lamont gazed absently at the door, while talking to Preston on the phone. He informed Preston that he needed his support with Lucas Sheppard, who was heading for his office. Preston agreed and after Lamont hung up the phone, he pictured Lucas Sheppard in his head. He trusted Preston's judgment and gleaming recommendation, but he must admit that Sheppard doesn't look like a detective. Well he was supposed to be the best and he was on the case, so Lamont had remained patient.

Lamont didn't have to wait for long, because the next day Lucas called to say that he had new information that Jake hadn't seen yet, and he would arrive shortly with his report. Lucas hadn't said much on the phone and Lamont was suddenly anxious to see the results.

Thirty minutes later, Lucas was seated inside Lamont's office, looking through his little notebook. "Okay, where do I start," he muttered more to himself, now studying his notes. "Okay, first of all Jake hit it on the nose. Peter Vel Haus has been using an alias to buy stock that mysteriously comes available at random.

"How does he know unless he has something to do with it?" Lamont asked, trying to imagine how Peter had access to such information first hand. "Obviously he's trying to accumulate stock, and the only reason that I can imagine is that he plans a hostile takeover. Still, Jake and the family jointly held the controlling shares, and Peter could never get enough to take over. "Barring some unseen catastrophe, there was no way anyone could get the family shares. Where is he getting the money? And what's his plan?"

"I'm coming to that" Lucas continued. "He's not buying the stock for himself; he's turning everything over to a third party." Lucas paused and looked at Lamont for effect. "Get this, that third party is none other than Anthony Carvoni."

Lamont looked directly at Lucas in disbelief. "As in Tony Carvoni? The Mafia Don? So Jake was right." Lamont whispered to himself. "So does that mean that Carvoni is finding some way to get stockholders to sell, and then he sends Peter in to scoop up their stock?

"That's what it looks like," Lucas sighed. "That's the bad news," Lucas hesitated flipping the page on his battered note book.

"What's the good news?" Lamont asked.

"That Tony is not being backed by the New Jersey mob. There was a rift between some of the bosses and pure chaos broke out between several families. Two hit men ended up shooting each other, and money was taken. And besides that the Jersey mob isn't looking to delve into a legitimate project this size. Their thing is gambling, murder, racketeering and the usual mob stuff."

"So what are saying? Carvoni is independent? Is that possible?"

"I don't know, but like I said after that rift they had in Philly and south Jersey a few years back, some of the rules were either changed or ignored by Carvoni, who's as eccentric as he is ambitious.

"What do you think his plan is right now?" Lamont asked, slightly dazed.

"It's really simply, I think Peter supply's Carvoni with the name of certain stock holders, and Carvoni coerces them to sell. Then Carvoni supply's Peter with the cash to buy the stock. It's an effective way to accumulate stock."

"There's no doubt now that Mob *is* trying to take over, or at least Carvoni's branch of the mob is." Lamont sighed deeply, sitting back in the chair now. "So Peter made a deal with the mob to get Cooper stock." Now Lamont stood and began pacing lightly. "Jake was right to suspect Peter all along and once I relay this news, I'm sure Jake will throw him out on his ass regardless. Why is Carvoni coming after Cooper industries? That's not the way the mob operates."

"Well like I said, Carvoni has his own eccentricities and his own little mini-mob in place."

"Can he do that Lucas? I mean he's still connected to the mob isn't he?"

"Yeah, but like I said he's kind of in no man's land here. He's in between the Miami mob and the New Jersey mob." Lucas paused then added, "But if he pulls this off, some one is going to want a piece of the action."

"That's the key word, if," Lamont stressed.

"There is the slim chance that he might abandon this project if he thought that it wasn't all that he hope it would be."

"What do you mean?"

"I mean that Carvoni is an excitement Junkie, and he's attracted to glitter, pretty girls, hustling and illegal contraband. In short he loves the life style of running the rackets. So the one chance you have is to convince him that running a business is a dull, un-exciting experience."

"Yes, I see your point. It is a vast wide variation from his usual pursuits."

"Then again, he could be planning to either raid the company and sell it for a huge profit, or have some a flunky like Peter run it for him. Cooper's is the most successful operations in the region, and is still turning a profit with this stock market mess. But with that said, I still don't see Carvoni running it as a legitimate operation. He's a control freak and if he can't run the company himself, he's likely to sell it."

Lamont nodded. "You're right Lucas; my guess is that he's going to raid the company. But there must be some way to stop him. I'm aware that he's powerful and well connected, but."

"Don't forget dangerous." Lucas added.

"Still, we can't just let him do whatever the hell he wants to do."

"Well he's got some of the local police, plus his soldiers and Capo, which makes it tough to beat him."

"Yeah, I'm aware that it's no easy task." Lamont shook his head.

"I can't believe how that little asshole just stormed into the area and set up operations almost overnight," Lucas said. "But the local police are useless, and as long as they got their generous donations they quickly look the other way. You know how money motivates people *not* to do things." Lucas shrugged.

"Now he's moving in on us, and we got to find a way to stop him, but how do we fight the mob? They look legitimate and blend right in," Lamont said with a sigh, and stood. He walked slowly towards the window, rubbing his chin thoughtfully. "There is possibly a more immediate problem that could arise with being associated with the mob. Cooper Industries could lose clout and contracts if the word got out about this mob connection."

"I don't think that's going to happen, Lamont. It's in Carvoni's best interest that the company continues to make money. That's more for him if his plan succeeds. So you can bet he's going to do what's best for the company right now. He's not stupid," said Lucas.

"And speaking of stupid, I got one more problem. Peter."

"Exactly," Lucas paused, looking at Lamont, "what are you gonna do about him, if I might ask?"

"There's not a whole lot I can do since technically he's my boss. Jake will handle this when he gets back. I really hate to bother him right now, because he's still grieving the death of his mother in law. I'm gonna just keep away from Peter until Jake gets back. I'll let Jake weigh all options and figure out the next move."

"I don't envy you or Jake," Lucas said, shaking his head. "And keeping away from Peter is gonna be an extra hard job seeing that he *is* your boss."

Actually Lamont worked directly for Jake, and Peter couldn't terminate him, but it wasn't necessary to reveal this information to Lucas.

Lucas opened up the shabby brief case and took out some papers. "I'm sure the two of you can figure out something. In the mean time, here's my report along with other evidence and information that you might want to ponder and use. I also got copies of stock orders and transfer slips, and I'll get your hidden camera set up in here like you wanted. You'll be ready when and if Peter tries anything else."

"Good," Lamont said taking the papers from Lucas. "Thanks Lucas, good job. I appreciate your suggestions and I definitely will heed your advice."

"Thanks," Lucas beamed with satisfaction and enthusiasm, apparently because he had impressed the young lad. He picked up his things and stood. "Okay then I'll be going. If you need anything else, a follow up or anything like that, get back with me."

"As a matter of fact Lucas, I'd like to get those reports about Peter until Jake returns. It's time to do some damage control. I want to know the next time Peter thinks about buying Cooper stock. The more I know about him the better I can deal with him." Lamont shook his head, and then added. "Peter was happy here once, and it's a mystery why he turned on Jake. You think maybe Carvoni might have threatened Peter?"

"I doubt it. It's no mystery to me why Peter is doing this," Lucas said with a pause. "Greed and need drives Peter, his greed for money, and his need to be number one. Add resentment and you have the formula that drives him. Plus he resents you, but he sold out long before you arrived," Lucas said.

"So you'd rule out duress?"

"Definitely. Peter's doing this for his own selfish reasons." Lucas shrugged.

"Yes of course you're right," Lamont said remembering that Jake was sure that Peter was guilty of embezzlement as well. "I'd like to meet Carvoni face to face," Lamont said.

"I don't know if that's wise. Thugs like Carvoni don't need any reason to hurt people, and he has no qualms about getting what he wants by using violence."

"You're right, it might not be wise. But now that I know about Peter's deal with Carvoni, I need to get more information on the deal that's cooking between them. Let's dig a little deeper Lucas. Find out about the deal between them. Maybe we can come up with something to stop them in their tracks. If there's something that we should know, let's find out about it like yesterday."

"You got it Lamont. I'll expand my investigation further," Lucas said enthusiastically. "I'll step it up, and before this is over I'll know which hand Peter uses to pick his nose, as well as the velocity and frequency of his farts." Lucas stopped abruptly. "Too much information huh?" He asked looking awkwardly towards Lamont.

"Maybe just a tad," Lamont said, lightly, "but it's good to know that you plan on being thorough."

Lucas left Lamont's office and he spotted Marcia and another young lady walking from the water cooler. An instant smile perched on his lips. 'Talking about your poetry in motion,' he thought. "Damn," he whispered under his breath, focusing on Marcia's bubble bottom and round perky breasts. "Look at those tits," he whispered to himself.

Marcia caught his eye and flashed him a sweet iridescent smile again. "Bye Mr. Shepherd, she said in a light raspy voice, and gave him a small *Miss America* wave, as she strutted gracefully to her desk.

Lucas was surprised that she spoke, and almost forgot to return her greeting. "Oh uh bye, uh Mar.. Marcia," he stammered and flashed a brief shy smile and walked quickly down the small corridor. He stepped onto the elevator in a daze, still entranced by Marcia's thoughtfulness and beauty.

He fought the urge to look back at her, afraid that the intensity of his gaze would expose his arcane lewd cravings. He was going to enjoy working for Lamont, because the atmosphere was uplifting and the fringed benefits were rewarding. "Welcome aboard Lucas, and enjoy the ride," he muttered, as the elevator rushed towards the ground floor.

Chapter Thirty Seven-
Crisis

Lamont's top priority was the Carvoni situation and now that Jake was back, he anticipated talking to him about a solution. He planned to drop by Jake's place this morning and fill him in. However his priorities changed when Candace called to inform him that Jake had suffered a stroke earlier. Lamont's knees almost gave way, and Candace's sobbing gave him a premonition of sadness. Lamont had listened to her words frozen, and from that point on, he was only interested in the state of Jake's health.

Candace was near hysteria, no doubt thinking the worse. Lamont sensed that the cause of her dismay was the combination of her mother's recent death, as well as Jake's present condition. From what he gathered, Jake had complained of chest pains the night before, but the pain subsided and he had gone to bed. The next morning the pains returned with more intensity and his left arm was numb. Jake had been rushed to the hospital. "Lamont, he looked so weak, and I just lost momma," Candace sobbed, unable to finish her statement.

"Try to remain calm Candace. I'll be there in thirty minutes," Lamont said. He called his siblings to break the news, then hurriedly dressed and rushed to the hospital. Lamont arrived ahead of the others and was told that Jake had a mild stroke, not a heart attack, and it wasn't as serious as they first thought. Still they were taking every precaution.

He called Marcia from the hospital and explained the situation, then asked her to cancel his scheduled appointments for the day. He waited in the hall next to the critical care unit. For now, only his wife was allowed inside, but Lamont managed to catch a brief glimpse of Jake lying helpless on the bed.

He shuddered to think what would happen if this family lost Jake. There was no way his business-challenged siblings could stop Carvoni from stealing the company. Jake had to pull through because if he died this family was dead. More importantly, he realized that he needed Jake.

A few hours later, the other siblings arrived and now gathered together, waiting to hear some news. Lamont kept a clear head and got coffee and sweet rolls for every one, but no one had an appetite. Candace and Cheryl drank coffee, but the others were just pacing around wringing their hands.

"I can't stand this," Candace said, breaking the silence amongst those present. If something happens," Candace started but burst into tears before she could finish.

Lamont moved to her. "It's not as bad as it sounds according to Dr. Joynes," Lamont said, touching her shoulder. "They're just making sure," Lamont said, feeling as if he had to try to keep everyone calm.

"Then how bad is it? More important, is he going to fully recover? Didn't the doctor say that there could be...?" She stopped. She couldn't bear to think about it."

Lamont hunched his shoulders. "Brain damage? Let's not jump the gun. Dr. Joynes said that there was a very small chance. It's too early to tell, but I'm guessing that Jake will recover." Lamont felt the attention of sad faces and silent voices, and was compelled to offer encouragement. "Come on guys, this is Jake. I know he'll make a full recovery."

They all nodded and made some half hearted gesture to show agreement. Lamont realized that he had to lead them. The thought intimidated him, because he sensed that his attempts to show leadership would cause more resentment. Still, that couldn't sway him, because regardless of whether they accepted or understood it, he had to do what was best for every one. "Look I think he's in good hands, and there's nothing we can do right now."

"Except pray," Ann exclaimed in a shaky voice.

"Yes, Ann, you're right. We can pray," Lamont agreed.

"God, why is this happening to dad? Why?" JJ's voice rang out with angry desperation. He stood off by himself looking messy with his rumpled clothes and uncombed hair. He turned away when Ruth moved close to comfort him. It was obvious from his eyes that he was under the influence of something.

"Calm down, JJ," Lamont said.

"Calm down? How the hell can I calm down? How can we just stand around doing nothing?"

"Because all we can do is wait, JJ." Lamont said.

"Why did this have to happen to him? Why?" JJ asked to no one in particular.

Cheryl moved closer to JJ and spoke. "JJ calm down and try to be patient. I'm sure they're doing all they can," Cheryl said slightly annoyed with her younger brother's whining. She whispered in his ear. "Pull yourself together JJ. We need you and Lamont as men of the family to be strong. If anything happens to daddy now I."

"Fuck you Cheryl," JJ said glaring at Cheryl and moving away from her. "Don't say that. Don't even think about shit like that."

Cheryl didn't respond because she saw the hurt lost look in his eyes. She knew then that he was still just a little boy who didn't want to lose his daddy. Unfortunately, he showed no signs of ever growing up. He was soft and he would never be like Lamont. The two brothers were as different as night and day, and right now Cheryl thought that was a good thing. They would be in trouble if Lamont was anything like JJ.

"Standing around like this it's stupid." Tears filled JJ's eyes and ran down his cheeks.

"JJ, you buck up and you listen to me." Lamont was in JJ's face and speaking firmly. "We aren't waiting for him to die. We're waiting for him to continue living. We're doing the only thing that we can do." Lamont said with a sigh, while looking around at all the sad faces. "We're here together, supporting him as a family, and that's the best we can do right now. We're not going to talk negative, so if you can't pull yourself together I suggest you leave." Lamont paused and an awkward silence filled the void.

"Jake's strong and he's got the best care, and that's a hard combination to beat." He looked at JJ directly and his mood softened. "Look, you think we all don't know how you feel. We do because we feel it too. We're all anxious and scared, but we're not going to lose hope or patience."

"He can't die, Lamont. Daddy can't die," JJ said, shaking his head, and fighting back the tears.

"Daddy's not gonna die, JJ." Ann spoke with quiet confidence, moving to JJ and clutching tightly to the bible under her arm. "The

Good Lord is not ready for daddy yet. I know this." Everyone was silent so she continued. "Daddy has done a lot of good and he's going to continue. I just know he's gonna make it. We must have faith."

"Yes, Ann is right. We should all have faith." Lamont spoke, looking around at the others.

"I think we should all go to the chapel and pray." Ann added, with renewed confidence.

"Really, Ann, what good is that gonna do?" Ruth asked with calm skepticism.

"Ruth!" Ann looked at her sister appalled. "How can you be so profane?"

"I'm not, and stop being so thin skin Annie. I don't want daddy to die, but ain't God gonna do what he want to do anyway?" She hunched her shoulders. "Ain't it all in a big book, already written down somewhere? You're born on a certain date, and you die on a certain date. We can do nothing to change that either way."

Ann looked towards Ruth obviously fighting to maintain control of her composure. "You are so wrong, Ruth, and it's sad. What you don't understand, Sis is that prayer changes things. Sure it's all in a book and predetermined to a point, but prayer is a way that parts of that book gets revised. Every book can be edited depending on the circumstances. That's the power of prayer, Ruth. Prayer edits parts of that book that you speak of." Ann was slightly offended at her sister's doubtful words, but remained civil and had only raised her voice at the end.

"Praying sure couldn't hurt," Cheryl said with a concerned frown.

"Yeah, "Candace added. "Let's do it. I just lost my mother and if I lose..." She halted in mid sentence. "Let's just go and do it." They informed the nurse on the floor as to where they could be reached then headed to the chapel.

After a short time, Lamont was anxious to check on Jake, so he left the others and went back up to Critical care unit. The nurse greeted him. "Oh Mister Cooper, I was about to send someone to get you."

"What? Did something happen?" Lamont asked ignoring her mistaken assumption that last name was Cooper. He was suddenly scared that bad news was forthcoming.

"Yes, but it's good news. Your father is conscious and he's asking for you I think. You're Lamont the oldest son, right?"

"Yes, I'm Lamont," he said excitedly. "He was asking for me?" He asked. It surprised him that he had not asked for Candace.

"You can go in briefly but don't excite him," the nurse warned.

"Okay then," Lamont said with relief as he entered the room. He saw Jake's eyes open and a ton of stress vanished from Lamont's mind. Jake seemed normal, except for a slight twist of his lower lip.

Jake spotted Lamont. "Lamont," he whispered.

"Hi, Jake. How you feeling?"

"Tired and bored." His voice was weak but coherent.

"You gonna have to take it easy for a while."

"I got things to do, Lamont. I don't have time for this."

"It's out of your hands, Jake, and I'm not letting you do something crazy."

He sighed wearily. "I don't want to be flat on my back leaving you to deal with that snake Peter by yourself. Peter is going to think that he has a clear field to take over."

"That's not going to happen, Jake. Not if I have something to say about it. We know that you were right about him now so he can't hurt us if we go on the defensive, which I already have."

"Good. I knew you'd get up to speed once you knew what was happening," Jake managed to say with some effort.

"Believe it, Jake."

"I do," Jake said. He studied Lamont briefly, scanning him and hesitating before continuing. "Do something for me."

"Sure Jake whatever you want."

"Get Preston up here."

"Hold on Jake. I know I said I'd do what you wanted, but it's not wise for you to talk business right now."

"I'm not. I want to have some legal papers drawn up."

"What kind of legal papers?" Lamont asked puzzled.

"I want you and Preston to have joint power of attorney. That way you can act as my agent and you'll be Peter's boss instead of the other way around."

"You sure you want to do that Jake?"

"Well if you don't think you can handle it I understand."

"It's not that Jake. It's just that it might rub a lot of people the wrong way. I am just a green rookie and."

"I don't give a damn who it rubs, or how hard it rubs them. This is a business decision, and I have to make it because I'm the only one who can. You catch on fast and I think you're ready, Lamont. Don't you?"

"Well I'm not really sure that I can fill your shoes Jake. I'm still green."

"I appreciate your honesty, and the fact that you're modest about your talents is the reason that I know you're capable. Besides, a green Cooper trumps an experience creep like Peter any day. And since I'm willing to gamble on you, you should be willing to let me."

Jake called him a Cooper, Lamont thought, while observing his father lying helpless on his back. In Jake's eyes he was a Cooper, and that meant something to him. He shook off any previous doubts about himself. He believed that he could do what was necessary. "Of course I can handle it, but I'll bet that you'll be back before I have to."

"Let's hope so."

"But you gotta rest first. You got to regain your strength."

"That's the hard part." Jake hesitated before speaking again, and now tried to get his words together. "Lamont, I."

Lamont was concerned now that Jake's manner had suddenly changed. "You okay Jake?" He feared that there might be some complications, perhaps even a relapse. "I'm gonna call somebody," Lamont said and started towards the corridor. Jake called out, and he halted in his tracks.

"Lamont, I'm fine." He managed to raise his hands in a gesture telling Lamont to calm down. "Sit over here; I want to tell you something, son."

Lamont moved to the chair next to the bed and sat. Jake's voice became stronger as he began to speak. "Son, I know that in the past I haven't done the right thing where you were concern, and I regret that. I let my personal feelings about." He hesitated, not wanting to say what he was thinking.

"Let's just say that I was influenced by things that I shouldn't have been influenced by. It clouded my logic and my judgment, and you ended up suffering because of it. I'm so sorry, Lamont. I'm sorry for you as well as me because I missed so much. I didn't see your first steps or hear your first words. At the time I didn't think about it, but now that I'm older, I realize that there are many precious things that I can never recover." He paused and took a deep breath. "I wish that I had been wiser and things had been different, but what has happened can't be changed."

"Look Jake, we all make mistakes and do things we regret. It's called being human, which means we're filled with flaws."

"Still, I was so neglectful and selfish and."

"And busy taking care of your family and growing your business. At least you cared enough to provide me support. It's not your fault that mom lied about you and the money for all those years. She's not so perfect or completely innocent herself."

"I know, but." His eyes were moist and he seemed overcome with emotions. Lamont had never seen him like this. "I was wrong and I'm sorry. If I had been a decent man I would have contacted your mother, and at least visited you from time to time. I'm ashamed of myself for being so selfish. I guess that's why I'm being punished now."

"Nonsense Jake, this didn't happen because of anything that you did or didn't do for me, and you're gonna pull through."

"That's not what I mean by being punished. I mean that you turned out to be such a class act, and so much time passed without me having the benefit of your presence." He hesitated again then looked directly at Lamont. "I love you Lamont, and I should have been there for you years ago.

"You're the best of my blood. You're special and you got more class than all of the rest of them. I love them dearly as well, but they've never shown any desire for responsibility the way you have. I know that's my fault because I spoiled them, and I loved spoiling them after their mother died.

Still I always hoped that at least one of them would show some spirit, and make a hard decision about something, or face some responsibility and see it through, even if it's not the right decision. I'd like to see them devote some passion to something they feel is worthwhile, or ..." His voice was faltering and his breathing was shallow. "At least I had hoped that."

"Easy Jake. Don't tire yourself out," Lamont said, feeling somewhat awkward and yet, elated about Jake's revelation. Jake had finally said the words and he knew now that Jake didn't just feel obligation and guilt towards him. Now at last he knew that his father not only loved him but liked and respected him as well.

Jake waved Lamont's concerns aside and continued to speak. "I lost so much time, and I missed so much by not getting to know you. I hope that I can at least stay around long enough to try and make it up to you." He seemed tired, but he was determined to continue.

"In some ways it was good that I wasn't there for you. It made you more independent, and better than you might have been had you been fed with that silver spoon I used on the others. I'm not justifying my mistake, but since it did happen, at least some good came of it." Now he sighed deeply and closed his eyes.

Lamont just realize how much he would grieve if he lost Jake. He had started out feeling merely an obligation to try and bond with the man who had given him life, but he had learned to respect and love him. He looked at his father and moved closer to the bed. Once again he recalled the words that his uncle Johnny had once said about Jake; *"Jake isn't special because he's rich, he's rich because he's special."*

"I love you too, Dad. You truly are a special man. I know that you've done everything possible to atone for your mistake," Lamont said through trembling lips. "As far as I'm concerned, you've more than made up for that. So you get well 'cause I need you, we all do." He wiped his eyes, took a deep breath, and walked out of the room.

Lamont felt good about having the love of his father, although he had once said that it didn't matter. The truth was that it mattered a lot. A father was hard to describe, and not having one was like not having an essential part of your spirit, and not knowing that it was missing. He had always needed a father and now he had one. He was deep in thought when he walked from the room looking straight ahead, and never saw Cheryl standing there beside the doorway.

Cheryl's facial expression reflected pain, and her hazel eyes were moist with tears. She stood frozen up against the wall in a single pose, and watched Lamont step on the elevator. She wanted to call out to him when he zoomed by, but she had been reeling from the conversation that she had just overheard.

Apparently, Jake favored Lamont over the rest of them and had given him his power of attorney. Strangely she felt slighted, even though she wouldn't know what to do with Jake's power of attorney if she had it. Jake had made his decision and she didn't know if that was good or bad. She did know that she couldn't do anything about it. Her one consolation was that he at least hadn't given all that power to Candace. That really would have been disastrous.

Chapter Thirty Eight- Comforting

Lamont had made his way from the critical care unit and headed down to the parking lot. He called Preston and informed him about Jake's request to see him. He planned to go back to the office briefly then return later to remain with Jake for a while. Now he noticed Candace sitting in the car trembling and he went to her. "Candace, are you okay?" Lamont asked, leaning on the car door, looking into her eyes, still red from crying.

"No, Lamont, I'm not," she replied "Lamont I don't know what would happen if I lost Jake."

"Good News, Candace, you're not going to lose Jake. He's conscious and I just talked to him."

"And he's going to make it then? I mean there's no brain damage or anything like that?"

"None, but he's tired and a bit weak."

She was silent briefly. "Lamont, I'm so relieved."

"Did you want to go back in and see him?"

"Lamont, I just can't face him right now. I just buried my mother and it's just too unbearable seeing Jake looking so." She was unable to continue. "Does that mean I'm a bad person?"

"Of course not. I understand everything you've had to face the past few days. Anyone would be drained. There's nothing wrong with that."

"Thanks for understanding; I'm not sure the rest of them would. If anything happened to Jake, I don't want my last memories of him to be his declining state of health. He's always been so strong, and I hate to see him looking as if he were about to."

"He's not going to die, Candace," Lamont said firmly. "Jake's fine, I just talked to him and he's gonna get through this. You should know him well enough to know that this won't stop him. You stop worrying about it."

She wiped her eyes. "You're right, and I need to be stronger. I need to go back up and stay there with him. I owe him that much." She wiped her eyes and started to open the car door.

"I just left him and he's sleeping right now, so he won't know you're there."

"I know, but I want to be there just the same." Her voice trailed away wearily.

Lamont could see that she was obviously tired. "Candace, I'd like to suggest something," he said.

"What?"

"Since he's sleeping now, why don't you go home and get yourself some rest as well? You can always come back later. He might even regain enough strength to talk when you returned."

She stared into his eyes. "You don't think I can't handle it do you?"

He shrugged his shoulders, but said nothing, while searching her face. He noticed that her lips were perfect shaped pouty little hearts, and her nose accented those lips with its own slanted arrowhead shape and flaring oval nostrils. Her large deep brown gorgeous eyes were filled with tears and redness. In spite of her comely beauty, he felt only care, concern, and respect for her right now. He was certain that she really loved Jake and was genuinely concerned.

Lamont now felt a different kind of bond to her. It was the kind of bond that came when two people cared about the same thing intensely. He was glad that his father had the support of this good woman, and he no longer envied Jake for that. A good man should have a good woman and he was happy for them both.

"You're right," she said, then paused and added. "Since he's sleeping I could use this time to freshen up."

"And get some rest," Lamont added. "I'll drive you home," Lamont announced, putting his previous plans on hold.

"I'm not going to argue with that suggestion. Thanks, Lamont."

"I'll pick up my car when we drive back later," Lamont said opening the door. "Scoot over."

Candace gladly did as he asked without hesitation. She got giddy when a strong man took charge. That's what she liked about Jake, and it was plain to see that Lamont was so much like Jake. A sudden feeling of warmth and security covered her, and she relaxed for the first time since this ordeal had begun. "Thanks Lamont," she said again and smiled for the first time.

They remained quiet for most of the drive until Candace broke the silence. "I never explained to you about being at that club that night did I?"

"You don't really have to explain anything to me Candice. But it did cross my mind as to why you were there, and flirting with me so boldly that night." He sighed. "Just my luck to run into my father's wife. That's why I don't buy lottery tickets," he chuckled, making light of the situation.

"Yeah, it was some coincidence that we had this mutual attraction, but then again maybe not."

"What do you mean?" Lamont asked.

"I mean that you looked so familiar that I was attracted to you. You carried yourself so confidently, and when you sang, that was the icing on the cake. I wasn't kidding when I said you could make money singing."

Lamont glanced at her skeptically, but didn't speak. He saw little point in discussing past emotions at this point.

"I was there that night because Jake and I were having some difficulties in the bedroom at the time and..."

"Whoa! Too much information," Lamont said quickly. "Look I'm not judging you, Candace. Let face it, you're a gorgeous woman married to a man much older, and I'm sure that there are times when he can't keep up with you. So let's leave it at that. I don't know and I don't care if you cheated or didn't cheat, it's none of my business and I'm not going to expose any secrets."

"There's nothing to expose." Her voice range raised an octave. "Sure I do some innocent flirting, just like every woman, but I never cheated on Jake. And believe me most of the time I'm the one who can't keep up with him. You wouldn't believe his stamina, and he doesn't need any drugs."

"Candace, please." He made a face. "Again too much information. It's great that you and Jake have a healthy relationship, but you don't have to convince me or give me a blow by blow." He caught himself and smile embarrassed. "No pun intended."

An awkward silence hovered between then until they arrived at the Cooper Estate gatehouse, where they were waved on. Once inside, Lamont parked and turned facing Candace. "Look for what it's worth I believe you. That night, I felt a strong attraction between us, and yet you were strong enough to remain faithful to your husband. I admit that I was angry that you lied to me, but now I can see that you had no choice. I respect the fact that you didn't cheat on Jake."

"Thanks, Lamont. That means a lot coming from you. I have a great deal of respect for you." Impulsively she leaned over and gave him a quick hug. "I'm glad you're finally in Jake's life, and believe me so is he. I don't know if he even knows it yet, but you're the best thing that could have happened to him. You're the most sensible of all these brats. " She made a face as she spoke. "Not that you're a brat, I wasn't talking about you. It's the rest of them.

Sorry to talk about your family like that but they are brats. The girls will never forgive me for marrying their dad." She stopped and looked at him sideways. "Hope you don't hate me for saying that, but I got to be honest, Lamont."

"Don't worry about that. I understand your side, and I appreciate your honesty. After all we're both outsiders."

She smiled. "You're the best Lamont." She reached over again and gave him a light embrace. Lamont reminded himself that this was his step mother and fought the urge to pull her closer. He was only human and holding a beautiful woman this close would stir the average man.

The smell and touch of her bombarded him with traces of temptation, but he fought valiantly and regained his power to resist her. "I don't know about all that, but I'm glad that I'm in his life, and that he's finally in mine," Lamont said, breaking from her embrace.

"You know I think you should stay at Cooper Estates while Jake is in the hospital. There's tons of space. You can move into JJ's old suite. It's got everything. I don't know why he even left."

Lamont suspected that JJ had left in order to keep his drug use and wild parties a secret. "I might just do that. It would save me a lot of driving back and forth. And it is close so maybe I could even spend more time at the office."

"God, you are Jake's clone. You and Jake with this work work work. What happen to that fun guy with the sexy voice that I met at the bar?"

"Certain things beyond his control made him grow up and he learned to focus on what was important," Lamont sighed.

"Grown ups have fun too. Don't you know how to have fun anymore, Lamont? Your fiancée looks like a fun girl. I bet she knows how to have fun."

He hadn't thought about Jane the past few days. "If you say so."

"She probably could stand to see more of you."

"Don't bet on it."

"Oh I see." She gave him a concerned look. "You guys have a fight?

"Yeah, something like that." He wasn't going to give her any more details.

"Well, Honey believe me that's just temporary. She's gonna come to her senses when she realizes how lucky she is."

"Well, you're probably right. But we'll see."

Ruth was already at the Cooper estate when Lamont and Candace arrived, and she stood in the foyer gazing out the huge window. She wondered how Jake would react when he found out about what she had done. She could only hope that her bad news wouldn't cause a more severe stroke.

At the time, she thought that she was being clever, but she had screwed up. Her decision to settle her hit and run case with that shady lawyer was a huge mistake. He had made it sound like such a sweet deal when he told her that everything would go away, if she gave up her shares of Cooper stock. It had seemed like a harmless solution, since she only had a few shares.

She had avoided paying any blackmail money by giving up her stock. She figured that she didn't need stock. However, she was having major doubts about her decision now. Jake once said that Cooper stock was more precious than money, and now she wondered if that's why that lawyer had settled for her shares of stock instead of money.

At first, she had felt so good about flaunting her resourcefulness in Lamont's face. It had given her a world of pleasure to prove him wrong, because he is such a smug know-it-all, and she had been aching to show him up. Now, she wondered if he had been right all along, and perhaps her actions had been harmful to Cooper Industries.

Suddenly, Ruth's attention was diverted from her inward thoughts and focused on Lamont and Candace sitting in her car. Her scornful eyes watched them share an embrace. "What a perfect match," she murmured into the window pane. "The bastard and the bitch. Damn those two," she groaned with sudden rage. "Sneaking around behind daddy's back while he's in the hospital. Probably been sneaking around the whole time."

She caught her breath suddenly. "What if Daddy knew? What if that's what caused his stroke?" She whispered to herself, eager to soothe her guilty conscience about her own deception. "I'd bet that their sitting out there plotting some strategy to take over now that daddy's flat on his back."

Ruth convinced herself that they were two of a kind, and filled with deception. Neither of them had ever fooled her. Since she was the only one who had witnessed the two of them together, she had to do something about it. Still she needed back up and that meant that she would have to form an alliance with all the others to pull it off.

The Cooper's had to unite against the non-Coopers, and she would willingly make whatever sacrifices are necessary. That meant putting aside her differences with Cheryl, but that wasn't a problem, because she wanted Lamont gone more than she hated Cheryl. Bitch that she is, Cheryl is her full blood sister. Lamont and Candace were just mangy strays. Lamont just happens to have Cooper blood and Candace just happened to have the Cooper name, but they were both here by default. The sooner they were gone the easier she would breathe.

Chapter Thirty Nine-
Back down

Lucas Sheppard had personally come to Carvoni's club to conduct his surveillance. Now he sat back in the booth close to Carvoni's office, sipping his beer and equipped with a small powerful listening device. He could hear the sound from the porn movies inside that office. He was turned on by the combination of those sounds and the pretty waitresses with the short tight dresses. He loved his job.

Carvoni's main henchman, Bennie, sat in the booth on the opposite side and paid little attention to Lucas. That was the advantage about being so inconspicuous, Lucas thought. His plain and homely appearance made him impervious to suspicion.

Shortly, Two Martin, the hustler and pimp, zoomed through the door towards Carvoni's office, apparently angry about something. Two spotted Bennie, in the booth and stormed up to him fuming. "Is Carvoni here, Bennie?" He asked.

Bennie gave him a quick up and down. "What's eating you, man? You upset about somethin'?"

"I need to see Tony that's all." Two ignored Bennie, but he was wise not to offend the big man right now.

"And now you see me," Carvoni said, standing in his office doorway holding a glass half filled with wine. "Come on back." He motioned to Two to enter ahead of him, and then followed him inside.

Now Lucas could hear Carvoni's voice coming through the ear piece clearly. He covertly turned up his listening device and checked the volume. He was getting excellent reception, and from what he could hear Two sounded like he was about to confront Carvoni about something. Two was upset and speaking very defiantly to the vicious mobster, which could be dangerous.

"Calm down namesake," Carvoni said, "sit and take a load off."

"No thanks, I'll stand," Two said, irately. "Why did you set me up like that Tony? What's the idea of cameras in the bedroom? What's that all about?" Two asked, still fuming. Lucas concluded that Carvoni had deceived Two and apparently had planted cameras without Two's knowledge.

"How are tapes of me having sex with Cheryl going to get you Cooper stock?" Lucas heard Two ask, and his ears perked up at the mention of the Cooper name. He listened more intently, recording it all in his expensive electronic device.

"Sit," Lucas heard Carvoni say in a no more nonsense voice that sounded like a threat. Apparently Two did as Carvoni wished, because Carvoni's tone was more pleasant when he spoke again. "What's the big deal? So you're a porn star, so what?" He laughed and Lucas could hear ice rattle in the silence that ensued. Apparently Carvoni was sipping from his glass.

"Why didn't you tell me that you had cameras in Cheryl's apartment? You been taping us having sex all this time? Thanks a lot," Two said sarcastically.

"Okay, so I took some pointers from you," Carvoni said chuckling lightly. "Or did you forget that you came up with the idea first. I just took some initiative and forged ahead. It didn't really involve you."

"Didn't involve me? But I'm the one being taped. You could have warned me so that I could cover my face."

"Naw, that wouldn't work."

"How do you know?" Two asked, raising his voice slightly.

"Because I do," Carvoni said, matching Two's volume and Lucas could hear the meanness in Carvoni's voice as he imagined his facial expression. After a short pause Carvoni continued in a calmer voice. "It was better that you didn't know. Things work smoother when people aren't under pressure."

"You don't trust me do you?"

"That's a given. I don't trust nobody, except maybe my cousin Bennie, and that's only about eighty percent."

"But I gave you my word, Tony."

"Right, that's a good one. I'm gonna take the word of a pimp, and trust you with important details while you rompin' in the sack with a broad built like that. Hell, she might give you temporary amnesia. So just be a good little boy, do what I tell you, and stop pretending that I have to answer to you. If you even thinking about a double cross, just remember that I know all about your little firebug mission on that freak's property on the fifteenth of February. You remember that little personal venture for revenge I'm sure. I'm not above using that information if I have to."

"You wouldn't do that because if you did Cheryl would have nothing to do with me. You don't want that do you?"

"Hey boy, don't act like you got the upper hand on me. If this plan don't work, I got plenty of other plans. If she decides to stop didling your dick, I can find another way to get what I want. I already have some footage so you better keep any thoughts about controlling this to yourself. You can't outsmart me on your best day."

Lucas could imagine Two's anger because he felt some animosity himself at Carvoni's seemingly racist's remarks. He hoped that Two wasn't foolish enough to take that bait and get himself killed. It sounded like Carvoni, as usual had the upper hand, and Two's nuts were in a vice. Carvoni would squeeze them with great pleasure, and the slightest provocation. Lucas surmised that Carvoni had incriminating information about some of Two's recent criminal activities, and revelation of those activities meant jail time. He was surprised to hear that Cheryl Cooper was involved with a low life pimp, like Two Martin.

"What do you plan to do with the tapes?" Two asked submissively now.

"Not that I have to tell you a damn thing, but I'm not planning on going into the video business." Carvoni continued speaking. "Look Namesake, I don't want to have a battle with you unless you make me. You can't win, but in the interest of getting along, I won't do anything to hurt you. You're my point man and I need you to keep on doing what you're doing. You've figured it out by now. I don't care what she knows or don't know about the business, it ain't about that. I just want some more tape footage. Don't tell me that it's gonna be a problem for you to keep poking this cunt."

"I don't mean any disrespect Tony, but"

"Good then," Carvoni said cutting Two's words. "There's no need to say anymore." After a brief silence Lucas heard Carvoni say, "You ain't gettin' whipped by this pussy are you?"

Two was silent but Carvoni spoke. "You know, if I didn't know better, Namesake, I would think you're falling for this rich little slut. That pussy must be real good huh? Do you feel like you want to protect her now?"

"Of course not. Hell if anything she's falling for me," Two said, but Lucas could hear the insincerity in his words. Lucas knew that Carvoni had detected that as well.

"Then we don't have a problem do we?"

"Of course I don't have a problem, TC, it's just that now that I know I'm being watched, I'm afraid that I might not be effective."

"So what are you saying? You giving me an ultimatum? Don't give me ultimatums. If you're having performance anxiety, I suggest Viagra and a nice wine. Forget about those cameras and hop to it because I want that footage."

"I know better than to give you ultimatums Tony. It ain't nothing like that."

"What do you think I ought to do?"

"Well why not just take the camera out and."

"I should stop taping? Is that what you're saying?"

"Yeah."

"Why? I'm supposed to halt my plans because you got the problems about that camera? No way." There was brief silence in the room and the faint sound of moaning filled the void just before Carvoni continued. "Two, my friend, you just don't get it, but it doesn't matter because it's gonna be done my way regardless. I can see that you got a soft spot for this chick?"

"I told you Tony, I don't. Can't you just believe me?" Two sounded uncertain and his voice had become loud again." Lucas saw Bennie hopped from his seat and peer into the office. After a brief check he returned to his spot in the booth just outside the office door.

"Okay, so you don't have a soft spot, but you better have a hard spot because the camera stays." He paused and asked once again. "You don't have a problem with that do you?"

"No, of course not." Two said again unconvincingly. "Later, man," Lucas heard Two say as he walked out the door with less arrogance in his stride. He walked past the booth where Lucas sat, moving like a man who had been beaten down. Apparently it was hard to make a break when you were obligated to a man like Carvoni. Lucas wondered what Two would do now that he was on the spot. He wouldn't trade places with Two for all the money in the Cooper's vault, even if it meant screwing some one like Cheryl.

Shortly after Two left the office Lucas finished his beer and was prepared to go and report to Lamont, but now he froze when he heard Carvoni talking to Bennie. "Cous, I think Namesake might be trouble."

"Two? Naw, Cous', he's cool," Bennie said, "He's a player. He'll come around. He won't let no woman turn his head. He loves all the women the same."

"You think so? Well let me tell you Cous' never underestimate the influence of intimacy. I'll bet you ninety nine per cent of the thugs in jail are in there because they did just that. Either a woman did them wrong and they offed em, or they offed somebody because of a woman.

Men do manly things just to impress women. And I'll bet you that all the men in prison thought they were in control. Truth is women are smarter than men when it comes to emotions and sexual influence. What's even more diabolical is that women don't mind letting men think they're smarter to get what they want.

"Yeah but I think Two got it together." Bennie offered.

"You think so? I think our lady's man has met his match. I think that lady has pussy whipped our boy so bad that he's gonna need intensive care. I can't trust a man who thinks with his Johnson. They're just too easily influenced by a hot mouth and a hot ass, and that's no good for business."

"So what do you plan to do about him?"

"Nothing for now, but I'm gonna watch him a little closer. If and when Two decides to double cross me, I'll be there to refresh his memory. I still got Peter, and I'm gonna set the righteous Cooper sister up next. She's got a husband with a record and an easy target for what I got in mind."

"Your think that will work? Bennie asked.

"Why not? Everything has gone like clockwork up to now. I set Jake Jr. up with the underage girl and that drunken sister up with Mattie the jumper. She's the best at hit and run scams.

Lucas felt a cold shudder run down his spine at hearing Carvoni's words. He had a full court press on to take over Cooper industries and apparently he was heading into the final stages. Lucas had to get back to Lamont with this vital information immediately.

Chapter Forty-
Changes

Lamont had planned to ride back to the hospital with Candice to pick up his car, but JJ had insisted that they ride together because they needed to talk. Candace understood. "Don't worry I'm fine," she said to him.

They arrived at the hospital and looked in on Jake, but he was sleeping so that gave them a chance to talk. They could return later to visit. The two brothers now faced each other from across the cafeteria table. There was an awkward silence between them mainly, because they hadn't talked one on one since the party.

JJ was the first to speak. "Lamont, you know things do happen and I'm sorry about what happened at the party the other night. I know you got pissed at me." He paused but continued when he noticed that Lamont was still silent. "I was high man and my judgment was bad."

"JJ, you're an adult so I'm not going preach at you, but I'm going to say this. You need to learn that life is not a continuous party. You got so much and you've been blessed. Why don't you settle down and get serious? I don't understand it. Jake wants you to be a big part of the company, but you just don't get it. Don't you want to be a part of the company?"

JJ breathed an impatient sigh, obviously fighting to control his temper. "Look, Lamont," he started slowly, "I'm not like you, and truthfully, I don't want to be like you, man. No offense you understand, but it's like you just don't know how to have fun, man. You're more like dad than you are like me. You're so serious and I wish it was the other way around.

I used to think you were really cool man, and I wished that we could be close. I remember the fun we had when we were together in the hospital, flirting with the nurses. We made a connection, and I thought that I finally had a brother who was so much like me. I thought we would be like..."

"Peas in a pod?" Lamont finished the thought with the question.

"Well, sort of. Yeah."

"JJ, we did make a connection, and I wouldn't trade that for anything. I love you even if I don't agree with some of the things you do. You have to understand that I was raised different, and my values are different."

"I understand that," JJ said impatiently. "I know you always had to work and I imagine that money was scarce, Lamont. But can't you see that's over and you got it made now. You don't have to beg for nothing or answer to nobody. We're rich brother, so learn to accept and enjoy it." JJ's words carried a tone of urgency.

"Look at all the people who ain't got a damn thing," he said with a brief pause. "I thought that you and me with our looks, and access to money were gonna team up, hang out, and screw everything in our zip code. All these women are out here and all we got to do is go and get em." JJ looked at Lamont and turned his palms up as he asked. "So what's wrong with that?"

Lamont could see JJ's disappointment. "JJ, I know you wanted that for me, but can't you understand that's not what I want? That's just not my life style. Can't you see how shallow that is man? You think that fun is about, flaunting your wealth and using it as bait to catch loose women.

You get high because you're bored, and you waste money just because you can. Obviously, you got a long way to go before you realize that people have fun without doing the things that you're doing. Unfortunately, you think that he who laughs loudest, or gets the biggest buzz, or fornicates with the most women is having the most fun."

"Look bro," JJ said patiently, "you have to understand that I almost died. You know? I could be dead right now. But I'm alive and I owe you for that, Lamont, and I will always be grateful. I like feeling alive, and having fun makes me feel alive, man. I'm spontaneous and I go with the flow, instead of worrying about the outcome before making a move."

"That can get you in trouble and as I recall it has." Lamont said stiffly.

"That was one incident and it's settled now."

"And since you're still doing the same thing, there will probably be more incidents."

"And I'll settle that when and if it happens." He gave Lamont another disappointed expression. "See, that's what I'm talking about with you, man. That's the thing that pisses me off about you sometimes. You always looking ahead and thinking negative."

"No, it's called caution and optimism. See brother I almost died too. I was nearly tried and executed for a murder that I didn't commit. Luckily for me that things happened the way they did. I appreciate life as much as you do, maybe more. That's why I'm cautious rather than frivolous. I heed warnings of disaster and it might pay for you to think about that once in a while."

"What's the use?" JJ threw up his hands. "We're never going to agree on this issue." "You do what you gotta do and I got to do the same. I'm gonna keep on living my life, because I don't plan to miss a damn thing," JJ said as he stood. "I'm going up to check on dad. You going up now?"

"I'll be up shortly, why don't you go spend some time with him?"

"Okay, Later bro," He walked away from his brother and moved swiftly to the exit and through the doorway.

Lamont realized that he suddenly didn't feel so good about his brother. He didn't like the attitude of that brash arrogant brat that he had just seen. It would only be a matter of time before that attitude got him into more trouble. He feared for JJ and wondered if he would ever grow up.

He once thought that he could get closer to JJ, but their personalities and priorities might make that impossible. They were too different and that saddened him, but he couldn't dwell on it. This was trivial in light of the many other problems he needed to solve, especially with Jake laid up and Peter working to help the mob take control.

Lamont returned to work the following day, and Marcia found it hard to hide her elation at his return. "How is your dad doing, Lamont?" She asked.

"He had a mild stroke but he's expected to make a full recovery. It wasn't as bad as they first thought."

"That's good news. I'm glad. He's such a sweet man. You wouldn't believe that he was such a tycoon just to see him."

Yeah." Lamont looked towards her. "I'm gonna be staying at the

Cooper Estate while he's in the hospital. I'll have to go pick up some things later, so cancel my afternoon appointments and you can go home early."

"That sounds like a plan to me," Marcia's voice reflected her elation. She was glad to have some time off. Now an idea came to mind. "Listen Lamont I was just wondering."

"About what?"

"Well since you owe me a lunch I want to make a deal."

"I'm listening."

"Since we'll both be taking off early today, why don't you let me fix you a nice dinner tonight?"

"Sounds good, and I'd like that, but I don't want to put you through that. I insist that you let me take you out to a restaurant instead. My treat."

"No, I insist. I want to do this, let me do it please. I can cook you know."

"I never said you couldn't," Lamont said with an amused smiled. "Okay."

"Great. How about eight at my place?"

"That's fine. You're still at the same place on Marshall Avenue?"

"Yes."

"Okay, then I'll see you at eight," he said and noticed that her smile was more pronounced and her gaze was more intense than usual. Maybe he was imagining it.

Chapter Forty One-
Bliss

Marsha went shopping earlier and spent the day in the kitchen, because she wanted everything to be perfect when Lamont arrived. She couldn't wait to impress him, and she buzzed about preparing everything with care. She was briefly distracted when the telephone rang. "Hello," she said.

"Hi Marsh it's me,"

"Lamont, are you on the way?" She asked, holding her breath thinking that he was about to cancel.

"Yeah, but I'm caught in traffic, so I'll get there as soon as I can."

"Okay then," she said weakly. He would be late but at least he was coming.

Lamont arrived thirty minutes late. "Sorry about being late," he said apologetically.

"I forgive you this time buddy," she said jokingly. "But don't let it happen again or you're in trouble. Now get in here."

Lamont saw a difference in her immediately and was strangely intrigued. He was in a good mood in spite of the problems that he face. He felt elated because now he knew how Jake's felt about him. "I didn't bring anything; I meant to get some wine."

"It's okay, I got alcohol, and I even got champagne."

"Champagne! Wow. Are we celebrating something?"

"Yes."

"What?"

"It's a surprise."

"A surprise? Am I gonna like this surprise?"

"Of course you are." Marcia said with loaded mysterious confidence.

Later, Marcia served a delicious well prepared dinner which Lamont enjoyed intensely. It surprised him that Marcia was such a great cook. He guessed that her cooking skills must have been the surprise she spoke of, and he did like it. Jane's meals were a joke compared to the feast he had just consumed.

Shortly, they relax on the couch listening to music and sipping Champagne. Marcia continued to play the perfect elusive hostess. "Care for some more pink Champagne?" She asked, pouring it before he could answer. "Might as well kill it now," Marcia said pouring the last of the liquid into her glass.

She inched closer to him on the couch, changing the subject the moment Lamont began to talk about business. "Lamont, can we forget about the office? Let's just enjoy this time. We got some nice jazz and a nice buzz flowing, we just had a good meal, so let's relax."

"You're right Marsh," Lamont said light headed from the champagne. His eyes were glued on Marcia's, and he studied her closer. She wore more make up than usual, and yet it enhanced her features, and made her gorgeous. She was great company, and her classic cheek bones, curvaceous hips, and full lips were suddenly exciting and tempting. Still he couldn't take advantage like that.

He studied her even closer now, and scrutinized her mysterious large eyes and pouty full lips. Her face was a perfect pattern it seemed. She looked extra sexy, and that threw him off guard. He seemed to listen to the music for the first time, while sipping the champagne. "That sounds like Hank Crawford on that Sax."

"Good ear." She smiled.

"He's my favorite."

"Really?" She gave him a subtle glance.

"You knew that didn't you?" He asked smiling easy.

"Lamont there are many things that I know about you." She flipped her hair off her face flirtatiously.

"Really? You been spying on me?"

"No, not spying. Just..."

"Just what?"

"Just noticing you." She paused and a sad look appeared on her face. "Unfortunately that's been a one way street so far."

"Marsh, you know," he started.

"I know, I know, we're friends, I know the speech by heart now Lamont.

Lamont paused suddenly, thinking that he was a prize hypocrite. Right now he felt like throwing that friendship speech out the window.

"I'm cool with where we stand so relax," she said with a limp wave and a mischievous smile. "Tell you what; you make yourself right at home, Honey," she said, getting up and moving towards the bathroom down the hall. "I'll be right back."

Something was different or maybe he was just high. He wasn't much of a drinker, but tonight he had drank more than he was accustomed to. Lamont sat on the couch trying to relax, but he felt puzzled by his restless anxiety. The intoxication sharpened his awareness and heightens his urges. Now he thought about luscious Marcia in that form fitting dress and was suddenly gripped by her sexuality. He had suddenly spawned a new attitude about this woman and she seemed new and different. Maybe she's been this woman all the time and he was different.

He glanced around the apartment and wasn't surprised that it was orderly, efficient, cozy, and neat. He was aware of her perfume saturating the air, and smooth sounds coming from the speakers. He relaxed in spite of his new found anxiety.

Marcia decided that he had waited long enough, and it was time to act. She was about to take a big risk, and her hands shook with her first step towards the living room, but she wouldn't back out now. Lamont might reject her again with his friendship speech, but she had nothing to lose. It was ironic that Jane's harsh criticism of her was the reason that she was about to take these drastic measures.

Jane's words were similar to words her sister Eunice had said, and she feared that perhaps she should be more aggressive. Maybe fear of rejection had made her a timid loser, with no spunk to fight for the man she wanted. Things were different now, and it was time to step out of the shadows and chase her man in the light.

She quietly glided towards him like an exotic dancer, until she stood next to him. "You like?" She whispered in her most sultry voice, as she twirled gracefully to the beat of the music. She stood there in sexy five inch spike heels, wearing wispy gauze lingerie that was slightly more than an illusion.

Lamont blinked repeatedly to get his bearing, because his head was spinning from the alcohol. "Marsh," was all he could utter, and his lightly dazed eyes observed her with a sudden growing and deep desire. He said nothing but his lust was quickly accounted for as focused in disbelief. Marcia swayed from side to side, looking delicious to him, in the sheer black negligee. She looked like a sexy lingerie model with luscious boobs, which seemed two sizes larger. Lamont was still stunned and at first he only stared. "Damn, Marsh?" He said again through a thick voice hoarse from lust. He watched her through hypnotized eyes, longing to taste her.

His random gaze scanned her shapely legs, which were made even shapelier thanks to the black spike heels. His lust increased, and his anxiety became uncontrollable as she moved closer. He was instantly erect, and urgency spread in his loins. He realized that he had been a hypocrite and a liar when he had proclaimed that he saw Marcia as a sister. What he felt at this moment wasn't brotherly love and brother lust didn't exist.

He captured the images of her in his head and sound logic became silly nonsense. He had crossed a threshold where reality was altered, and sensible perception was lost. His passion burned and this new sexy Marcia lit flames that grew with rapid intensity. He wanted her more than he had ever wanted any woman. He was so hard that it scared him and he wanted to be all over her at once. He prepared to take the solid foundation of their deep friendship to another level.

He stopped resisting the idea of making love to her, and plunged into the sheer pleasure of indulgence. Why the hell had he been resisting the feelings that he had for this woman? Was he sick? If so he was cured now because he released his mind from logic, cast out all doubt and suppressed any excuse as he relished the sight and smell of her. Now only a slow-burning soul deep craving, fed his passion and lust driven imagination. Her incredible tight body caused him to salivate, and he feared that he would embarrass himself by drooling if he opened his mouth. He strain against his pants and twitched with more desire than he had ever felt.

She was suddenly on his lap and her mouth was on his. "Marsh.

What are we doing Marsh," he said trance-like and hoarsely while returning her kisses and capturing her hot tongue.

"You know what I'm doing, silly bo-oy," she murmured sexily, continuing to kiss his lips. "You know about the birds and the bees." She was writhing and moaning lightly

His lips parted and her hot probing tongue once again found haven inside his warm mouth. As their hot tongues met, their bodies gave passions the reins. Their mutual groans and hot kisses transformed from sweet to frantic. Lamont for the first time was out of his head with passion. Perhaps his slight intoxication and his new sensual awareness of this soft sexy woman had caused this transformation and submission. "God Marsh, you're so sweet, and you taste so damn good."

"Not as good as you feel." She moved from his lap and sprawled on the couch next to him and pulled him on top of her. She rubbed his crotch and undid his fly while he worked the buttons of his shirt. Mutual lust clutched them and guided their sequence of action. Their passion raged out of control as they fondled, caressed, kissed and even bit into each other's flesh.

"Shit Marsh," Lamont said in a voice hoarse and low with passion. His pants were down and he was stiff against her crotch. He felt her heat radiate from inside. "God you're so hot," he whispered, while covering her with kisses.

"You make me this way," she said amidst his onslaught of kisses. "And you got a piece of hot steel yourself, she said, moaning deeply. "Oh Lamont, I've waited so long, but I'm glad."

Lamont realized that no words could express his passion. Only action could express and soothe this deep core burning soul lust. Now that neither of them could wait any longer, he slipped slowly inside of her, with gentle concern. Her fire surrounded his throbbing center and bathed him with a joyous release of extreme mind bending passion. "Oh Marsh, baby."

They made love urgent and brief on the couch, without much foreplay because none was needed. The cat-and-mouse game that they had played for months had been perpetual foreplay. Now the long burning fuse had finally burned down to the dynamite and the explosion was being processed.

Their brief passion on the couch had only been a prelude of the splendor yet to come. Shortly, he picked her up from the couch and carried her to the bedroom, where the lust between them intensified. Their world became a series of screaming mutual orgasms. Lamont realized that he was making more noise than Marcia with each orgasm, and he feared that her neighbors might call 911. Incredible newfound passion cascaded through him like a pounding jack hammer with each orgasm. The raw intensity of his passions made him aware and indifferent about all self control.

Marcia was in a deep trance as well and lovingly pulled him deep inside her, draining his passion with hard steady strokes. She relished her saturation of endless joy. "Oh Lamont baby, right there, my darling, it's so fucking good. Damn." Marcia cried out several times during their love making. "I knew it would be this way. I knew it would." She whispered in his ear, clutching him closer.

Lamont was thinking about all the ways he wanted to please this wonderful woman. At first he thought the alcohol had affected his logic, but he realized that the alcohol had only suppressed his inhibitions. He had wanted to get with her all along, but for some reason could never admit it. His excuses didn't make sense.

He hadn't used a condom and the thought of disease and pregnancy had entered his mind briefly, but he couldn't break this passion spell. He had condoms but it wouldn't make sense to use one now. Besides, this was Marsh and he was sure that she was okay.

Finally they were spent and shock waves remained between them as they lay side by side, breathing heavy and bathing in the afterglow of their abundant pleasure. The world and their sanity returned, and they drifted off into a motionless deep sleep, satisfied and spent.

Lamont awoke just before dawn and realized that he had to travel to Richmond and get ready to go to work. However, before he could stir Marcia closed in with a thousand kisses. "Been waiting for you to wake up," she said.

Now he realized that her hand was stoking him and to his amazement, he was instantly aroused. "Damn!" He exclaimed with surprise. He wasn't about to leave just yet. "I can't be still horny after all we did last."

"You tell him that," Marcia said, holding his erect penis in her hand.

Lamont looked at her and even without make up she looked sexy as hell. He didn't know what was happening, but right now she was top priority and work would wait a few more minutes. Besides, he could use his lap top and work from home if necessary. He didn't want to do that since Jake had put so much confidence in him. He would report to work late.

This was so unlike him, and he couldn't believe he was thinking that way, but he had never felt anything like this before. Suddenly he longed for her and he started the ritual of foreplay, relishing her soft skin. "Oh Lamont, I love you so much." He heard her moan as he probed deep inside her. He had uttered something incoherent in response and the steaming passion gave him goose bumps. He twitched uncontrollably and wanted to laugh out loud with every stroke.

"Damn, Lamont," she squealed in reaction to his quick steady motion that sent his liquid passion deep inside her. "Ooh OOH, Lamont babee, give it to me." Her eyes were shut tight, and her concentration shifted to that one happy spot that had now become the center of her being. She voluntarily tightened up around him and felt his throbbing intensify and swell within her. Her nipples grew harder and her nerves tickled her skin. "God, Lamont." She moans breathlessly.

Lamont felt as if he was having a seizure with each renewed spurt inside her. There was something about her body that was instantly familiar and making love to her became as natural as breathing. This experience with her was like a wonderful long running Déjà Vu that suspended his breathing, and gave him slow motion pleasures. Like magic, Lamont instinctively knew how to please her and he shared their mutual intense pleasures. "Damn, why can't I get enough of you? It's too good Marsh," Lamont said, lunging deep into her with each syllable.

She cried frantically as she reached another orgasm. "Yes Lamont yes. Babeee." Marcia wasn't sure if she had heard correctly or just imagined what she wanted to hear? Right now it didn't matter because her renewed passion vibrated aggressively in her ears and made her unsure of any spoken words she had heard. She was only sure of the steady joyous passion and its continued frenzy.

Shortly, Marcia rolled away satisfied. "God I can't believe this. It's just too damn incredible." "OOOWeeee. You are something, Lamont Savage, but I can't take you no more. Get away from me you nasty man. That thing is dangerous and it's still hard," she said in a voice that reflected surprise. "Don't we have to go to work?" She gave him a naughty expression. "You on Viagra or something?" She teased.

"Yeah, it's called Marcia Dawson."

"Well don't over dose big boy; it'll be here when you want it." She paused and stared at him adoringly. "You're gonna have me on drugs, you know that? But I don't mind."

"Drugs," Lamont said, smiling amused. "You talking out of your head, woman."

"No I'm not. I'm probably gonna need strong pain killers if you're gonna be that aggressive with little ole me all the time." She lapse into a southern accent once more. "I might already be in pain, but I'm too numb right now to know," she said, bursting into a loud laugh.

Lamont thought her humor was timely as always and joined her in laughter. It was a happy satisfied laugh that releases some inner tension that he hadn't been aware existed. He pushed aside all negative feelings and enjoyed this rare moment.

Yes he had broken his own rule, but he told himself that Marcia was different and he couldn't deny her any longer. Rules were made to be broken, and who better to break them with than Marsh? She was always a great friend, and now she had become a great lover as well. He wasn't going to spoil this by seeking flaws in their new relationship as lovers because even now he didn't want to end it.

This would only change thing between them if he let it, but he wouldn't let it interfere with their working relationship. He knew her well enough to know that she felt the same way. They were close, so what was wrong with taking it another step? What was wrong with being friends with benefits?

He justified his actions, but he knew that it was more than just another step, but right now he didn't care. Marcia was wonderful and she made him feel something that he had never felt. He knew that this hadn't happened because he was on the rebound, because he had never wanted Jane this intensely, or been so drained, in spite of her sexy nature. Frankly he should thank Jane, because his life would have been ruined had he fulfilled his commitment to her. Because of Jane he was free to discover Marcia's soft side. He could stay in bed with her all day and not just to make love. She was smart and insightful and not full of herself. He looked forward to the next encounter, which would be very soon.

Chapter Forty Two-
Summit

Cheryl had been feeling depressed since hearing her father's conversation with Lamont at the hospital yesterday. She sat on a reclining chair absently watching television and listening to the water running in the shower. She heard Tony singing low inside the shower, as she pondered Jake's words. She found it hard to accept Jake's negative assessments of his own family, and she felt sorry that she had overheard that conversation.

She once believed that Jake saw her as special, but now believed that Lamont had gained Jake's favor. Now it seemed that the rest of them were clumped together, and declared worthless. It wasn't Lamont's fault and she wanted to be fair to him, but Jake's crucial words had stunned her.

Was Jake right to think that way about them? Had she or any of her siblings ever taken any responsibility? What good were any of them without Jake's money? Could any of them survive without money and become productive in society the way that Lamont had? Probably not, because even now she had been ready to quit school and have an abortion. Damn, Two and that busted condom. She never meant to get knocked up. Maybe she was just a loser.

Her other siblings were just as bad, she thought. Ann was the only neutral one, but that was because her head was wrapped around bible quotes and couldn't seem to grasp the real world. Ruth is a jealous hearted loser who would be homeless if it wasn't for Jake's money. JJ is a womanizer who cares only about parties and proving his manhood.

Lamont on the other hand was so well adjusted and ready to take responsibility. Maybe that's why Jake was so fond of him. She wished that Jake could be that proud of her, which gave her mixed feelings about Lamont. She liked him, but she felt an urge to hate him because Jake held him in such high esteem. That wasn't Lamont's fault.

Suddenly she was hit in the midsection by a jolt causing her to jump with a start. "What the hell was that?" She asked herself, and wondered if her baby had just kicked. That was impossible, since she was only about six weeks pregnant at the most. Was it her imagination or a sign? If so what the hell did it mean? Surely it wasn't meant for her to keep this baby because that didn't make sense. She was pregnant by a man who would likely be the worst father in the world. Tony was a player at best and a pimp at worse and he had zero fathering skills. Besides that her father hated Tony for attempting to blackmail him, and she couldn't blame him. In fact just a few short weeks ago, before the booty call, she couldn't stand Tony either.

Things had changed, making him a major part of her life. He had certainly become the only man in her life. Still she never thought that she would become pregnant by him, but that damn broken condom had put her in this precarious situation.

Maybe Jake was right and it was time to face responsibility for the first time in her life. She carried a delicate life inside her, and thus far her main goal was to destroy that life. Maybe this pregnancy was her ultimate test of character. She recalled Jake's words to Lamont. 'If one of them would make a decision about something and stick to it, I could live with that even if it was the wrong decision.'

She felt another kick. "But that was impossible." She said aloud and held her stomach. She didn't know a hell of a lot about pregnancy, but she knew that babies don't kick this early. Either her mind was playing tricks on her or this really is some kind of a sign. Maybe this is a special kid, and a special pregnancy. She was suddenly not so anxious to be rid of this innocent new life.

She came out of her thoughts now as Tony enters the room in his bathrobe, flops down on the sofa, and flips the channel to the music videos. Her emotions are all over the place, and she wants to peel off that robe and make love. She needs to know that she matters to someone, because right now she feels rejected and unwanted. Wild raunchy sex would make her feel totally accepted, and she always counted on Tony for that.

Feeling deep hunger and neediness for intense emotions, Cheryl slid on the couch next to Tony and began kissing and nibbling on his ear. She is sure that with his active libido, he would never turn her down. She once wondered if he's as horny with other women. Then again, he has seemed distant these past few days. Maybe he was involved with some one else. Maybe he was tired of her and was seeing other women. She was ready to find out, and continued her attempt to seduce him.

"No baby, not here," Tony said, seeming distracted.

She is instantly annoyed that he put her off. "Oh, and why not here? You find that television more important?

"Of course not. It's just that I want us to do something different and I think that we should go to a motel." Unbeknownst to Cheryl, Tony is still paranoid since discovering that hidden camera in the apartment, and he senses that there might be other hidden cameras. He hated the fact that Carvoni is spying on him.

"Tony don't be silly. Why should we blow money on a motel when we have this huge place with all the modern comforts?"

"Well for one thing it would be more romantic. Don't women want men to be more romantic? We can get a nice suite and order room service. And the way you spend money, I can't believe you're worried about money. I tell you what. I'll pay."

"I kinda wanted to stay here. This is home and it's got everything we need. Large flat screen, bar filled with liquor, comfortable and cozy queen size bed. Me! What else could you want? Besides, I don't feel like getting dressed or driving anywhere." She pauses, and then asks, "And when did this arrangement become a romance?" She paraded around in front of him, sat on his leg, and blocked his view of the TV. "If we stayed here we can get started now," She said in her teasing bedroom voice, smothering him with baby kisses, and letting her tongue slip between his lips.

He pulled back. "But if we went somewhere, we would have the excitement of a different surrounding, and we might discover some new moves," he said standing and easing her gently from his knee. As if on cue there is a knock on the door and the doorbell chimes. "Plus there wouldn't be any interruptions," Tony adds, while nodding towards the door smugly.

"Damn, who can that be?" Cheryl asked as she looked at him puzzled. "And why the hell couldn't they at least call first?"

"Hey don't look at me. I'm just visiting, remember?"

"Shut up silly." She chuckled and playfully sticks out her tongue and walks to the door. She looked through the peephole, and then moved away from the door. "It's Ann and Ruth. They never visit me. God, I hope daddy's okay. If something was wrong why didn't they call me?"

"You want me out of sight while you find out what they want?"

She gave him an apologetic look. "I'm sorry Tony, but I would appreciate that. I don't want to have to expl..."

"He held up his hand. "Don't give it a second thought. I'll do this for you but you got to do something for me."

"Okay, okay," She says, anticipating what he wanted. "We'll go to a motel after I find out what they want." He smiles with satisfaction and goes back inside the bedroom and shuts the door.

Cheryl was anxious about what to expect as she opens the door to greet her sisters. She looks into their blank faces for clues as to what's on their minds. "Ann, Ruth, what are you two doing here? Is Daddy okay? Did something happen?"

"Daddy's doing fine. He'll be home tomorrow," Ruth said with impatience and seemed irritated as she looked from Cheryl to Ann.

"Come in and sit down." Cheryl said automatically. The sisters stepped inside her apartment and sat. Ann was calm and quiet, but Ruth seemed anxious and restless. "Well are we going to get down to it or not?" Ruth said, and looked purposely to Ann.

"Yes." Ann clears her throat to speak. "Cheryl we have a slight problem. It involves Lamont."

"Lamont? What about Lamont?" Cheryl asked.

"He's a sneaky, two faced phony bastard, that's what? Just like I always knew he was." Ruth erupts, and twists her face in a scowl.

"Ruthie, please," Ann admonished. Then she continued. "Ruthie thinks that Lamont and." She pauses unable to finish what she is about to say.

"Damn Ann I'll say it if you can't." Ruth said irritated. "I think Lamont is screwing Candace behind daddy's back. And I think that both those sneaky asses are out to grab dad's company. Lamont is a snake and Candace is a gold digging bitch. We all know that. I saw the two of em getting all cozy after we left the hospital yesterday. Now that Lamont is on the scene and Daddy's in bad health, she's trading Daddy in for a younger version."

The sisters discuss the situation back and forth and Cheryl realizes that this would take a while and Two is hiding out in her bed room. She couldn't make him hide out all day. She also didn't want him hearing about all the family's secrets, but she wanted to resolve this situation. She let out an impatience desperate sigh, and listens to Ruth whine.

Cheryl figured a way to kill two birds with one stone. "Listen, I'm hungry," Cheryl blurted out. "Let's go down to that little restaurant, have some lunch and continue to discuss this."

They all agreed and Cheryl moved towards the bedroom. "Let me get my purse." She opened the door, glanced in and saw Two reclining on the bed, watching television with the sound off. He smiled and gave her a thumb up and she mouthed the words, "see you shortly." Then she was gone.

Two had heard their discussion about their latest so called crisis, and dismissed their problems as minor. They were so far from the real truth that it was sad. Carvoni is the real culprit here, not Lamont, the half brother, or Candace, the pretty young stepmother.

What would they do if Carvoni got his way and took Cooper's company? What would Cheryl do if she uncovered his secrets? No doubt she would probably dump him for starters. Eventually, she would likely seek some sort of revenge, he was sure.

Suddenly he wasn't proud of himself for the things he had done in the name of survival and revenge. He was part of Carvoni's nasty plan to invade and control Cooper Industries, and he had burned down her friend Rasheena's place in an act of revenge.

It had all been so complicated. Rasheena had helped Cheryl set him up and Cheryl still had those tapes and pictures of him. He didn't dare get on her bad side. Since he couldn't extract revenge on Cheryl, he went after Rasheena.

Carvoni had discovered his part in the arson and now he had no choice but to follow orders obediently. That's why he had seduced Cheryl, and at first he didn't care. Now he is concerned about the damage that Carvoni might cause to her and the Cooper family.

He wasn't supposed to care or be concerned, because Tony "Two" Martin never cared about any one except himself. However, he did care about Cheryl and he didn't want her hurt, especially by scum like Carvoni.

He had fought his feelings but he could no longer deny what he felt and this rattled him. It was dangerous for guys like him to get involved with women like Cheryl Cooper. He had made a living hustling and using women, and he had no idea how to treat any woman decent. It was even more confusing when the woman was as complicated as Cheryl. He hoped that he wouldn't regret his involvement with Cheryl, but due to the bizarre circumstances, he felt that inevitably he would.

Chapter Forty Three-
Conference

Lamont concluded his brief meeting with Peter and Lawrence Preston and gathered his reports. The two had informed Peter of Jake's decision to give Lamont a share of Jake's power of attorney with Preston. The two would be acting in Jake's behalf.

Peter is obviously humiliated, thinking that this is Jake's way of punishing him. He felt that Jake had no right to give an unproven apprentice authority which should have been his. He felt snubbed and cheated out of something he had earned.

He was Jake's right hand man and such power rightfully belonged to him. His inner anger was ironic because he neglected the fact that he could no longer be trusted to look out for Jake's interests. Yet he felt that he was entitled to consideration because he had worked close with Jake, and knew company business operations. Besides, on the basis of Lamont's screwed up reports, he should have been fired, not promoted.

Of course, he knew that Lamont hadn't really screwed up, but no one else knew that, and therefore Lamont should have been tossed out based on what they knew. Peter is miffed that the other executives are going along with Jake's erratic decision, and he labeled them all as wimps for submitting.

Now, he was expected to go along as well, and to play and work along with Lamont as a team. Jake had some nerve to think that he should just sit back like some passive fool, and offer aid and comfort to his enemy. Because of such rejection, Peter started spinning a plan inside his head. He wanted Jake and his people out on their asses, and he was anxious to try a plan that had just popped in his head, that could speed up Carvoni's takeover.

He is proficient at forging Jake's signature, since he had done it on numerous occasions with Jake's blessing, and now he could use that skill to his advantage. The big man couldn't waste time signing his name to piles of paper documents, so Peter had done it for him. Now it was going to cost him.

Peter put his own sinister thoughts on hold and listened to Lamont, who sounded eager to make an impression. Peter hoped that he was overeager just enough to fall flat on his face.

"I want to meet with the directors of the various departments to brief them on what has happened as well as on the direction we need to take from here," Lamont said.

"And what direction would that be?" Peter asked cautiously, trying to sound neutral.

"Well for one thing I'm going to start with having an open dialogue with the union. I want them in on some of our power meetings."

"Don't be foolish, Lamont," Peter blurted out bluntly. He was still simmering about Lamont's access to authority over him, and had lost his sense of diplomacy. "I mean union and management don't travel in the same circles," he said, now aware of Lamont's stare. It's like asking cats and dogs to play nice."

"Well that's because no one has ever tried hard enough to change it."

"Change it? But they're going to expect." Peter stopped abruptly, and opted instead to submit. Why was he trying to give Lamont good advice, he thought. Let him fall on his ass with this hair brain ideology. "Okay, you're in charge." He paused and sighed impatiently. "So what else is on the agenda?"

Lamont was openly annoyed with his attitude. "Look, Peter I know you're not happy about this situation, and you think that you should be calling the shots. Maybe you should because I'm not on your level when it comes to running the business. But Jake made his decision and I'm going to honor it. I regret if that's a problem for you, but I'm not going to apologize or question Jake's motives. So you decide if you're going to work with me or not. If not then you should exercise your options."

Peter's eyes narrowed. "What's that suppose to mean? Are you asking me to resign?"

Lamont didn't bat an eye. "Or you can take voluntary retirement if you feel uncomfortable with Jake's decision. Maybe you should consider those options. Of course you would get a portion of your pension and the other benefits." He threw up his hands. "But hey, I'm not personally asking you to resign. I think you're a valuable asset to the company and your input would be constructive.

On the other hand, if you're unhappy here and if you're going to spend every day resenting me," Lamont said then paused and shrugged his shoulders. "Do the math and make your call. Jake gave me a job to do and I'm going to do it. Are you going to do yours, Peter?"

Peter said nothing at first because he was infuriated by this young green upstart, and he stewed mildly as his rage rose towards his boiling point. This punk kid was in his face offering him veiled threats and bad options, and he had no choice but to take his abuse. He wanted to yell racial slurs and spit in his face. However, he had invested too many years to be lured into losing all he had at stake by this green punk brat. That's exactly what they wanted him to do but he wouldn't give them the satisfaction.

He had to maintain self control because he feared Carvoni's wrath and he couldn't leave if he wanted to. He was Carvoni's inside man and he feared upsetting the formidable mobster. Besides, Carvoni would take over soon. In the meantime he believed that Lamont would prove himself to be incompetent. He might just help rub golden boy's face in the dirt. He wasn't about to leave now, he would stay around and enjoy watching this amateur fall on his face.

When that happened Lamont would come to him and beg him to save his father's company, after his miserable failure. Then everyone would see just how dumb he is. Most of all Peter would gloat and hold this colossal blunder, over Jake's head. "I don't think I will have any problem doing my job. After all, I am a professional and I can live with Jake's decision." Peter was finally able to say with some reluctance.

Lamont didn't show any surprise as Peter suspected that he would. Instead he gave Peter an easy smile. "Good, Peter. I think you're a valuable man and I'm glad you're not going to do anything rash."

Peter just nods but says nothing.

Preston glanced at his watch. "Well, I guess we'd better get going if we're going to make the meeting on time."

Lamont checked his watch. "Yeah," he said, tucking the reports inside the briefcase.

"Anything there I need to see?" Peter asked, looking curiously to Lamont.

"You'll get to see what's in here along with everyone else at the meeting I've called this morning," Lamont said sternly.

"Maybe I could offer some suggestions. You sure I can't glance over them now?"

"I'm sure," Lamont said, starting towards the door. "Shall we gentlemen?"

Peter moved slow and reluctantly towards the door, feeling insignificant and helpless.

The meeting convened ten minutes later, and Lamont updated every one on Jake's condition, and briefed them on administrative changes. He passes out copies of his reports and financial statements. "The last time I passed these reports around, they were seriously flawed. And even though I have some theories, I can't explain how that happened. I apologize for that turn of events. But these reports are valid and updated. You'll find balance sheets, sales projection sheets, project proposals, projected income, stock options and possible future investments, as related to in depth studies of these various documents.

"These reports are also based on factual in depth studies of the company's growth rate, business practice and past earnings according to specific economic trends. I suggest that we study these reports with a fine tooth comb, find any hidden problems that might need mending, and nip them in the bud."

Peter studied the reports with close scrutiny, hoping to see the work of a green amateur. He stood ready to pounce aggressively on any mistakes, miscalculations, and unsound theories. To his surprise and disappointment, the reports were not only accurate, but sound, creative, and logical about directions in which to go based on the information at hand.

It was apparent to Peter that Lamont had gotten help from Preston no doubt. There had always been an intimate closeness between Preston's lips and Jake's ass, Peter thought. So it's only natural that Preston had inherited the son's ass to kiss as well.

Peter was annoyed that the group accepted Lamont's proposals, and even enlightened him as to the soundness of his proposals. None of them showed any hostility or resentment of the blatant favoritism so evident by Lamont's newfound authority. Peter couldn't stomach the way they treated him with kids' gloves, and praised his executive skills. He had seen enough praising to turn his stomach and his nausea deepened at the sight of this obsequious band of spineless monkeys.

Peter had hoped that this meeting would be disastrous for Lamont, but it was more like a coronation that lifted him to royal status. For a brief moment Peter felt like perhaps he should take his pension and quit. On the other hand, he couldn't just go away that easily. He would stick to his earlier plan to give Carvoni the advantage, and the control he wants by forging Jake's signature.

Once he convinced Carvoni that his plan would work, Carvoni would owe him. That would mean not only a bigger cut in this deal, but he could finally be rid of Jake and Lamont. Then as a bonus, he could even get Carvoni to make his freaky lesbian wife disappear. He had discovered quite some time ago that Amanda had a lesbian lover. He wanted out of his marriage, and he wanted Amanda to suffer as well. So why not get Carvoni to take care of his little problem? He would be rid of her and never have to get his hands dirty.

Lamont and Preston left the meeting together and went to Lamont's office discussing various strategies. Lamont was pleasantly surprised to see Marcia and Cheryl inside chatting when they arrived. Marcia moved towards them quickly and consciously. "Hi, Lamont, Mr. Preston. I let your sister in, she said she wanted to chat with you and, I knew you would be right back. Hope I didn't upset your schedule or overstep my bounds," she said looking into Lamont's eyes.

"Oh of course not Marsh. Never," Lamont said with a quick smile.

She returned his smile. "Okay, I'm out." She left reluctantly, wishing that Lamont had been less business-like to her. Their recently shared intimacy made her feel closer to him now, and she wondered if he had similar feelings. He made no indication other than his brief smile and haunting glare. She knew that he felt something.

It had only been three days ago that they had first made love but that had been enough to last until now. She thought that it was just too good to last. She hopes that Lamont doesn't think that their intimacy was a mistake.

Lamont often said that office relationships were dangerous and unwise, all odds were against any relationships with the boss, she thought. She wanted to think that they had something different because they had a special connection.

Perhaps she dreamed too much, but she wanted him to show more affection now that they had slept together. She understood that he had to concentrate on his work, and couldn't carry on with her in the office, but she wished he would at least give her a sign. A lecherous glare, a quick wicked wink, or a fond little pat on her butt would be nice.

In all fairness to him, he wasn't purposely ignoring her, he just been so busy since Jake's stroke. She had to be less selfish and give the man a break because his world had changed dramatically. He had gotten a major promotion, dumped Jane, worked on several projects and attended meetings.

Maybe she expected too much, but she couldn't help herself. She had wanted him for so long, and now that she was this close, she wants everything to go right. She remembers his cries of love during sex, and she clings to that. On the other hand, maybe she had forced the issue with her sweet seduction, and given him no choice. She had been fierce and maybe now he regrets yielding to temptation. She took a deep breath and tried to cast her paranoia aside.

That wasn't easy to do because suddenly it seemed that every woman here wanted Lamont. She had already heard Linda and the others talk about jumping Lamont's bones, and she knew they would relish the chance. Every day she heard various girls' comments about Lamont as well. Maybe Lamont had also heard things and wanted to keep his options open.

"Ahem, excuse me, Marcia," Lucas Sheppard said clearing his throat, and observing Marcia's cleavage from his side of her desk.

Marcia was suddenly aware of the male voice speaking to her and jumped from her daze, startled by the presence or the little man. She recognized him and smiled cordially. "I'm sorry, I didn't see you. Mr. Shepherd, right?"

"Yes, Marcia, sorry to startled you." He smiled showing a row of coffee stained teeth.'

"Oh don't worry about it. My head was in the clouds," She said with a brief wave and an apologetic smile. "He's in a meeting right now. Would you mind waiting? "

"No, I don't mind waiting; I'm good at it now." In fact, Lucas was glad to wait because it gave him the chance to study this beauty, and revisit his arcane cravings that Marcia brought to light. Even now his deep passions stirred, and Marcia had officially replaced Candace Cooper as his main sexual object.

"Would you like some coffee?" She stands and moves towards the coffee counter nearby. "I'm about to have another cup."

"Yeah that would be fine." He is fascinated by her display gorgeous legs gliding gracefully towards the coffee pot. He inhales her flowery scent and turns his head to get a full frontal view of her backside and tiny little waist. Lord Jesus, that was a sexy woman, he thought. She was so sweet that he got a sugar rush from being in the same room with her.

She reminded him of a perky Halle Barry with that bright smile and sparkling eyes. She had a behind that would put Beyonce to shame and pretty brown skin that made him want to die licking milk chocolate. He had no doubts that Lamont was banging her. Hell he was only human, how could he resist?

Marcia felt his eyes on her, but wasn't offended. Her experience at the Outreach Center had made her aware that older men liked to watch pretty young girls, and frankly she felt flattered that he appreciated her assets. He seemed so sad and unloved, and she sensed that he had no one special. He seemed like a nice man, but she guessed that he probably lived for his work. That was such a shame. "Here you go, Mr. Shepherd," she said, handing him a Styrofoam cup filled with coffee. "Here's some cream and sugar, she said handing him several packets. "You have to fix it the way you want."

"This is fine just like this."

"Yuck, that's like mud."

"Well it's an acquired taste. And besides black is beautiful," he chuckled, while reveling in the warmth of Marcia's positive attitude. He sipped his coffee and smiled. Yes, I can wait, he thought to himself. Take your time Lamont, take your time. I'm having a most wonderful day, a most wonderful day. Any day was a good day when a man with his looks and bad skin could talk to a pretty woman and not be treated like discarded waste, or road kill.

Chapter Forty Four-
The Report

While Lucas waited outside Lamont's office enjoying his coffee and Marcia, Cheryl was talking to Lamont about the discussion that had taken place with her sisters. She had come here without their knowledge because she felt obligated to Lamont.

Ruth's story was too far fetched, and it was obvious that she disliked Lamont, so she had come to hear his side. Now she got to the point. "Ruth thinks that you're having an affair with Candace, and claims that she saw you making out in the car with her yesterday."

"What," Lamont said focusing fully on Cheryl. "Why would she accuse me of something like that?"

Cheryl hunched her shoulders. "Why wouldn't she? Don't forget this is Ruth I'm talking about. And that's not all of it," Cheryl paused for a dramatic effect. Ruth also thinks that you and Candace are planning to take over the company now that daddy's in the hospital." Cheryl couldn't conceal the amused smile she wore.

"That is beyond ridiculous," Lamont said, shaking his head in disbelief. "It's always some new drama with her isn't it? Does she have rocks in her head?"

"Of course she does," Cheryl said and paused briefly. "Well for what it's worth, you know I don't believe it for a minute, especially if Ruth said it. She's batting a thousand when it comes to misreading signs."

"First I wouldn't even know where to begin to take over a company as complex as Cooper Industries. That's the last thing on my mind. And as for Candace, she was all to pieces the other day," Lamont said, looking Cheryl squarely in the eyes, "and I gave her a hug to console her. That's probably what Ruth saw. I guess that was enough to send that twisted imagination off to the races. Jumping to the wrong conclusions is Ruth's special talent."

"You got that right and it didn't take you long to figure her."

"It doesn't take a genius to see that." He paused and seemed to be in deep thought. "Cheryl, does she honestly think I would do that to Jake?"

She gave him a soft look. "It's hard to tell with Ruth. She's so damn mean that no ne knows what she's thinking.

"But do you think anyone else believes her?" Lamont asked concerned.

Naw, of course not," she said without hesitation. "It's no secret that Ruth is wacky." She paused and gave him a look between puzzled and suspicious. "But I have seen the way you look at Candace."

"She's a pretty woman and she's nice to me." He shrugged defensively.

"So you think she's pretty?" Cheryl asked seeming with disbelief.

"She is, but not as pretty as my gorgeous sister." Lamont added playfully.

"Nice save." Cheryl said with a knowing nod. "You are smart aren't you?"

"Well what can I say," he said brushing his hair with playful vanity. Now he became serious. "Look Cheryl, a man sees a pretty woman he looks. That doesn't mean he's going after her. I'm sure you notice handsome men and they notice you. So what? And no way would I go after my stepmother. It's ridiculous." Lamont felt slightly awkward and a little deceitful. He had once entertained thoughts of sleeping with Candace, even after finding out that she was Jake's wife. That was in the past, and lately his concentration was on his sudden new relationship with Marcia.

"You don't have to convince me. You got my support. I believe you, Lamont, and I'll try and talk to our crazy sister. We don't need false rumors floating around."

"No we don't, not with all the other stuff that we got to worry about. I'm glad to hear that I have your support, and I want you to know that I'm here representing Jake. I don't have his savvy or experience, but I do have some, and I'm gonna be outright in seeking all the help and advice that I can get. I want to do it for Jake and I'm ready to enlist anybody and everybody who is willing to help me." He looked purposely to Cheryl now.

Cheryl paused and there was an awkward silence. "Ruth would really be in a tizzy if she knew what I knew about you though."

"Oh, Like what, Cheryl?"

"I know that daddy gave you power of attorney. He thinks a lot of you." Cheryl's tone was upbeat and neutral now. She realizes that Jake had to trust Lamont because he certainly couldn't trust any of them.

"Well that was a business thing," Lamont said, "and I'll tell you about it sometime, but right now I can't."

"That's not a problem," Cheryl said. "I understand but I didn't mention this to the others."

"Thanks, I don't think that would go to well." He pauses, still thinking about Ruth's blind accusations and now he could appreciate what Candace was going through with the Cooper clan. Any type of bonding must have been elusive with her because all of the girls were envious, even Cheryl. The daughters all held some resentment towards Candace because she's an outsider. He too is an outsider, and was also the object of resistance and suspicion. However, Ruth's unfounded, blind accusations crossed the line.

Ruth was no doubt the evil sister, but she came with the territory. He might never gain her support, but he felt as if he had Jake and Cheryl on his side. Lately, he is no longer sure about JJ, and Ann was too hard to read.

Lamont decided that instead of worrying about his relationship with the Coopers, he needed to initiate a plan to put everyone on the same level.

"You know what Cheryl; I got an idea that might rein in the family's fears." He gave Cheryl an amused look.

"Something is going on in that head of yours. You got that same expression that daddy gets."

"Yeah, I do and anybody who has objections to what I am about to propose is beyond reach as far as I'm concerned. Even Raging Ruthie would have to consider my proposal."

"Sounds delicious, please tell me more." Cheryl said, curiously.

"I haven't worked out all the details or ran this by Jake yet, but meet me for lunch and I'll bend your ear with some details."

"I can hardly wait."

****

A short time later, Cheryl left the office and stopped to exchange pleasantries with Marcia before going gracefully on her way.

Lucas Sheppard was still sitting there sipping the coffee and stealing furtive glances at Marcia. Now his eyes jumped to Cheryl, who was as gorgeous and sexy as Marcia. He is glad that he waited patiently, because now he was getting a bonus. He had watched in awe as the gorgeous woman stepped through the door of Lamont's office and said something to Marcia. He knew that she was Jake's daughter because he had seen a photograph of her in Jake's office. He didn't know she had such a sexy body.

His eyes scanned and saved to memory, the essence of these two feminine creatures. Now he watched Cheryl in astonishment as she waved to Marcia on her way to the elevator. "Bye now Marcia, don't work too hard," Lucas heard her voice ring out with the soothing power of a deeply moving song.

"Can't help it, Cheryl," Marcia replied lightly, "Your brother is a slave driver."

Lucas remembered the conversation that he had overheard in Carvoni's office. Two Martin and Carvoni had discussed Cheryl, and the cameras that they had in her place. That low life pimp was screwing Jake's gorgeous daughter, and the thought of it filled Lucas with instant jealousy. "That lousy bastard," he said under his breath, continuing to watch Cheryl as if in a trance. His trained watchful eyes could only concentrate on Cheryl's graceful jiggling buttocks and proud walk. His senses returned with a start when he heard Marcia's soft wispy voice say his name. "Mr. Shepherd, Lamont will see you now."

He smiled. "Lucas, please. Call me Lucas," he said hoarsely.

"Lamont will see you now Lucas," Marcia said flashing an obligatory smile.

Marcia was on Lamont's mind now and he recalled their recent sexual encounter as Lucas entered the office. Recently all of his urges and free thoughts were channeled towards Marcia, and his emotional involvement with her. He had made things complicated, because he was being a hypocrite who was involved with a coworker, although he had preached against such relationships. Now that he had crossed that line himself, he found a need to make excuses. It was difficult to break things down to cold hard technicalities with her. She was almost too good to be true, which concerned him slightly. Most things that are too good to be true aren't true.

Still, he couldn't justify sleeping with her, but he didn't really care. He was confused about where they were gong from here right now, and he tried to keep busy and not think about it. Yet he yearned constantly to be with her and he would probably continue to break his own rules and remain indecisive.

He couldn't get over how right it seemed with her. Making love to her was fulfilling and different from anything he ever felt with any woman. He thought about the intimacy and even recalled it often.

"Hello, Lamont. How's Jake doing?" Lucas asked, interrupting Lamont's thoughts.

"Hi, Lucas," Lamont said coming out of his reverie. "He's stronger and he's home," Lamont said with a brief pause. "What's up? You said you had some urgent information for me."

"Yeah I do, and I gotta say you might not like it." Lucas hesitated briefly, and then added. "It's bad news about your siblings."

"Bad news?" Lamont asked with heightened interest.

"Yeah, JJ, Ruth, and Cheryl. I stumbled on this among a few other things while following up on Carvoni and his relationship with our boy, Peter." Lucas took a small tape from his brief case. "It's all on this tape here and you can listen when you get time, but I can go over everything that's on the tape."

"Okay, let me have it then."

"Carvoni went after the two youngest and most vulnerable Cooper kids, and set them up with two separate cons to get his hands on their stock."

"What," Lamont said with a look of total disbelief. "I thought something like this could happen. I knew that stock wasn't safe. How did Carvoni con them, Lucas?"

"It was a master stroke," Lucas said shaking his head. "First he got a professional jumper to fake the accident with Ruth. He knew she drank heavy, so he waited until the opportunity presented itself and took advantage. She was so loaded at the time that she had no sense of what was going on."

"Yeah I talked to her right after and I know that's a fact," Lamont said reflectively.

"He bribed the bartender to double up on her drinks on the night in question, and she left there good and drunk. Carvoni even bragged about how easy it was, and how it disappointed him that neither of them presented a challenge."

"Incredible, but what about JJ?" Lamont asked. "That girl that accused JJ of rape was part Carvoni's scam?"

"I'm afraid so," Lucas said with a nod. "Carvoni took advantage of your brother's weakness as a ladies man. He claimed that JJ was less of a challenge because wanted to screw anything with a pulse. When Carvoni found out that JJ was dating Roxanne Perilli, he bribed her and her mother to set JJ up. The girl and her mother are promiscuous addicts so it didn't take much to convince them."

"So are you telling me that the girl is not underage?" Lamont asked with a scowl.

"She's over twenty one and very experience and Carvoni knew that. The charges would have been dropped if the lawyer had done a full investigation. That's why Carvoni moved so fast to prevent that from happening."

"I see, and once the settlement was made, there was no more need to investigate," Lamont said, regretfully. "Carvoni has been a step ahead of us the whole time. The con was to get Ruth and JJ's stock by getting them to go for the settlement. And he knew that he could scare them into doing what he wanted. Damn that man is the Devil," Lamont said pounding his fist on the desk.

"The slimy little bastard moved fast, applied pressured, and got Ruth and JJ to hand over their shares. Now he has thirty percent of Cooper stock and he's closer to controlling Cooper Industries."

"Damn, he's relentless," Lamont said with a deep sigh. "What do you think his next move will be?"

"That's easy; he needs fifty one per cent, so he's gotta go after your other two sisters. Whatever their weakness, believe me he's going to find it and exploit it to the fullest."

"Yeah, that makes sense. Cheryl and Ann are next on his list, Lamont said in a voice that seemed strained.

"Well, your sister Ann's husband has a record and I heard Carvoni mention using it to get Ann's shares. It wouldn't surprise me if he tried to set up the husband for some kind of black mail." Lucas paused and gave a pained expression. "And he's already got a plan in motion involving Cheryl's stock. I don't know if you know it or not, but Cheryl's keeping company with a pimp by the name of Tony Martin, they call him."

"Two Martin," Lamont cut Lucas off.

"Yeah, you know him?"

"Oh yes, I know him," he said with a sigh. "He's a real snake. You're sure about this?"

"Positive. From what I head, Carvoni's taping Two Martin and your sister having sex. The only thing I can figure is that he plans to use it to blackmail Cheryl in order to get her stock. Just to be sure about the relationship, my guys spotted Martin going in and out of her place a couple of times and they recently checked into a motel for a couple of days running. But the coup de grace is that Carvoni owns a club that Two is running."

"So Two Martin is working with Carvoni to set Cheryl up," Lamont said through clenched jaws. "He's persistent as hell."

That's it in a nutshell. Two Martin's action is the heart of Carvoni's plan to get Cheryl's stock."

Lamont was unhappy after he heard Lucas' brutal report, and he had to figure out some strategy to outsmart this ruthless mobster. Right now he couldn't think of a thing. "Thanks Lucas," Lamont said in a gloomy voice. "Stay on this for me and get back with any new developments."

"Will do," Lucas said, then let himself out, leaving Lamont deep in thought, no doubt trying to figure out what he had to do next.

Later Marcia did some reports and watched the door of Lamont's office, debating whether to go in and see what he was doing right now. Lucas had left an hour earlier and so far he was inside his office alone. She replayed their lovemaking in her head a thousand times, and she was horny just thinking about the things they had done recently.

Now, she imagined going into his office and doing it on the desk. She saw it so clearly in her mind and she whimpered aloud. Suddenly she was aware of making an audible sound, and she pretended to clear her throat. She shuffled through some paperwork and looked around quickly for furtive knowing stares, but the three girls in the surrounding desks were busy at work.

She calmed down and reminded herself to be patient, but she suddenly had no patience. She was hooked on Lamont and she wanted him to feel the same vibrancy that she felt. It was torture being so close to him and pretending that things were business as usual. She wondered if it was the same for him.

Chapter Forty Five-
Sure Deal

Peter Vel Haus was in a terrible mood when he arrived home later that night. He felt humiliated and couldn't shake the image of Lamont and Preston's smug taunting faces. He wanted to think that he had imagined it, but the recent images constantly played in his head. It was totally unfair for him to be submitting to Lamont. It's an ultimate insult and worse than being terminated. Too bad that he didn't have rich relatives to give him an unearned authority.

Then, as if that wasn't bad enough, he couldn't come home to relax and have any peace of mind. Amanda had made his home a hellish haven and was preparing to run off with her lesbian pal and sue him for her fair share. As far as Peter was concerned, the bitch didn't have a share, fair or otherwise. On the other hand the bitch would tie him up in court and try to bleed him.

He relaxed and had a drink alone as usual. Amanda was in her room and stayed there most of the time when he was home. He suspects that she had on occasion brought her lover home. He has detected an unfamiliar perfume from time to time. She made a chump of him just as Jake had done. Today had been an ultimate agony of mental pain.

Any so called love, if it ever existed, had long gone the ways of smoke into clouds. The only thing real and genuine now was the despicable contempt that he held for her. She had blatantly disrespected him and thought little about it. She had hit him with the lowest of low blows and cheated on her with a woman. That stung deep.

Peter remembered the night he had busted her and her lesbian girl friend leaving the Omni Hotel. Even now he saw the image of Amanda and the tall black haired women locked in an embrace, French kissing in the parking lot. She hadn't shown him that kind of passion in three years. He had been patient, thinking that she was just cold.

He sat there nursing morbid thoughts and obsessing about Amanda's death. Peter could see it in his mind and he felt elated about killing Amanda and her freaky lover. The problem was that he didn't have the stomach to commit murder. However, he didn't have any reservations about having someone else do it, and it was time to cash in on his association with Carvoni. He can scratch Carvoni's back and Carvoni could scratch his.

Thirty minutes later Peter enters the Carvoni's office and sat nervously, thinking about making his proposal. He felt like his plan would solve Carvoni's problem and his own. He was spurred on each time he remembers how Jake, Lamont, and Amanda had walked all over him. Now he was here to offer Carvoni his prize in return for a personal favor. He would let Carvoni do his dirty work for him.

Carvoni was an impatient man who hated impromptu meetings, so he addressed Peter directly, when he noticed him hesitating and fidgeting in the chair facing him. "So tell me what you meant when I talked to you earlier over the phone. You said you might have a way to get the last of the stock I need, and that you needed a favor in return," Carvoni spoke, holding his stubby hands out palm up. "So spill. What's this great plan you got?"

"Well like I said I can get you controlling stock in the company."

"How, Peter?" He asked impatiently. "Old man Jake got the controlling shares."

"What if I could get my hands on them and deliver them to you?"

"Don't play games. Can you do that or not," Carvoni growled with a glare.

"I can," Peter said with trepidation.

"Again, how?"

"Well as a loyal and devoted employee I got access to certain information."

"And you can deliver that stock to me?"

"I think so."

"You think," Carvoni said annoyed. "What do you mean you think? Are you wasting my time, Small Fish? You called me and I assumed that you had something positive in mind. Now do you or don't you?"

"Yes I do, and yes I can deliver."

"How come you didn't tell me about this before then?"

"Well, I didn't think of it before and."

"Never mind," Carvoni said, throwing up his hands, interrupting

Peter. "I don't doubt your ability, but start from the beginning and explain to me exactly how you're gonna pull off this scheme."

Peter began to explain. "I can forge Jake's signature and with those skills, I can authorize the sale of Cooper stock, then jump in and acquire blocs of Cooper's stock before it hits the trading floor. Leave the details to me. It can be done. Then I'll make that stock available exclusive to you. You'll have your controlling shares and Cooper Industry."

"You're sure about this?" Carvoni asked skeptically. "It seems too easy."

"We'll have the element of surprise, which always makes it easy."

"It's crazy and simple enough to work," Carvoni bit on the cigar, and rubbed his chin wearing a slow wicked smile. He wanted to believe that it was possible, and that Peter could pull this off. Still, he wasn't going to assume anything. "Okay Peter, we're going to go with your little plan. Now get to the bottom line. How much cash are we talking to make this thing a go?" Carvoni said, glaring directly at Peter.

"Peter swallowed hard, realizing that he had taken a deep breath for the first time since he finished explaining his plans. He hadn't actually considered an exact price for the stock, because he was set on revenge and hadn't thought about money. However, he thought about it now and he frantically did the math inside his head. "I can manage to get you the 21 percent that you need, for five hundred thousand. I'll work with this broker that I know. He can arrange the whole thing for a small fee. He will see that the stock never trades on the open market."

Carvoni scanned him suspiciously, no doubt wondering if this man was cheating him. Still, if he got what he wanted, and if this geeky little nerd had enough nerve to cheat him, he could live with it. Frankly he didn't think the little nerd had the guts. "You got yourself a deal Peter. How soon can I get that stock?"

"About five days from now. That will be first thing Monday, no later than Tuesday. I'll get back to you before then to confirm it."

"Yeah you do that." Carvoni paused and tasted the meatballs from the bowl sitting on his desk, then pushed the bowl away. "Now what was the favor you wanted in return if this thing works? More money? President of the company? What?"

"What I want is simple. I want to get rid of my wife," Peter said calmly and without hesitation.

"Why is that? Not that it matters, cause if that's what you want, then you got it."

"Because that perverted bitch has put me through hell," Peter said with fire. "She's a dirty," he paused as if it hurt to say the word but then he continued. "She's a lesbian and she's been lying and denying me for years while she's spending my money and cheating on me with women. I'm sure that she's even had sex with them in our home," Peter said.

Carvoni sat silently, seeming to contemplate his words. "A lezzy huh?" I know that pain," Carvoni said low and almost inaudible. "Okay, Peter, I can certainly understand that and the hit is on. It's done," he said with a jubilant wave of his hand. That would solve your problem."

Pete believed that the heartless man sympathized with him. "Thanks Mr. Carvoni," Peter said, rising from the chair and moving towards the door. Before he could reach the exit Carvoni called out.

"Oh Peter, there's a couple of things we need to get straight. This broker you got, his fee will come out of the five hundred thousand so you work that out," he said looking Peter directly in the eyes.

Peter wanted to protest but he knew that was a bad idea from the look in Carvoni's beady little eyes. Peter sensed that if he didn't submit to Carvoni the deal was off. "Okay Mr. Carvoni, his fee will be covered as you wish."

Carvoni smiled. "Good. And last thing Peter." Carvoni's demeanor became dead serious. "I look at this as a promise to me. That's very important. If you don't pull this off like you promised, I'm gonna be very disappointed, and very angry with you."

Peter's stomach dropped, when he thought about the consequences if he failed. The reality of Carvoni's verbal threats and cold icy glare reminded him that this is the mob. His quest for revenge had put him in a position where failure was no longer an option. Deep depression and desperation ripple through him as he left that office. His perspective had changed and his plan had to work now, because it was a life or death matter.

The following Monday morning, Peter paid fifty thousand dollars to acquire Brian Banks, his shady stockbroker, to help swindle a large bloc of Cooper industry stock. Brian had upped his original fee from thirty thousand to fifty thousand, claiming that he would be taking a bit more risk, and that more people would have to be involved. Peter had no choice, so he agreed after griping about it briefly.

Peter presented Brian with the forged documents and the cash. Carvoni's men waited with Brian in his office, and stood guard on the cash while Peter phoned Carvoni with an update. Peter was nervous, but he felt confident, because he had the element of surprise. The main thing is that he would get his revenge once Carvoni got control. The Coopers would be out, and Amanda would be the eliminated. That was the icing on the cake.

Meanwhile at the Cooper office building, Preston was with Lamont in his office discussing strategy. "Sheppard just called," Lamont said looking at Preston. "A shady stock broker name Brian Banks put in a forged sell order for a large bloc of Cooper stock. There was also a market order issued for the exact amount of stock along with that sell order. It also bore Jake's forged signature," he paused and gave Preston a look before continuing. "And that market order was a day order," Lamont said

"That removes all doubts," Preston said. "Now we know that an insider is involved, and my money is on Peter. He must be desperate to think that such a hair brain scheme would work."

Lamont gave Preston a knowing look. "You're right, what was he thinking with that day order? At least an indefinite order would have avoided suspicion. We know that he's forged Jake's signature in the past, and that day order is proof that Peter knew exactly when the stock would be available.

"Exactly." Preston said.

"Maybe he thought that he could get away with it because Jake was not here on top of things," Lamont said shaking his head. "He outsmarted himself with that one day order. That leaves no doubt about it being issued by someone with knowledge of the stock's forthcoming availability. That's enough circumstantial evidence to implicate whoever forged Jake's name."

"And know that was Peter." Lamont concluded

"It's good that we moved fast and had our security team on the look out for all Cooper stock trade orders. That made it easier to track Peter down."

"Yeah, Sheppard suspected that Peter might do something devious and cautioned me. He was right." Lamont said, giving Preston an approving nod. "And you were right about Sheppard. He's good."

"Yes, he is. He doesn't look like much, but he's a damn genius when it comes to detective work," Preston finished with a sigh and now changed the subject. "Anyway I've made calls, and notified the securities exchange commission as you suggested. The stock deal is dead, and the only thing left now is what to do about Peter?"

"We're not going to do anything. We're simply gonna present the facts to the authorities, and to our board, and wait. Then no one can accuse me of any self serving manipulation or file any lawsuits."

"Well in light of the evidence, I don't see how anyone can blame you, but I do see your point. Better safe than sorry."

"Yes, and the authorities will likely file charges later, but for now I trust this board to pursue a course of action. I know they have high regard for the interest of this company's stockholders Trust me, once we expose Peter's actions, the board will render a unanimous decision to ask for his immediate resignation.

Chapter Forty Six-
Departure

Peter had been stunned when he discovered that the stock deal had been quashed, and then he got word that the board was asking for his immediate resignation.

Now he collected his things from the large desk, he looked around the huge office that had once been his prize trophy. He felt totally dejected, and angry about everything and with everyone. He had been unsuccessful in his underhanded scheme, but he didn't feel bad about what he had done, only about getting caught. He deserved more, he thought. He had guided Jake through important decisions, and now he was being tossed like snot tissue.

He asked himself how did a green kid like Lamont checkmate him. It was a fluke, he thought, not wanting to believe that Lamont had been savvy enough to outsmart him. The damn kid was lucky, that's all. There had to be a way to make him pay.

In the midst of packing, Peter became aware of Lamont's presence in the large office. "What the hell do you want," Peter said with open hostility now, seeing no need to fake his feelings any more. "You here to gloat about your victory?" Peter sneered as he turns back to the desk and continues to gather his things.

"No, I'm here to ask you some questions."

"I don't have to answer any of your damn questions," he said with a sneer.

"I know you don't, but I'm still going to ask," Lamont said with a deep sigh, twisting his mouth to the side. "Why didn't you continue to work with Jake? Why did you have to make a deal with Carvoni?"

Peter froze at the mention of the name, remembering suddenly that he now had to deal with Carvoni. He realized that he had not only failed to deliver on his promise, but he had gotten fired as well. That meant that he was useless to Carvoni now. Fear suddenly took hold and Lamont became the last thing on his mind. His concerns now focused on how the mobster might retaliate now that he had failed on the stock deal, and lost his usefulness as an insider. Peter shook nervously, realizing that he was in deep trouble, and his life was in danger.

"I don't know what the securities exchange commission is going to do, but I'm not pressing charges because you did work with Jake closely, and in spite of what you tried to do, he did consider you as a val."

"That's mighty white of you," Peter said with a sarcastic burst, cutting Lamont off. "You can save it Savage. I don't need your damn gratuitous bullshit speech" He grabbed his box and headed for the door.

"Hold on a minute Peter," Lamont said, catching up to Peter and standing between him and the door.

"For what?" Peter asked with predictable irritation, as he stopped and faced Lamont.

"Security check."

"Get serious, Savage." He tried to get past, but Lamont block him.

"I am serious, Peter. You know the drill. You're no longer trustworthy, so I need to check that box. You understand we can't have you stealing any files from here."

"This is an outrage. You can't hold me here, and I would never take any files from here...

"Chill out, Peter," Lamont said calmly. "I'm a compassionate man, Peter, but not to the point that I'm gonna let you walk out of here without checking that box. So suck it up and sit your ass down," Lamont said with a firm expression, and significant increase in volume.

Peter clenched, he had never seen this side of Lamont. He wasn't brave enough to defy him, so he pouted openly, while moving to sit in the small chair.

Lamont opened the door. "Come on in guys," he called out.

Wendell, and Jimmie, entered with serious official expressions, looking first to Lamont, then to Peter.

"Okay guys, I need you to search this box and this man, and then escort him from the premises."

The two security guards nodded, and then proceeded with their search while Lamont looks on.

"Be careful not to bruise him, or break anything that belongs to him," Lamont said while staring directly at Peter. "We don't want to damage his personal property or inflict bodily harm."

The men completed the search, took all of Peter's identification badges, and then escorted him from his old office. As Peter lumbered towards the elevator surrounded by the security guards, he felt intense humiliation at the loud whispers, distinct murmurs, and open observance of nosy peering former co-workers. God he wanted revenge, but for now he just wanted to get out of there as quickly as possible.

When Peter arrived home Amanda was talking on the telephone and didn't bother to acknowledge him. He guessed from her body language, tone of voice, and silly giggle that she was talking to her Dyke girlfriend. Lately, she purposely flaunted her freaky love affair, and purposely disrespected him.

Peter ignored her and quietly climbed the stairs, because right now he had more grave and serious things on his mind. The mere thought of Carvoni's wrath filled him with fantastic trembling fear. Carvoni had made it clear what failure would mean, but in his desperate need for revenge, Peter had cast caution aside. Now, he had no job, no wife, and if Carvoni has his way, no life. The only thing left for him to do was run.

It no longer mattered what Amanda did or didn't do. He was done here, and she could have her Dyke and her new life. She would be surprised and pissed when she found out that she hadn't yielded the bonanza she expected from this marriage. Half of his assets would amount to a meager sum.

He would take the hundred thousand dollars in his safe deposit box and disappear without a word. Amanda and her Dyke friend could have this house and the mortgage that went with it. That was all the settlement she would get from him, and it was far more than she deserved.

He suddenly had renewed energy, and his nervousness turned to excitement with the idea of starting a new life. He needed to move immediately, because Carvoni had gotten the bad news by now, and there was no doubt that his henchmen were on the way.

For the first time since the stock deal fell through, Peter felt hope replace his stress. He went quickly to his secret place in the den, and took his safe deposit box key from the drawer. He went back upstairs and packed a small duffle bag, while Amanda continued to talk and giggle on the phone. She didn't even turn to acknowledge his presence.

Bennie along with Mario and Angelo pulled up to Peter's house in the large green SUV. They got out and marched cautiously to the front door. "Remember, guys," Bennie said, looking to the two men standing beside him, "Tony wants this done. He's furious about what happen with that stock deal and he was clear about what to do to the little man. We can't let him escape. Got it?" The two men acknowledged with a nod and they proceeded to enter the premises.

Peter was in the midst of packing, and was startled by the sound of the front door being forced open. He heard Amanda distinctly shouting angry protests, "What's the meaning of this? Get out! You can't come in here and." her shouting was abruptly halted and her angry complaints turned to feeble pleas. "No, please don't"

Peter heard three hiss-like sounds in rapid successions, and recognized them as muffled gunfire. He froze momentarily unable to gain his bearings. He knew that Carvoni's men were in the house and those shots had ended Amanda's life.

Now the silence and its implications filled him with aggressive fear. He heard them stirring about and he knew that he was next. His heart raced at the thought of Tony's men coming for him. He went numb, aware only of the warm urine running free down his left leg. He had to go now or he was dead too, but he couldn't use the stairs. He stuffed the safe deposit box key inside his jacket, left the bag, and fled to the window and opened it.

He heard footsteps at the top of the stairs, and jumped without hesitation, twisting his ankle when landing on the small grassy patch below. He saw Bennie coming towards him and he instinctively started to run. His toes burned and his shins ached, but his surging adrenaline blocked out his pain. He ran fast and wild through neighbors' yards, too terrified to look back. He put a great distance between himself and those horrifying men, and even though they were now out of sight, he still felt threatened. They were determined to kill him to appease Carvoni, and right now, he wished that he had never heard of Tony Carvoni.

Peter hid out for hours in a large junk yard, inside one of the hundreds of cars. Now he emerged from the back seat of an old wrecked Toyota near the back fence, feeling sure that he had made good on his escape. He still had his credit card, and he breathed easier as he formed an escape plan. He'd get a room, buy a change of clothes, then go to the bank to get his money and leave the country.

Unfortunately for Peter, Carvoni's men were a step ahead of him all the way and caught up with him later when he pulled the rented car out on the highway. Peter hopped out and ran, but Carvoni's men caught up to him before he could get into the thick brush, on the deserted roadside. He begged for his life in vain, and Carvoni's men were determined to carry out Carvoni's wishes.

It was sundown when Carvoni got the word from his cousin Bennie that Peter had been properly dispensed. Carvoni's men had set things up to look like a murder-suicide. Carvoni's one regret was that he had to find another insider.

Carvoni had a slight change in the original plan, since Peter's little fiasco had failed to jumpstart his takeover, and Peter had gotten fired. If Peter's plan had worked, he would be in control right now. However, trusting that loser had turned out to be a big mistake. He wasn't about to make another with a loser like Two Martin.

If Two didn't get his act together, he would give him the same treatment that he had given Peter. He still owned that wannabe pimp, and maybe it was about time that he reminded that two bit hustler who was boss.

In light of Peter's failure, he needed Two to deliver on his end. Tony had the feeling that Two was thinking independently, which meant that he might be harboring thoughts of double crossing him. That would be so unfortunate for him. Carvoni didn't want to take him out but he would if he found it necessary.

Two's subtle defiance had thrown a major monkey wrench into his plans to use Cheryl to discredit her father. However, in order to do that, he needed more quality footage of Cheryl and Two, having freaky sex. The footage he had now was too grainy and Cheryl's face wasn't as clear as he needed it to be. Two hadn't screwed that Bimbo in her bedroom since finding that camera there last week.

He hoped that Two hasn't suddenly grown a conscious and lost his objectivity. It will be too bad for him if he is protecting the hot little bitch, because that would be the cause of his demise. Nobody was going to stop him from getting his way, and once he surprise Jake with his tape, he would take control.

Yes, Peter's little fiasco had failed, but once he got Two Martin in line, Cooper Industries would belong to him, and no loser pimp or bimbo brat was going to derail it.

Chapter Forty Seven-
Connections

Upon hearing the news about Peter and his wife, Lamont felt a fleeting sense of guilt, thinking that Peter's death might have been a result of his actions. According to the sketchy details on the news report, the couple was found inside the home in close proximity, and all the evidence indicated a murder-suicide. Lamont sensed that Carvoni was involved.

Lamont thought it was logical to believe, that Carvoni had ordered a hit on Peter because he had failed to carry out his job. Peter was responsible for Carvoni's acquisition of so much stock, and his rewarded was death. Carvoni was a cold hearted monster, lacking morality and convention. He was a dangerous animal, because he was a vicious cold hearted killer and a devious underhanded strategist.

Thanks to Lucas Shepherd's report, Lamont knew all about the depth of Carvoni's wicked mind. He had set up Ruth and JJ with twin evil plans out of Satan's handbook. Now, Lamont was uneasy about what Carvoni might do to get his hands on Cheryl and Ann's stock.

He could almost feel Carvoni breathing down his neck. That cold blooded schemer was launching an all out attack with dirty tricks, cons games, and murder. Jake wasn't back on his feet, and Lamont felt that it was his responsibility to keep his father's company out of the hands of the mob. How could he win against Carvoni? He had to find out.

He picked up the telephone and dialed. "Hal come up to my office right away." There was no reasoning with Carvoni, but he wasn't going to sit still like a weakling. Five minutes later Hal was inside the office.

"Yeah what's up, man?"

"What do you know about Two Martin's connection with Tony Carvoni?"

"Carvoni?" Hal thought briefly then said. "I know Two is Carvoni's bitch, and he's into him for some big bucks. He runs a little club for him and he would shine Carvoni's shoes, kiss his prick, and pick lint from his pubic hair. Why do ask?"

"Can he contact Carvoni?" Lamont asked without responding to Hal's question.

"Yeah he can. Why?"

"Because I need to arrange a meeting with Carvoni."

"Carvoni?" Hal asked raising his voice two octaves higher and shaking his head. "Hey, man, don't go doing nothing crazy. That bastard is a cold-blooded snake hearted terrorist, man. He'd off his own family members if they farted too loud, or if he could make a profit. All that mattered to him was the almighty dollar. I think it's that Napoleon complex thing, you know."

"I'm not stupid, Hal. And I'm not planning on challenging him. I just want to talk."

"Well unless you make some deal with him where he can see some profit, you can forget it. Talking won't do you no good."

Lamont was getting annoyed with Hal. "Just the same, Hal, I want to meet with him. Can you get Two set up the meeting or not?"

"Yeah, but..."

"Good, I want you to get in touch with Two, and then get back to me. And I want to do it right away."

"Like when?"

"Like yesterday."

"You serious?"

"As a widow's grief. Get on it for me."

"Okay, you got it." Hal stood there mumbling and shaking his head for a moment. Then he turned and hurried towards the door, almost running into Marcia who was on her way in "Hi Marcia."

"Hi Hal," Marcia said as she enters Lamont's office and closed the door behind her, and moved close to his desk. "Hal was in a big hurry. He going somewhere?"

"Yeah, I sent him on an errand." Lamont shot her a quick smile, and then looked back to his computer.

"Busy?" She resisted the urge to kiss him.

"Swamped." He looked up from the computer screen. "Look I'm sorry I haven't been able to get away for lunch recently, but with this stock thing you wouldn't believe all the crap coming at me now," he said, forgetting that she knew nothing about the stock fiasco.

It didn't matter because she was more concerned about what she was about to say. "Yes I would. I'm your assistant. Remember me?"

"Yeah I remember you," he smiled warmly.

She felt like his smile was a sign. "Do you remember anything else? Anything you'd like to do to me or with me?"

"Lots of things and I'm gonna get back to you, but I can't get into that right now. We really do need to talk."

Marcia didn't like the sound of his voice or his attitude. "Is this something that I should be worried about, Lamont? Have you forgotten about..?"

He didn't let her finish. "No, of course not Marsh, it's just that..." He was impatient with her now.

"What?"

"Things are hectic here, and I need to work on some things alone. I hardly have any time to spare anymore. Maybe this is all unfair to you. It's complicated.."

"What's complicated, us? If you're throwing hints Lamont, believe me I get it." She hadn't meant to sound so angry, but frustration overwhelmed her. "I won't make any demands on you, if that's what you're thinking." She hated herself immediately for saying that, and yet she couldn't control her words or actions. "Am I a burden to you now that we've had sex, Lamont? I don't expect any special treatment or anything like that." She hated the way she sounded, and now she felt like the pathetic creature that Jane had depicted her to be. Still, she continued pleading her case. "I'm a good woman and I won't bug you about things."

"I know you're a good woman Marsh. You're the best."

"But?" She asked, seeming to anticipate his negative reaction.

"But I don't want to lose such a good friend."

"Oh Lamont, get real. Are you still preaching about that? How I'm I ever going to think of us as just friends after all the steamy passion we've shared? How are you ever going to think that again? Do you know how wonderful we are together? Besides who in the hell wants to be friends? How can you deny how explosive and insanely passionate we are together? I don't know about you, but I've never felt that way with any one before. What the hell is wrong with what we have? Don't you see that we don't just click, we go bang? You think we could go back to just being friends, Lamont? Wake up, man, what we have is real."

He sighed, not knowing what to say. "Marsh. I," he stammered weakly, unable to think.

"Are you tired of me already?"

"What? You know better." He rubbed his face and sighed again. "Actually I'm thinking about you Marsh. I don't know what I want right now. I know you love kids and you want to get…" He paused as if he was afraid to say the word. He changed the subject. "I don't want to hurt you, Marsh, and I have to admit that this thing between us is so dramatic that it scares me. What we got is almost too good. It's so."

"Wonderful, passionate and peaceful with mutual understanding," she said finishing his sentence.

"Yeah it is. But I feel guilty about it."

"Why, Lamont? That makes no sense."

I feel like I'm taking advantage of you. I think that you might feel pressured to submit to me because I'm your boss. You don't have to do me any sexual favors to keep your job." Lamont realized that he wasn't thinking straight, and his words sounded foreign even to him. Everything seemed as if it was crashing down on him. This crisis with Carvoni, his dubious relationship with the Coopers, and now this new thing with Marcia left him totally confused.

"God, Lamont, I can't believe you're saying this to me. I don't appreciate being insulted and regarded as a shallow, cheap office slut, Lamont. Is that how you feel? I thought that things between us were deeper. You seem to forget that we have a history. How can you think that I'm the kind of person who is so incompetent, and so insecure that I have to sleep my way up? Do you think I'm a prostitute?" She asked fighting back tears.

"No, of course not, Marsh. That's ridiculous. I don't think anything like that about you, and I never will. That's not what I'm saying, Marsh," He said sighing deeply. "I'm sorry if I'm not making sense." He couldn't even explain to her right now. He had hurt her unintentionally and everything was all wrong.

She cut off his confused murmurs. "My motives are simple Lamont. I happen to think that you're a handsome, intelligent man, although right now I'm rethinking your intelligence." She sighed deeply and softened her tone. "Lamont, you're the kind of man that any woman in her right mind would want, regardless of whether you're the boss or the janitor. Furthermore, Mr. Duffus, can't you see I've always loved you..?" She stopped abruptly. Suddenly she couldn't fight off the tears. She was too embarrassed to stay there or go to her desk, so she bolted to his private bathroom and slammed the door.

He heard her words ring inside his ears, while he sat staring stunned, and wanting to kick himself. What was he doing? She was in love with him. He wanted to tell himself that he had done nothing to encourage those feelings, but he knew that he had always encouraged her.

He recalled all those late nights at the center, when just the two of them had worked together, chatting over coffee. After a grueling day, he had often anticipated, and never refused those great neck massages she gave. He remembered the subtle long glances, and how they often finished each other's sentences.

He realized that they had much in common, and he felt closer to her than he had ever felt to anyone. She knew everything about him, so why was he being so standoffish with her? She's a great friend, a sensational lover, and unlike any female he had ever known.

He cut his thoughts, and walked from his desk to the bathroom, and listened to her soft sobs coming through the door. It bothered him deeply that he had hurt her, and each sob rippled painfully through him. He cursed himself for his abundance of stupidity, and scarcity of understanding.

He was holding back with her because of his horrible experience with Jane's deception, and that was unfair to them both. If he didn't get on with his life and start to trust again, then Jane was in control of his life. He couldn't let that happen.

He shouldn't deny someone who is worthy, just because he once gave his trust to someone who was unworthy. Marcia was nothing like Jane and he trusted her completely, and desired her immensely. At that moment, he only wanted to protect, comfort, and love her.

The more he thought about Marcia, the less vague he became about his feelings for her. He had been confused about what to do so soon after breaking up with Jane, but he realized now that she was special in every way. "Marsh, are you okay?" He asked feebly, listening helplessly to her muffled sobs.

She wasn't just some rebound romance, they had a history together, and he now wanted to preserve that history. He could finally admit to himself what he had been afraid to admit before. He had asked her to come aboard at Cooper Industries not so much because of their friendship, but because she fills a void in his life.

He needed her for many reasons, and the last thing that he wanted was for her to quit. He felt fulfilled and comfortable with her around and now he knew that she was the most important person in his life. He needed to tell her that now.

The loud constant ringing of the telephone interrupted his thoughts and at first he absent mindedly expected Marcia to answer it. Then he realized that she was still in the bathroom bawling because of him. He walked quickly to his desk and picked up the phone. "Hello." It was Hal on the other end. "Already? Man that was fast. Tony's club? So he talked to Carvoni and he agreed? Okay. I'll be there in ten minutes. Bye Hal."

Lamont hung up, wrote a note and slid it under the bathroom door. "Marsh, Sweetheart, I have to go but I'll talk to you when I return. I promise everything will be okay. I understand now. Please, Sweetheart, stop crying. I love you too." He hurried from the office without hearing a reply from her.

Marcia heard his outside office door close and she now tried to pull her together. She thought that she looked a mess as she glanced at herself in the mirror. She straightened her hair and dried her tears. "Don't lose it now girl," She told herself.

She stepped out of the bathroom, and noticed the note on the floor, and picked it up. She could see that Lamont had written it. She picked it up, moved to Lamont's desk, and sat in his chair. The slight scent of his cologne still hung in the air and she savored recent memories of them together. Now her eyes focused on the sheet of paper containing the message that Lamont had scribbled.

Marsh: sorry I hurt you. Things are going to work out. I promise. Trust me. I have an important meeting, so hold down the fort until I return.
Love Ya
Lamont.

She wipes her eyes and read over the note several times. She wants to think positive, but she had been irrational and had made a scene. Now he would probably solve all his problems by firing her.

What had she done? She admonishes herself. Why had she tried to force his hand? Not only was she going to lose him, it was possible that she would lose her job, and not even get any references.

Chapter Forty Eight- Face Off

Lamont briefly forget about Marcia, and headed straight to the Italian Stallion club after leaving the office. He sat across from Carvoni, who sat behind his large desk. He saw only one bodyguard present, and he guessed that Carvoni didn't see him as a threat, in spite of his reputation as a black belt in martial arts. Lamont wasn't here to start trouble, and Carvoni knew this. His black belt in martial arts was useless here and would accomplish nothing. He was only here to talk and not to act.

Carvoni seemed amused, while studying Lamont's grim expression. "So you want to talk do you?" Carvoni asked smugly. "I hope you ain't so foolish, or so arrogant that you think you're gonna talk me out of my shares of stock," Carvoni said, still studying Lamont from his side of the large desk.

Lamont hated being here, and wanted to finish his business as soon as possible, and part company. That's why he had wasted little time getting to the point. Now he wasn't satisfied with Carvoni's response. He had to try and reason with Carvoni, even though he found it to be a difficult task. Carvoni was the lowest form of human species, surrounded by the essence of conspicuous scum. Yet he felt that this meeting was necessary because Carvoni had something that belonged to the Cooper family.

"Mr. Carvoni, I'm willing to pay twice what you paid or twice the peak market value, from the time you obtained possession, whichever is higher. Any way you look at it, that's a free and clear profit. Once again I'm asking you to consider selling them back. "

Carvoni scanned Lamont's features and shot him a smile that seemed to ask: *Are you out of your mind?* Instead he played the role of diplomat. He had nothing to lose. "Hey, no need for formalities here, Lamont. Call me Tony." He paused and look towards the daunting thug standing next to the counter by the window, completely ignoring Lamont. "Vito bring us an espresso."

"No thanks, Vito," Lamont turned slightly to the man Carvoni had spoken to. He turned back to Carvoni. "You didn't answer my question, Mr. Carvoni."

Carvoni chewed on his unlit cigar and looked at Lamont, sighing loudly and shaking his head. "Do you have any idea how long I've planned this? Did you really think that you would come in here and convince me to sell? You really have one colossal ego, Dude." He paused briefly and sighed before continuing.

"Now let me get something straight so you'll have no doubts about my intentions." He stood up behind the desk, stretched his Five feet three inch frame, and came around to the front of the desk and sat. "I now have thirty percent of Cooper Industries. I worked hard to get that stock, Lamont, and there's no way I'm gonna turn around and hand it over to you for any price."

"You call swindling people work? That's not work, Carvoni, that's stealing. That's called dishonesty. I know you setup my brother and sister, and then moved in. I know you're working on a scheme to get the rest. I know all about the hidden camera in Cheryl's apartment and I've informed her already, so that part of your plan is dead. No telling how many other people you've cheated and swindled just to get your feet in the door of Cooper's."

Carvoni was surprised that Lamont knew about the camera, but he kept a straight face in spite of his frustration. He wouldn't give him the satisfaction of knowing that he had foiled a major part of his plan. He smiled without mirth. "You're a funny guy, Lamont. You calling me a thief, and saying I'm dishonest. The only difference between me and so called legitimate businessmen, like you, are our lawyers. And as for your little company, I plan on owning it all now that I've got my feet inside the door. Neither you nor Jake Cooper can stop me from getting what I want, and I will get what I want. And you know why?" He didn't wait for Lamont to answer. "Because like your own Malcolm X once said: I will use any means necessary."

Carvoni stood now as Vito approached with the espresso, and took the cup from his hands. Vito resumed his position of guarding the door. Carvoni took a sip, and then continued to speak. "You see, Lamont, I don't worry about rules because I make my own. I don't worry about people's opinion of me because their opinion is what I say it is, and they jump when I say jump. They don't sigh, belch, laugh loud or fart unless I give the thumbs up. You got that?" He sipped his espresso and gave Lamont a confident glare.

Lamont's sudden inner rage filled him with an urge to grab the little pip-squeak, lift him from the floor, and body slams him into a wall. However, he was a businessman and not a thug, and he was here on a mission of diplomacy. He couldn't let his personal hostility, or his temper effect the outcome. Besides, there's no telling what would happen if he were to take such drastic violent action against this known Mafia Don. Still, his rage didn't prevent him from expressing his inner bitterness towards Carvoni verbally.

"Carvoni, I understand that a man in your position is always seeking more money and more power, but in the past your main source of income has been the rackets and prostitution. Things that don't require so much specific skills and hard work. You got to see that the sacrifices required in business wouldn't be worth your free time, and you might even lose revenue."

"Are you saying that I'm not up to running a corporation?" He didn't give Lamont a chance to answer. "Are you calling me stupid or something? You're real sassy, you know that boy."

It took all of Lamont's will power to calm down right now, but he had to think of Jake and the company. "I'm not saying or insinuating any such thing. I'm just saying that running a company would be a great departure from the business that you're in, and you might not like all the extra time and work that's necessary to keep it going. And if you don't like business, let's face it; you're not going to be any good at it, which means that you're going to lose money, maybe even lose the business itself."

"Look, Lamont, I can see that you're one of them educated Niggers. I see what you're doing with them two dollar words, but you can't talk me out of this. I'm not stupid, I'm not lazy, and I've made up my mind. Besides I can hire people to do the work for me. In case you didn't know, I'm pretty good at doing that."

"Why Carvoni? Why Cooper Industries?"

Carvoni wore an expression that seemed to say: I'm-glad-you-asked-that-question, then held up one hand and counted off with the other. "That's easy. One, because it's there, and two, because I got my foot in the door already. And three, if a black man can run it I can too. Let's face it; you spooks are never really tightly organized and always easy to unravel." He chuckled. "You're just a bunch of pretenders who think with your johnsons and are always ripe for the picking. So why not?"

Carvoni's last remarks irritated Lamont past the point of holding his temper in check. He suddenly felt a rush of nervous energy and nothing could hold back what he was about to say to this little Napoleon-like creep. "Look here you power hungry little bastard," Lamont said twisting his face into an expression of total disgust. "Your stubby little foot might be in the door, but your crooked little ass will never cross the threshold, I promise you that."

"Maybe you won't have anything to say about it." Carvoni shot back, matching Lamont glare for glare.

Lamont wanted to crush him. "You don't impress me, and your squeaky dwarf's roar sure as hell doesn't scare me. There are ways to deal with your kind, it's been done, and if you pursue this, I will dedicate my life to toppling your greasy little garlic saturated ass."

Carvoni's mouth was frozen open by the mere shock of Lamont's boldness. "Who the hell do you think you're talking to, boy? I'll have your black ass. You have no idea of the misery I can bring you. You got too much attitude."

Even though Lamont realized that he might have gone a bit too far, he couldn't stop the diarrhea of the mouth that now took control. "First of all I don't think any observer in their right mind would have no difficulty in establishing which of us most resembles a boy. Secondly, the name is Mr. Savage to you, Half Pint. I'm not worried about your threats because that works both ways. I might get to you first," Lamont said, then as he stood. His attention suddenly focused on Vito, who put his hand inside his jacket. Lamont realized that the thug stood ready to pull his weapon and he was suddenly in defense mode.

He was confident that he could pulverize this crooked little bastard and his lone henchmen easily, but the consequences would affect more than just himself. He couldn't risk that. He calmed down and tried to find the voice of reason again. "Look, Carvoni, you can understand that I'm a little upset. My father worked hard to establish this company and naturally I want to see it continue."

"All things come to an end." Carvoni's voice was ice cold, his own anger still raging. He wasn't used to gettin back talk from any one.

Lamont was sure that he had just blown whatever chance there might have been. He was a fool to think that this creep would listen to reason, and he had been an even bigger fool to go off like that. Still he wasn't backing off, because Carvoni was an insatiable pig. "Okay, I can see I'm wasting my time." He looked from Carvoni to Vito, whose hand was still inside his jacket. "I might not win but I'm gonna fight you all the way. Be prepared for a fight."

"In that case, maybe I should get rid of your smart ass right now, and save myself some needless battles. Ain't too much fight left in the old man, and once you're outta the picture, those soft ass little brats will fold up like a dollar store umbrella in a compactor." He looked directly into Lamont's eyes with an icy threatening glaze. Lamont knew that Carvoni was a power hungry little bastard, who would do anything to get what he wanted. Still Lamont couldn't show any sign of relenting. "People know I'm here. You'd never get away with it."

"Maybe, maybe not." He smiled slyly. "But in any case it won't be today. That would make me a real bad host wouldn't it?"

"You are a bad host Carvoni. The case is closed on that one." Lamont brushed by him, like a quick graceful cat, bumping him purposely as he headed out the door. He felt the sudden rush of adrenaline, and realized that if he had remained in that room with Carvoni another second, he might have tried to take him and his henchman apart. Then he *would* be in serious trouble.

He had to find another way to get Carvoni's stock, or Carvoni would eventually end up with control. That bastard had Ruth and JJ's stock, but not Cheryl and Ann's shares, and he had to make sure that he didn't, because if he did, it was over.

After putting a distance between himself and Carvoni's place, Lamont felt overwhelmed. He didn't know what else to do in order to stop Carvoni. He would talk to Jake later, but he wouldn't tell him about his disastrous meeting with Carvoni.

Even though his visit to Carvoni had put things in perspective for him, it had also put Carvoni on alert. Carvoni now knew where things stood, and Lamont prayed that his visit hadn't made matters worse. Would Carvoni now speed up his timetable, and force Lamont to do the same? Lamont had lost the element of surprise, but it was his mistake and he had to correct it.

Although Lamont wasn't responsible for Carvoni's acquisition of shares, he felt the need to resolve the problem. It was dangerous and uncomfortable that Carvoni had so many shares, and just having him as a major stockholder could eventually be disastrous, even if he doesn't gain control. He felt frustrated and fresh out of ideas, and he couldn't shake the haunting fear, that Jake's company was facing debacle.

Chapter Forty Nine-
The-Sibling

Tony Carvoni was still smiling and gloating about the impending takeover of Cooper industries after Lamont left. He had them on the run and he was ready to move in. He would force everybody's hand with his next move. Once Bennie and the boys returned he would put a contract out on Lamont, and get his smart ass out of the picture. Nobody talks to him like that in lives.

His smile disappeared when his sister Marie walked in the door. Even though there was no way that she could know for sure, she might suspect that he was responsible for the death of her lesbian lover, Amanda Vel Haus. His guys had done a great job to make it look like a murder-suicide.

He felt at ease now because he observed sadness and not anger in his sister's expression. Instead, he was delighted at the aromas emitting from the covered basket she carried as she entered his office. It seemed that nothing had changed, he thought.

Since he openly rejected her life style, she constant tried to bribe him with food. Since she was here with the basket, he assumed that she knew nothing about his part in her lover's death, and he was pleased. She was the world's greatest cook without a doubt, even better than their mother. He loved everything she made for him.

It might seem strange bringing food to a restaurant, but the Italian Stallion was a restaurant in name only. It served mainly as Carvoni's headquarters and pickup spot for his prostitutes. They only served grilled food, and booze, and it was common knowledge that Carvoni was a ravenous eater.

Maria's attempts at bribing him with her great dishes had become a habit, and while he enjoyed her great dishes, there was no way he would allow her to embarrass the family. The best he could do was of-fer her a job at his place, but she refused to give up her own business.

He paid her for doing special dishes for family outings, but other than that, he had nothing to do with her. He would never allow her to attend any family functions or bring one of her freak girlfriends. Things might have been different if she wasn't so open with her freaky behavior. She seemed proud to be a dyke. Even now she was dressed in those washed out jeans and plaid shirt, and her beautiful head of lustrous hair was so short that it destroyed any illusion of femininity.

Now his thoughts settled on the aroma wafting from the dish, and attacking his olfactory senses, and compelling him to salivate. He recognized the odor of his favorite dish right away. She had out done herself and his toes curl at the thought of her culinary magic. He observed her smile as she came closer. She was continuing to try to get on his good side, and he guessed that it was because she wanted to attend the family reunion, at the end of the month.

He loved her, but he had to practice tough love as long as she was confused about her sex. She had to choose between the ones she loved and the life-style that she lived. She had to decide if she wanted to be with family or freaks, and he was sure that being hard on her would force her to change.

Now he concentrated on the smells and their overwhelming promise. He had to give her an **A** for effort and in the long run, her persistence was beneficial to him. He got to test all of her great food with no strings attached. She was trying to wear him down with all this good food and frankly he had been deceitful about it. He had given her the impression that he might reconsider, but he had no such intentions. "HMMM, is that delightful smell your famous homemade spaghetti sauce?" He asked.

"Of course," she said with a smile. "And with my very special brown sugar garlic butter bread."

"What's the occasion sis?"

Maria smiled and sat the huge basket of food on his desk. "No special reason. I made more than I needed for my customers, and I didn't want to serve it as leftovers. I can't eat it all, or I'll blow up to be a queen size Barbie." She looked around. "Where are Bennie and the guys?"

"Angelo and Bennie went to do some collecting and Vito went to get my cigars," Carvoni said, uncovering the dish with a wide smile. "Nobody cooks like you, Sis,'" he said with a pause and looked at her suspiciously. "I know what you're up to."

She anticipated what he was about to say. "Oh Tony, I'm not trying to bribe you anymore. I'm through begging, and don't worry, I'm not coming to the family reunion if you don't want me there. I've accepted that I'll always be an outcast, and I have to live with that." Her eyes teared up now. "Amanda's sudden death has shown me that life is too short to for constant drama. I was feeling depressed after hearing about..." She cut her words and fought back tears now. Then she changed the subject. "Any way I always cook a lot when I'm depressed.

"Yeah I heard about what happened with that chick. That's the one you were involved with wasn't it?" Tony checked her face for a reaction, with a clandestine glance, and notice her sad look. "That was something the way that husband went off like that," he said quietly.

"I still can't believe she's gone. She had planned to leave him and go away with me. He must have found out and." Abruptly she changed the subject. "Any way I started cooking and couldn't stop. I got enough to feed an army for a week." She took a piece of garlic roll and dipped it into the sauce and chewed it slowly. The glazed looked in her eyes suggested that her mind was elsewhere.

Tony didn't know what to say. He wasn't about to be a hypocrite, by pretending to sympathize about her lover's death. He disapproved and he stood by that. "Well you know, Sis, sometimes things happen for the best."

"Yeah maybe you're right," she said, fighting back a sob. She pulled a handkerchief from her purse, and then wiped her eyes and mouth. "Well the only thing that can be done now is to make sure that she gets a decent burial."

Tony decided to change the subject. "You'll be alright."

"Yeah, I know I will." She gave him a hard look and sighed.

"Look I know what you're about to say and..."

"No Tony, you don't. I told you I'm not gonna beg. You don't accept my life-style, and I'm okay with it. I would love to have the family's blessing, but that's not going to happen, so I'm moving on."

"You're calm about it, and that's a good thing."

"Yeah, well it's time to accept that some things will never change."

"That's a dramatic turnaround. The last time I saw you, you were so pissed."

"Well, you had your goons throw me out of my own mother's birthday party. I felt that I had a right to be there, and I was hurt because I thought I was family too. Hell, Ma won't even talk to me. The last time we spoke it was clear that she wanted nothing to do with me."

Tony couldn't respond because he was eating the spaghetti like there was a time limit to finish it. "Hey I had nothing to do with that. That's between you and ma."

She watched him in silence briefly. "Actually you did Tony. You convinced mom to." She couldn't finish the thought so she changed the subject. "But I forgive you both, even if you don't forgive or accept me."

Carvoni wiped his mouth, took a breath, and then sipped the wine from his glass. He felt awkward at what he was about to say. "Look, Maria, I didn't approve of ..." He didn't finish the sentence. "I'm.. You know. Sorry for your lost anyway. But, like I said, maybe that's a sign you need to heed. Maybe it's a message from God that he doesn't want you involved in that kind of life."

"Oh Tony." She shook her head exasperated. "When have you ever cared about what God wanted? And I don't know what kind of message you think Amanda's death could be, but I'm not buying it. It was just something unfortunate that happened, and unfortunate things happen whether gay and straight people. That nerdy husband was suspicious, and I guess he just flipped in the end. Those nerdy timid little bastards always pull this kind of shit," Marie said raising her voice slightly in anger. "He should have just killed himself and left her alone, damn him."

Convinced now that she had no suspicions about his involvement, Tony breathed a sigh of relief and took another fork full to his mouth. He purposely changed the direction of the conversation. "This is great, Sis, I think this is your best yet. You've really out done yourself. And this garlic bread is about to give me an orgasm."

"Glad you like it. Bon appetite," she said, seemly amused.

"I still say there was a reason why you two aren't together...."

"Tony, please don't preach. It's not your strong suit," she said moving away.

"Okay, okay. No more lectures."

She turned to him misty eyed. "Still I wished that we were close like we use to be, but don't worry, I know that won't happen. You've made your feelings clear."

"Well damn, Sis, can you blame me. An Italian beauty like you who is such a great cook should be a wife and mother, and giving Ma grandchildren. Besides, no woman can spit a baby." He held up a fork full of the food and shook his head. "It should be a law that a woman, who can cook this good, must have a man."

"Every female doesn't want to be wives and mothers and at the service of men."

"Why not? Why wouldn't you? See that ain't natural right there."

"Did you ever stop to think what I want? Do you even care what I want?" She asked slightly annoyed.

"I thought about it and you know what? I think that you don't know what you want. Some way you got mixed up, and now you're all confused about what you really want. I think you can be helped though."

"If you mean that you think I can be straight then that's where you're wrong, Tony. I can't be helped, even if I wanted to. Neither one of us can be helped now." She gave him a mysterious sad look.

"I don't need help. I'm straight. What are you talking about?" He asked with an annoyed scowl.

"I know you're straight. That's not what I...Oh never mind." She changed the subject. "Besides, you and Carla have the boys, so Ma will just have to be satisfied with at least three grand children." She stood and gave him a sad look. "Good-bye Tone."

"Good-bye? You going somewhere, Marie? You talk like we're not gonna see each other again."

"Would you even care?"

Tony noticed the obvious sad look in her dark radiant eyes. "Of course I care, you're still my sister. And you're a great cook." Tony thought that she looked suicidal, but what could *he* do? He had tried his way but apparently that wasn't the answer. He didn't know any other way and he didn't have the patience to learn. Maybe she was beyond help. He had to let her go. He wasn't going to interfere any more. Perhaps it was better to just leave well enough alone, and let her continue to be the person that she wanted to be. "Good-bye, Sis, and good luck. I'm sure gonna miss your cooking."

"Thanks," she said sadly, and walked out the door fighting back her tears, knowing that this would be the last time she would ever see her brother. Shortly she sat behind the wheel of her car feeling sad that their relationship had ended with tragic lies.

Marie knew that Tony was responsible for Amanda's death and she had been unable to forgive him. She had been talking with Amanda on the telephone when Bennie and the others entered the house. She had heard everything, and she had recognized her cousin Bennie's voice during the ruckus. She recalled his cold words. "Tony said to do them both and make it look like murder-suicide."

Tony was a liar and a schemer. Still, she knew that it would be futile to confront him about his actions, because he would never admit the truth. Her brother was a miserable creepy mobster who hurt people and escaped justice for his deeds.

She had made sure that he wouldn't escape this time, because she knew his Achilles heel and had forged forward to pierce it. She had served him her own brand of justice in a tasty tempting meat sauce. She knew that his insatiable gluttony knew no caution and would never resist food, especially from her.

It was fitting that his greed had become the instrument of his demise as it so often did with evil men like Tony. He got exactly what he deserved and she wasn't sorry. "Bon Appétit, motherfucker. And may your dirty little ass rot in Hell." The words came with a rush of jubilation and relief as she sped away from the Italian Stallion knowing that the world had seen the last of Tony Carvoni.

Chapter Fifty-
Termination

It wasn't until later that evening that Lamont managed to calm himself down. The encounter in Carvoni's office earlier had left him nursing an unhealthy rage. He had other things that needed to be done and couldn't spend much time worrying about how he would handle the likes of the little Napoleon-like mobster. He didn't have the stock he needed and therefore Cooper Industries was safe for now.

He had invited Marcia to meet him in his own apartment, since he had moved back after Jake returned home. Jake had invited him to stay longer, but he was more comfortable in his own new place. He liked the simple atmosphere provided by his place, which was just right for a private get together between Marcia and himself. His feelings about her were clear and it was time to end her suffering and remove their unresolved issues.

Marcia arrived at Lamont's apartment, not knowing what to expect from him, but she wasn't expecting good news. She stood there at the door, reluctant to ring the bell, but finally forced herself to follow through.

Lamont opened the door immediately, wearing a strange look that made her uncomfortable. "Hi, Lamont." She tried to make her voice sound light and nonchalant, but didn't pull it off.

"Hello Marsh." He smiled timidly. "You look good." He stepped aside and allowed her to enter, and she sat on the couch, and looked towards him. He also sat on the couch a few inches from her. Marcia sensed that he was unusually serious and guarded. Apparently there was something heavy on his mind. It wouldn't surprise her if he had sworn off women altogether. Many men have taken such actions once they'd been burned by bitches like Jane.

She renewed her dislike for Jane, because if Lamont now distrusted all women, it was Jane's fault. What if he never trusted women again, herself included? What would she do then? Now more than ever, she regretted failing to whipped that worthless skank's ass when she had the chance. Damn her.

Jane wasn't worth thinking about right now, and she concentrated on Lamont, wondering why it was so urgent that he see her tonight. She remembered her words earlier, and was prepared to for whatever news Lamont was about to break, even if he fired her. "You said that you wanted to talk. Well here I am," she said, nervously, then spread her arms out and dropped them at her side. "I assume it's about us right? You want to know why I acted like a damn fool today."

"Yes Marsh, it's about us and what happened today, but I also know why you acted like you did."

"Let me guess," Marcia realized that her voice was on the verge of cracking, but she continued speaking anyway. "You want to put me down easy right? You're gonna tell me that it's not wise for us to get involved in a relationship, because you're my boss, and you don't have feelings for me."

Marcia hated herself for even bringing up that possibility. She didn't want that thought in his head. She was saying the things that she thought he was about to say to her. "Hell you probably are thinking about firing me as your assistant." She half expected him to protest such a thought as absurd, but his facial expression confirmed her fear. "Oh my God. I'm right aren't I?"

Lamont sighed deeply, stood and moved away from the couch. They were both feeling tension. "Look Marsh."

"Damn it Lamont. Answer me. Am I going to be working as you your assistant or not?"

Lamont hesitated and looked her in the eyes. He sighed deeply and twisted his mouth to the side. "Well, no."

Suddenly his words faded out and her head was filled with constant ringing. She gasped, "Lamont how could you be so..." She was overwhelmed and unable to form a complete sentence. Her legs went numb and rubbery, and the floor was suddenly rushing towards her face. She heard Lamont's voice call out her name from far away, and everything turned black.

Lamont moved quickly to prevent her from hitting her head on the floor, then picked her up and laid her on the couch. He then dashed to the kitchen, and returned instantly with a glass of water. "Go on drink it," he urged. "You okay?"

Marcia looked around, groggy and puzzled as to her whereabouts. Then the look of recognition flashed on her face. "Oh," she groaned as she sat up.

"Easy, Marsh," Lamont said and forced her to lie down.

"No, get away from me, Lamont. I never thought."

"Chill for a minute and listen would you?"

"I've heard all I need to. You had your fun, and now you're ready to cast me aside." She was incoherent, and unable to speak cohesively. "I never thought you were."

"Damn it would you listen to me? Would you just stop jumping to conclusions and just listen? Can you do that please?"

Marcia was surprised and a little frightened that Lamont had raised his voice at her. "Yo..You don't have to yell," she said timidly, while pouting openly.

"I'm sorry," he said more calmly. "You're right. I apologize for yelling, but you're jumping to conclusions and I need you to hear what I have to say. So please just listen."

She folded her arms and gave him a sideways glance, sighing deeply. "I'm listening," she said, trying to maintain her anger.

Lamont began. "Look, I was green and I felt like a sacrificial lamb when I first came to the outreach center. But I got lucky because you were there for me, and I probably couldn't have gotten anything done without you.

"Greg lacked the total dedication necessary, so you were my life line in a sense." He paused and looked directly at her. "Then there was Jane. You probably won't believe this, or even worse you'll probably think I was stupid when I say this." He sighed briefly and continued. "Frankly I was star struck with Jane. I apologize to you a million times for that, because I fail to see what I really wanted because of that."

"You thought she was a star so I guess that made me what?" Marcia asked timidly. "Chop liver?"

"Frankly I don't know. I was like an enchanted child I guess. Jane knew how to push all my buttons and she was relentless as we now know. I hadn't planned to become engaged, but I was such a wimp. I let her blind and bully me." He paused. "I guess what I'm saying Marsh is that I was so involved with winning her and being in her world that I failed to face reality or see the real Jane.

In turn I also failed to see the real you. I constantly denied what I knew was inevitable and I can't think of any sane reason why I did that. Jane wasn't what I wanted, and I so many doubts constantly in my head."

He threw his hands up as if he expected her to interrupt. "I know I know. Why did I get engaged? Like I said, I got stupid with Jane. Blame it on society, peer pressure, confusion or just plain hot sex. I only know that something nagged at me throughout that relationship and I instinctively knew that something wasn't right."

"It didn't seem that way to me. You seemed so happy and you two..."

"I know, but guess what, when I had something buggin' me and something to get off my chest, I never confided in Jane." He reached out and grabbed her hands. "You were my solid connection to the real world. You gave me comfort in those times, Marsh, when I wasn't blind, dumb, and infatuated by Jane's star quality. Hell she was hot and on TV," he added sarcastically. "It was an ego trip to know that I was getting down with a local TV star. I didn't realize that I was so shallow. But I found out that Jane cheated and suddenly all the blurry unclear logic was erased and I saw her for who she was. My feelings for her have died completely, so I'm sure that they never had any solid base."

"How can you be so sure now, Lamont?" Marcia shrugged.

"Because like I said my feelings for her died instantly, and real feelings of love are deeper, durable, and die harder than that. There's no chance of resuscitation, because now I have you." He came to within a few inches of her, and peered into her eyes.

"Now that we've been together, I know beyond a doubt exactly what I want, and need. I'm in love with you, Marcia Dawson, and I don't plan on wasting one more minute fighting something so obviously inevitable. You're just so easy to be in love with that I see why the expression is falling in love."

Marcia's stunned eyes locked with his and all the anger that she had tried to build up fizzled flat. Her glistening eyes gazed and her expression was an uncontrolled smile. She tried to say a thousand words at once, but the only thing that came out was, "Oh Lamont." She went into his arms, speaking his name over and over, holding him tightly.

"Marsh," Lamont grunted, but she didn't acknowledge his words, so he called out her name once more.

She finally acknowledged. "Yes, Lamont darling?"

"Loosen up a bit, you're stopping my circulation," He said jokingly.

"I don't want to ever lose you," she said.

"You're never going to, unless you squeeze me to death."

She ignored his sarcasm and pulled back from him, and looked into his eyes. "But Lamont, why are you firing me?" She asked.

"You're look so cute when stretch your eyes like that." He said teasingly and ignoring her question."

"Stop, beating around the bush. Answer my question."

"I never said I was firing you. I said you would no longer be working at Cooper Industries as my assistant, and you won't"

"I..I don't understand. Wh..what are you saying then? What are you talking about?"

"Actually I'm saying, Dear One, that you're too valuable to be an assistant. So I'm promoting you to executive consultant."

"Executive consultant? You mean I'm not fired? You're giving me a promotion?"

"Yeah, and a raise goes with that. Like I just said, you're too smart and too valuable to be a glorified secretary."

"But what if some body complains that you're playing favorites?"

"I'm sure they will, but I know you'll justify your promotion by doing a good job."

"Oh Lamont honey, I could kiss you," she said beaming with joy.

"What do you mean you could?" He asked playfully and pointed to his lips. "There better be some hot lips here before I count to three," he said puckering his lips out comically. "One, two.."

"My pleasure," she said and moved to him before he finished counting. She covered his mouth with tiny baby kisses. "You're the sweetest man, and I'm the luckiest girl on this planet. Thank you, thank you, and thank you."

"You're welcome honey and you deserve it," he said with a glaring look in his eyes, and now his mood became serious and he pulled her closer. "What was I thinking? You were right there under my nose all this time and I was unconscious. You're perfect."

"Yeah I know. Ain't you glad you finally came out of your coma?" She batted her eyelashes, and patted the back of her hair playfully. "I forgive you. Men are sometimes blinded by a flash of light, made by trash in flight."

"Well I'm awake now and that won't happen again."

"It better not." She kissed him more passionately. "Now make love to me, Lamont." She whispered hoarsely into his ear.

"I'm already ahead of you, sexy." He pulled her closer and kissed her hard, sending his tongue inside her willing mouth. "Making love to you makes me want to laugh and sing all at once."

Shortly, they lost themselves in layers of sexual bliss. Marcia cried out joyously, and Lamont expressed the waves of equal pure pleasure surround him. "You're not leaving here tonight, you know that," Lamont said in a voice thick with passion in the midst of their torrid love making. Her answer had been to hold on tighter, and lose her self in the complete bliss that she had now come to expect.

Lamont woke earlier than usual the next morning, and feeling hornier than ever, while spooning Marcia, who purred passionately. He didn't understand how Marcia left him feeling so drained one minute and perpetually horny the next. The previous night's passion should have been enough, but now he was in a full state of readiness as he kissed the back of her neck, and moved closer. He could hear her low lusty groans that signaled her awareness to his rising passion.

"Oh yes," she responded as she pushed her backside up against him. "OOH, Lamont, Baby. You feel so good, ummph." Marcia was wide awake now.

"You feel gooder," he said with a laugh.

They made love, and afterwards Marcia fell asleep while Lamont took a shower. Shortly he returned to bed and flipped on the television. Instantly he heard Carvoni's name mentioned, now he focused his attention on the screen with some annoyance. He studied the image of the Italian Stallion, and the crowd of reporters, photographers and spectators gathered outside. Was he being haunted by Carvoni, he wondered. It seemed that lately Carvoni was everywhere, taunting him. Yet in spite of his dislike for the unpleasant little mobster, he was compelled to look and listen with interest to the news story with morbid curiosity. Something about the announcer's tone alerted Lamont that the story contain some element of tragedy.

A recent picture of Carvoni popped up on the TV screen and Lamont was confused by the commentator's words. He thought that he was misinterpreting the narrator's words so he listened more closely, and waited to hear the correction. The story was repeated and more pictures of Carvoni popped up on the TV screen.

Marcia turned over and observed Lamont's taunt expression. Her smile was replaced with concern. "What's wrong baby?" She asked.

"Wait a minute, Marsh," He said making a shushing gesture with his finger to his mouth. "I want to hear this."

She turned and squinted at the screen. "What's going on?" She asked in a hushed whisper now.

Lamont listened a few minutes more, and then turned to her. "Carvoni, the Mobster. If that story is correct, he's dead."

"Carvoni?" Marcia was puzzled. "Who is Carvoni?"

"He's a mob guy," he stopped in mid sentence. "Never mind, it's complicated, but according to that news report, he was found dead in his office yesterday. They think he might have had a heart attack. "I was there yesterday," Lamont said to himself. "I need to see if this information is correct. This is a miracle, I can't believe this. I got to go check this out."

"Lamont, what's going on? Who is this Carvoni? Why are you happy about some one's death?" She turned to face him as she asked this question. "I've never seen this side of you."

"Sorry baby, I know it's morbid and I'm not happy to see anybody die, but frankly it might take a lot of pressure off of Cooper Industries." He looked into her eyes. "Baby, I know you don't know what role he has played in the life of Cooper Industries, but I promise to tell you everything after I find out if this will change anything. Hopefully it will change things for the better." He was up from the bed. "I got to go."

"You're leaving now?" She said obviously disappointed.

"Sorry, babe, we will spend more time in bed, I promise." He kissed her hurriedly and moved from the bed to dress. "I'll make it up to you in spades later."

"You better."

He scribbled something on a piece of note book paper and handed it to her. "Here's my IOU. Now you got it in writing."

"You crazy man. Get out of here." She giggled like a school girl, and felt happier than she had ever been.

"Why don't you take the day off and go get some of your things and bring them here. I would love for you to spend a few nights."

"That sounds good to me. You're sure about that?"

"Yes I'm sure. I'm sure about many things now.

"Okay whatever you say my love," she said as she kissed him and watched him leave.

Lamont arrived at his office an hour later, and after calling Jake to inform him about the latest event, he called a meeting with Lawrence Preston, Lucas Shepherd and Hal Atkins. He didn't know how Carvoni's death would affect his shares, and he needed to discuss strategy with these three men.

He needed Preston's advice about the legal aspects, and Shepherd could speculation about the possible heir to Carvoni's empire. Hal could also get information about the workings of Carvoni's organization by talking directly to Two Martin. He could surely pick up some bits and pieces.

"Gentlemen," Lamont said, looking at the three sets of eyes trained on him, in the small conference room, "I need your expertise. As you know Carvoni is dead, and while he is no longer a threat to take over, we've still got problems." Lamont looked directly at Lucas. "Lucas who's most likely to replace Carvoni, and what do you know about him?"

"Well I hadn't really given it much thought. For some reason I thought that Carvoni would be a constant thorn," Lucas said almost apologetically. "But right now his chief Capo and henchmen would probably fill in on a temporary basis."

"That would be Benito D'Amato," Hal chimed in. "Alias Bennie the Creep. He's Carvoni's cousin and he's likely to take over.

"That name sounds familiar." Lamont said, pondering to himself briefly, before turning to Hal. "What do you know about him, Hal? Is he as ambitious as Carvoni?" Lamont asked.

"I don't know for sure, but most of those guys are. I can sure find out," Hal said with a pause. "Do you think he might be more reasonable and less ambitious, and maybe easier to deal with?"

"Anything's possible." Lamont said hopefully. "If he's a henchman like Lucas says, he might not share Carvoni's ambition to venture into big business. It's also possible that that the other mob families don't know about his project, because of past disputes. If that's true, then we won't worry about them getting involved."

"Hal I need you to check with Two Martin specifically and get an update on Carvoni's operation from the inside. He does owe you right?"

"Yeah me and Two cool. It's his ex partner, Eye Ball Willie, who's still holding a grudge.

"Okay then." He paused then looked to Lucas eagerly. "Lucas check out this henchman's past, maybe there's some way we can make a deal with this guy. Jake doesn't care what it costs. We got to get that stock, and this might be our one chance, if we move fast," Lamont said.

He turned to Preston who had been sitting quietly taking it all in. "Preston I need you to find a loophole and standby with a plan B. We need to know if we have any legal roads and."

"That's going to be impossible, Lamont," Preston said, raising his arms. "Even if Carvoni did something illegal we can't prove it and since he's deceased we can't bring charges against him."

"I know," Lamont said depressed. "Still just do some research. You never know."

"Okay then you got it."

The meeting with the three men was over in less than an hour, and they all agreed that Lamont had to regain that stock, even at an excessive price. To accomplish that, he had to convince the new mob boss to sell and the question now was; would the new guy be willing to sell? Lamont realized that his only option right now was to wait and see if Carvoni's death would create positive result for Cooper Industries.

His mind was in a cloud about the problems he faced, and he didn't hear the door open at first. Now he became aware of another presence in the room and assuming that it might be Marcia, he spun around in the huge executive chair. "So you decided to come to work after I gave you the day off, and..." He cut off his words, and was stunned, upon seeing the tall male figure standing just inside the door. His heart was pounding like the hooves of run away race horses, and butterflies ran free inside his gut.

He knew that this meeting was inevitable, and he had wondered how he would react when it finally occurred. He didn't have to think about it for long, because his anger erupts with sudden aggression as he looked into the smirking face of Greg Jones.

"**Greg, what the hell are** you doing here? You have no business here so please leave." Lamont's anger had nothing to do with Jane. He was angry because Greg had been an underhanded, untrustworthy, two faced snake. He and Jane had made a fool of him and she was Greg's burden now. She was bad news and it was good riddance.

"Why are you here Greg?" Lamont repeated. He and Greg were far from being friends, and any chance of that happening had been totally destroyed. That was okay with Lamont because he didn't need a lot of friends, only a sidekick. Some guys needed a posse, and a multitude of admirers.

Hal was Lamont's sidekick in spite of the fact that they had little in common. It was just one of those things where opposites worked well together. Hal wasn't a spit and polish sterling character, but he was a quality friend. Hal had made a living doing things slightly outside the law, in the past, but he was different now. Hal fell short on some things, but he was a proven, loyal and trustworthy friend.

Lamont looked into Greg's face. "I'm gonna ask you once more, Greg. What do you want here?"

"I want to tell you in person that you're a dirty low down son of a bitch."

Lamont looked at him as if he had just presented him with an impossible riddle to solve. "Oh I'm low down? After what you did? You must be here looking for a fight. Is that it?" Lamont was aware of the smell of alcohol on Greg's breath when he moved closer. "You been drinking this early or are you coming off a binge from the night before?"

"Ain't none of your damn business what I do," Greg said raising the volume of his voice. "You ain't my boss and you never controlled me, or stopped me from doing what I wanted. I took off when I felt like it and worked when I felt like it." He cast Lamont a sly grin. "And wore your fiancée's ass out," he said with a short laugh. "That was so satisfying in so many ways. You were paying me and I was laying your woman." He broke out into hysterical laughter.

"So is that why you came up here? You wanna rub my nose in the fact that my ex is trash, and that you're a two faced low life trash collector? You really are a piece of shit without class, honor or morals. Oh you got me good. Greg. Feel better now?" Lamont said sarcastically and began to clap his hands.

"I applaud you. You won yourself a real prize. A blue ribbon slut. You did good, and your momma gotta be feeling real proud. So why don't you leave me along and go enjoy your prize?" Lamont asked, giving him a cold stare, and curling his top lip. "But go sober up first. You look and smell like a homeless piece of shit."

Greg's face twisted into an angry scowl. "Don't play high and mighty with me. You sneaky bastard, you got me fired cause you got all bent outta shape when I took your lady. You got pissed and went to Bob Pierce. I know you did."

"What?" Lamont twisted his mouth and sighed impatiently. "Earth to Greg. The job was temporary, Greg remember?"

"That ain't got shit to do with him putting somebody else from outta town in the same temporary job. Then they just let me go."

"Well I'm not surprised; everybody knew that you were a lazy shiftless bastard to begin with." Lamont hunched his shoulders. "What did you expect? Nobody's that blind. You didn't like to show up, and you never worked when you did show up."

"I did what I had to do. That job didn't take a hell of a lot of concentration, it wasn't rocket science."

"No, but you had to show up and do something."

"No, they were watching me. You told Pierce that I was a goof off didn't you?" Greg inched around to Lamont's side of the desk.

"You are a goof off Greg, and you're not even good at that. You didn't want that job anyway, so what's this all about? Did Jane cheat on you already? Are you pissed about that, and now you're here looking for a fight? I don't have anything to do with you, Jane or Pierce. My guess is that your work was sloppy and incompetent, and it didn't take long for Bob Pierce to see that you're worthless. So why don't you go sober up and tighten up your Resume?"

"Or what rich faggot? What the hell you gonna do? Whip my ass?" Greg got into a stance. "You think you the only one who knows that Karate shit? I got a black belt too, and I was top in my class."

"I got better things to do than to fight you, Greg."

"Ha. You punk ass fag! This job got you all soft, just like a little bitch. You probably gonna call your boyfriends in security on me ain't you? That's what you sissy ass motherfuckers do. I always did think you walked kinda funny, and got irritable every twenty eight days."

"I'm not gonna repeat myself." Lamont's jaw worked, and a prominent vein was present in his forehead. "Are you going on your own power or not?"

"Yeah, I am," Greg said, while throwing a punch to Lamont's jaw, catching him off guard. "But first I'm gon whip your soft ass," Greg smirked.

Lamont saw stars briefly but regained his composure. Greg was looking for trouble, and Lamont had no thoughts about calling security. Drunk or not he was done taking Greg's taunting and verbal abuse. It was time that he and Greg had it out. "Okay Greg, you want a fight, you got it."

Lamont charged into Greg and wrestled him to the floor. He delivered a couple of hard blows to Greg's midsection before he could recover. He hopped to his feet and into his fighter's stance along with Greg. He ripped into Greg with combination punches that caught him by surprise. Greg was hurt but he countered, and scrambled away to regain his balance. Lamont closed in and threw a lightning fast combination to Greg's head and mid section, hoping to end this battle quickly. Greg was either too stubborn or too drunk to go down. Instead he charged Lamont head first.

Greg's anger caused him to lose his equanimity and fight smarts. Lamont tried to use that to his advantage as he sidestepped Greg's charge, and chopped him across the back of the neck. The blow wasn't as effective as he anticipated, and it only angered Greg. Greg suddenly spun and charged throwing several hard blows that connected with Lamont's jaw and mid section. Lamont nearly went down, but he was more angry than hurt.

Greg had played possum and Lamont had let his guard down, which allowed Greg to set him up for that basic sucker combo. He had made the mistake of assumption, and Greg had made him pay. Apparently, the alcohol in Greg's system wasn't affecting his acquired reflexes. Lamont knew that he had to fight Greg with full concentration.

Greg saw Lamont stagger from his blows and overconfidence crowded his actions. "Now I'm gon' whup your rich little punk chump ass. I told you I was head of my martial arts class. Hell not even that teacher could take me on my worse day." He moved in like a stalker about to pounce on its conquered helpless prey. He threw two more combinations to Lamont's head and midsection, and saw Lamont's knees buckle. He felt a rush of warm self satisfaction deep inside his gut, and thought that he could move in and finish him.

Lamont had taken a clue from Greg and now he played possum. He knew that Greg would become overconfident, and then he would have him just where he wanted him. One more step, he said silently to himself, while watching Greg's feet come closer. He waited to make his moves. *Right now*, he said to himself as he stepped towards him, planted his feet, and shot two quick hard combinations to Greg's face and head. He then locked into a flurry of punches that ended with a powerful solid uppercut to Greg's jaw, which sent him sprawling backwards.

Greg lost his balance and landed on the floor a few feet away. He shook his head as if he was trying to regain his memory. He was in a stupor, and at first it seemed that his anger was gone. Suddenly his raged returned and he glared at Lamont with cold eyes. "You asshole, I'm gonna kill you," he hissed, while reaching inside his pocket and pulled out a long switchblade knife. "As much as it would give me great pleasure to tear your ass apart with my hands, I don't have time." He rushed swiftly towards Lamont, holding the knife tightly.

Lamont removed his jacket, wrapped it around his arm, and took his stance. He could se that Greg was filled with an angry frenzy, and Lamont knew that he had to disarm him. He reacted quickly, kicking at the knife when Greg slashed at him, but missed it by inches.

"I'm gonna cut that face of yours like ground meat."

"Talk talk talk, when do we fight?" Lamont said, taunting Greg even more. He knew that he had a better chance of disarming Greg if he was angry. "You call me soft, but look who needs a knife. What's the matter, Gregory, can't finish the job without a crutch? What will your ex class mates think? The head of the class had to cheat. Tsk tsk tsk, it's so shameful."

"You asshole." With those words he rushed towards Lamont and slashed at him again, this time catching a piece of the jacket. "Ha, got close that time didn't I," Greg said, seeming pleased.

"Close don't count, you jerk. Can't you do anything right, Gregory?"

Lamont's words angered him more. "Why you smug little piece o shit, I'll slice your ass up like a slab of fatback meat."

"Make up your mind Gregory. Are you going to slice me up like fat back or ground beef?" Lamont taunted, while glaring at Greg with scanning eyes. "Enough speeches, Greg. You're one of those people who talk a good game; cause talking is what you do best."

Greg came in swinging so wildly that Lamont had to keep moving to avoid getting cut. He threw some blows to counter Greg's actions, but Greg held the knife tightly, and Lamont couldn't knock it from his hand.

"Drop that knife." A voice rang out from the doorway, and they looked towards the source. The two security guards, Wendell and Jimmy were standing there at the door with their weapons drawn. Wendell spoke again. "You heard me mister. Drop it or I'll drop you."

In the brief instance that Greg turned to the door, Lamont stepped in and grabbed Greg's knife hand, wrestling furiously to pry the knife from his fist. Both men became oblivious to the guards, who now stood looking at each other, puzzled about what they should do.

Lamont and Greg wrestled around on the floor grunting and vying for the upper hand. Finally the knife came loose and skidded across the slick polished tile floor. Jimmy picked it up, but he and Wendell could only watch the two men struggle. Lamont clearly had the upper hand and he punched Greg one last time and watched him fade to the floor. "You forgot one thing, Greg," Lamont said breathlessly. "You were head in your class, not mine."

Wendell was the first to come over. "You alright boss?"

"Yeah Wendell, I'm good."

"You're nuts. That's what you are." Wendell's voice boomed. "Why'd you go and jump him like that? We had him in our sights. You could have got hurt bad, man. This Nigger had a knife."

"Hey, Man, chill," Jimmy said, giving Wendell an admonishing look as if to say; *'you don't talk to the boss like that man, so shut your mouth.'*

"You're right and I'm sorry guys. I should have let you handle it." Lamont paused and tried to smile. "But you know sometimes you have to taste the wine yourself to see if it's right. Know what I mean, Wendell?"

Wendell hunched his shoulders. "Yeah I do." He said reluctantly. "But don't be doing no crazy shit like that, especially when you got me and Jimmy here for that. We here for you man. Let us do what we suppose to."

"I got it, don't worry, I've learned my lesson," Lamont said, holding his hands out palms up. "Thanks, Wendell."

Wendell shook his hand then looked down at Greg, who was in a semi conscious state. "What do you want us to do about that? Should we call the police and have it locked up?"

"Naw, just get this trash outta here. He's stinking up the place like a fish market garbage can," Lamont said with a scowl.

The two guards lifted Greg off the floor and walked him towards the door. He was silent now almost trance-like as he went willingly with them, in a stupor.

After they left Lamont washed in the large bathroom adjacent to his office. Luckily he had this facility. He had a couple of bruises on his face and for the first time he felt the sting on his arm and saw blood. He had a cut, but it could have been worse, just like Wendell said.

Wendell was a straight talker and he was right. The next time he would leave it to them, and sadly enough there might be a next time because Carvoni had left his evil legacy. Now he had the mobster's cohorts to deal with, and there was no guarantee that they would be any better than Carvoni.

Lamont realized that he had to get some clothes so he called Marcia and asked her to bring him some clothes. Marcia was inquisitive when she arrived and saw his face. "Lamont what happen to your face? Have you been in a fight? Did somebody beat you up?" She seemed close to hysteria.

"I'm fine. I just had a run in with Greg."

"That jerk did this to you. That bully."

Lamont explained what had happened, and she noticed that he was holding a bandage over the cut on his arm.

"I think you should go downstairs to the clinic and get a tetanus shot. There's no telling where that jerk's knife has been." She shook her head. "I always knew he had jackass in his genes, but I never thought he would be stupid enough to pull something like this."

"I recall that you said that he was a jackass once or twice. I should have listened to you."

"It's not your fault, Lamont. Greg didn't kiss your ass, but he was on good behavior in your presence. With me it was constant sexual harassment. He was a real creep."

"Oh baby, why didn't you tell me? All you ever said was that he was a jackass. I would have fired his ass for that. You could have."

She interrupted. "Because I was handling the creep and you didn't need that extra conflict. It was no big deal, just a lot of dirty talk and remarks about my breast and butt, along with what he could do with me in the sack, stuff like that."

"Sorry you had to go through that."

"I told you it was no big deal, honey. He's not the first jerk I've ever met, and I've always been able to handle guys like that." She gave him a wide thirty two point smile. "But it's more fun handling guys like you." She gave him a mysterious pixie look. "You know you can still rescue me if you want to." She said smiling mischievously.

Lamont knew what she wanted and suddenly he wanted it too. He was standing there in the bathroom in his underwear, preparing to change into the suit she had brought. Now he discarded that suit and pulled her into his arms. "You know we got a few minutes to take care of some pressing business."

"I know, but are you okay? I mean you know how wild I get and your bruises...."

"What bruises? He kissed her hard on the mouth and probed inside, seeking her tongue with renewed passion.

369

She pushed against his crotch. "My goodness. Maybe you should get into more fights."

"You like my weapon pretty damsel?"

"Oh yes. I like. I like a lot."

For the next forty minutes, the private bathroom in the executive office became a private love nest, filled with the essence of two lovers coupling with fierce, reckless passion. In those few moments, there was no Cooper Industries, Cooper siblings, Tony Carvoni, Greg Jones, Jane Curtis, or important decisions to make.

Chapter Fifty Two-
Rescue

The next day Lamont got a buzz from his new secretary, Linda Lassiter. "Mr. Savage, there's a Benito, D'Amato here to see you.

"D'Amato, where have I heard that name, before?" Lamont asked himself, thinking that the name sounded so familiar. Hal mentioned it at the meeting yesterday, but he had heard it before then. Lamont's attention focused on the words coming through the intercom. *"I told you that you needed an appointment."* Linda's words stopped in mid sentence. Now Lamont heard her yell at some one. *"Hey wait a minute mister. I'm gonna call security."*

Lamont stood as his office door opened, and the large man entered wearing an expensive suit and dark shades. He was unmistakably Italian, and Lamont guessed that he was Carvoni's replacement, and wondered why he was here. Maybe he's more ambitious, and is here to pressure him into giving up more stock. Well he had a losing battle on his hands, Mafia Don or not.

"Sir I'm gonna have to ask you to leave. We don't conduct business like that here. You can't just barge in here."

The big man said nothing while coming closer to where Lamont stood. In spite of Lamont's recent bruises and soreness from his fight with Greg, he was prepared for action. He watched the big man take off his shades and glare at him. Strangely there was something familiar about him. Suddenly, to Lamont's surprise the big man's mean scowl transformed into a smile.

"Lamont? Ha ha ha, I thought that was you," he said still smiling. "I almost didn't recognize you in your high powered office and expensive suit. And what's with them bruises?"

Lamont gave him a puzzled look, thinking that the man was either deranged, or simply trying to scare him. "Look buddy these tactics aren't gonna work. You might as well forget it."

"You don't remember me, Lamont?" He asked seeming genuinely surprised. I'm crushed," he said sarcastically.

Lamont made a face. "Remember you? Mister I don't know you."

"Aren't you the same Lamont Savage who ran the Outreach Center in Norfolk?" The big man asked with a serious expression.

Lamont blinked surprise. "Yes," Lamont said less hostile now.

"You still don't know me?" The man's expression showed anticipation. "Gained a couple of pounds, and I got a new hair style, but I'm the same person."

Lamont looked him over and there was a brief look of recognition. "Wait a minute. It can't be. Butch?" He asked with mouth wide open. "Is that you, Butch?" He asked again, slapping his forehead. "Oh course I didn't put the name together Butch D'Amato.

The man smiled and moved quickly to Lamont and surrounded him with a bear hug. "In the flesh. But a little more of it these days. I see you doing real good, man." He looked around at the office nodding approval. "Good for you. I understand that Jake Cooper is your old man and.."

The door to Lamont's office flew open before Butch could finish. Wendell and Jimmy now stormed in with weapons drawn. "Get back Mister. Now!" Wendell said, while moving to within a few inches of Butch.

"Hold on fellows. Put the weapons down. It's all right. This is an old friend of mine."

"You sure, Mr. Savage?" Wendell asked, still eying butch with a look of disbelief.

"Yeah, Wendell."

Wendell gave him a brief disappointed look. "Okay Mr. Savage. After the other day, I just wanted to make sure." He turned and motioned to the other guard. "Come on Jimmy."

After the two guards left, Lamont looked Butch over. "Man, you've come a long way yourself. Nice threads."

Butch looked Lamont in the eyes. "I got a second chance and managed to get myself together. After you stopped me from doing something stupid at the center that day, I realized that I couldn't give up. I owe you and Greg big. I'm grateful to you both for saving my life that day. Thanks."

"Hell, we didn't have a choice, man. I thought you were gonna shoot everybody including yourself."

"Well I was out of my mind. Angeline had left me and I was popping pills and." He changed the subject. "You know, man I don't want to talk about it. You look great, Lamont, except for that black eye. What happen? Somebody got *bored* at a *board* meeting?" He chuckled at his own joke."

"Long story, man and I hate to *bore* you."

"I get it nice pun." Butch changed the subject. "How's Greg doing?"

Lamont made a face. "Greg and I don't talk anymore."

"Sorry to hear that, man. You guys seemed like a good team." Butch said but it was obvious that he wanted to talk about something else. "Look Lamont I got a reason for being here."

"I figured that when you busted in. What's up?"

"I understand that you might be interested in buying some Cooper stock back."

"How did..?"

"I took over for Tony. He filled me in on this project months ago, but I had no idea that you were related to the Coopers."

By the same token, Lamont didn't know from Sheppard's report, that this was the man that he and Greg had wrestled with, and disarmed at the Center that day. Apparently, Butch had been living a double life for a long time. "Yeah I heard about Carvoni." Lamont said without any show of sympathy. "Well I guess it happens, heart attack huh?"

"Naw," Butch said with a dismissive frown, "there was nothing wrong with Tony's heart. Tony was a Pit Bull. He was poisoned."

"Poisoned? Carvoni was poisoned?" But who would do that? And how could they get that close?"

"Would you believe his own sister?" Butch shook his head. "Damn shame too. I love them both, but they weren't as close as they used to be. I won't bore you with the reasons cause it's personal. Things just got outta hand."

"So what happened?"

"The murder weapon was her special meat sauce. She spiked it with those damn poison mushrooms. She knew how Tony loved her meat sauce and could eat it seven days a week. Even though they had drifted apart, she still cooked for him and brought it over from her restaurant.

I'm lucky I wasn't there because I would have probably eaten half of that deadly recipe myself."

"That's a shame. So where is his sister now?"

"She's in custody, on suicide watch. She slit her wrist, but botched the job. One of her employees found her in a pool of blood, in her up-stairs apartment and called 911. That's so sad. We were all close once," Butch said with a sad expression and a deep sigh.

"Really?"

"Tony C and his sister Marie and me are first cousins."

"What?" Now that he had mentioned it Lamont could see a resemblance.

"Anyway, enough about me and the family. I'm here to do you a big favor, cause you did me one, that I won't forget."

"You're gonna do me a favor," Lamont said with caution.

"Yeah. I want to do this right away because I'm temporarily in charge, and don't know how long I'll have the authority. I want to get this done while I still do. Now that Tony's gone, there might be some power plays, maybe even turf war."

Lamont cast him a look of disappointment and didn't really know what to say. He certainly wasn't about to offer congratulations for his promotion. He knew that Butch had to be a killer in order to even hold such a position. He had prevented this man from committing suicide a few years earlier, but now Butch was still determined to commit suicide, only now he was proceeding in a more complex and gradual manner. He had become a vicious mobster, and that was a twisted success story.

"Don't give me that look, okay. I gotta do what I gotta do."

"Sure you do Butch," Lamont said nervously, realizing that he had been glaring at Butch with disdain.

"Anyway, at least something good is going to come from this for you. That stock my cousin swindled from you, I'm gonna let you have it all back. I'm gonna do some good and let you keep your company. For a reasonable price of course."

"Really? Why would you do that?" Lamont asked cautiously, waiting for the other shoe to drop.

"Weren't you listening to me? I owe you man. That's the main reason, but I also have to admit Tony's scheme is too ambitious for our style. Quick and easy profit is the way to go. I don't have time for apprenticeship, babysitting and stock market gambling. My people are happy with easy profit, minus complications. This is a win-win situation. I get to make a good impression with the bosses by offering Tony's investment profit as a peace offering and patching up family differences. See where I'm going with this?"

"Yes of course," Lamont said, still unable to believe that this was about to happen. Right now Lamont wanted to pinch himself and jump for joy, because getting the stock back was about to become a reality. He cautioned himself that this seemed too good to be true. Was there a catch? He didn't know, but he wasn't about to waste time or let this opportunity pass. "Okay Butch how much are you asking?"

Butch smiled surreptitiously. "I did some checking and I know the stock is up forty per cent since Tony bought it. I'll sell it back at the current market price plus twenty per cent flat rate bonus. That shouldn't be too hard to take."

"That's more than fair and I can live with that."

"Great, then we have a deal."

Lamont agreed that they had a deal, but he wouldn't believe it until the stock certificates were actually in his possession. He had to act immediately. No doubt Jake would approve because Butch's price was well within the perimeters of the guide lines that he had set. "I'll issue you a cashier's check for the total shares. Would that be okay?"

Butch frowned "Truthfully, Lamont, I'd rather have the cash. You understand I like to avoid any paper trail."

"Yes of course. What was I thinking?" Lamont said. "Okay that can be arranged." Lamont picked up the telephone and dialed Jake, because only Jake could authorize large cash transactions. "Hello, Jake. I just got some news that will make your day. We can get the stock back but we got to move now, and got to have cash," Lamont said and tried to briefly explain his connection to Butch.

"I don't care about the details, explain later," Jake said excitedly. "If this guy is for real you make the deal immediately. If he is for real, than we're getting a bargain. I would have paid ten, twenty times that if I had to, so get it done quickly son. I'll have the courier there with the cash in less than an hour. Great. Good Job son. And believe me, I knew you'd come through. Thanks."

Lamont hung up the telephone feeling overjoyed. He sensed that Jake must be feeling the same, because his voice had vibrated with joy. It appeared that the old Jake was back and that made Lamont feel joyful. Now Lamont turned to Butch and shook his hand. "We got a deal and the money will be here within the hour. Thanks Butch. This means a lot to me."

"Hey, it's the least I can do," Butch said, looking around the office.

Now awkward silence haunted the room, and Lamont gazed at the slow moving clock, and nursed his anxious need to finalized the transaction, and break his ties to Butch. That made him a hypocrite, because in spite of Butch's role in the salvation of Cooper industries, when this deal is done, he was done with Butch.

A lot has changed since that day at the center, and as far as Lamont was concerned, Butch could have chosen a more righteous path to pursue. He had thought that Butch had gone straight that day when he left the center. He had sworn that he would get his life together. Lamont never suspected that he would do it by hurting people.

Ironically, Butch's endeavor into his chosen life had provided Cooper Industries with the solution to its most severe crisis; and allowed the company to recover all the lost stock. That was noble in a sense but it didn't make up for his senseless indecent actions. Lamont was torn between his aversion for the man's life style, and gratitude for his affable action.

Three hours later the transaction was completed, and thirty percent of Cooper Industries stock no longer belonged to the mob. After the transaction, Butch announced that he had one more meeting to make and left. Lamont breathed a sigh of relief, because now he was sure that he would never see the big man again. Strangely he had gotten the feeling that Butch felt the same way.

Epilogue

When Bennie/Butch D'Amato left Lamont's office, he drove back to the club where Two Martin nervously waited. Two had no idea what to expect or what Bennie would do, now that he was in charge. He had never had any dealings with the big ugly goon, one on one. Even though he knew very little about Bennie, he knew for sure that the big man killed without remorse or regret.

He might even be worse than his cousin, now that he was top man. What was worse than an empowered killer, Tony thought. Bennie might be out to prove that he could do a better job, and he just might come down hard on every one as a way to show his strength.

Two couldn't worry about that now. All he could do is make this meeting with him as he had requested, and not read anything into the meaning of this promotion for Bennie. The truth of the matter is that he had no reason to suspect that Bennie would do anything different from his infamous cousin. When this meeting was over, he would know for sure where he stood, and what was going to happen with the tapes of Cheryl and him.

Shortly Two Martin sat in Carvoni's office looking at Bennie with astonishment. He still wasn't sure that he had heard him right. "I don't understand. You're giving me these tapes? Why?" Two asked looking dumbfounded at the video tapes now in his possession.

"Let's just say that it's about completing a payback of a debt I owed. It ain't got nothing to do with you. You're just the recipient of my overflowing good will."

Two didn't understand what the big ugly dude was talking about, but he wasn't going to argue. It was a second chance for him and now he looked at himself. He's been scamming for years and had nothing to show for it. He wanted to do right and he wanted to be with Cheryl, but that meant he had to consider change. "Bennie, about the Two Plus Two Club?"

"What about it?"

"I was wondering if you would let me buy you out."

"I like you Two, but I don't know. I'm giving you the tapes. Don't get greedy on me."

Two decided to leave well enough alone. "Okay fair enough," Two said dejected.

"Tell you what I can do though. For as long as I'm in charge, I'll give you a raise and if you can manage to save enough, I might consider letting you buy me out."

"Fair enough," Two said with a smile. Two had never been ambitious about doing the right thing for anyone other than himself, but lately he wanted to be more responsible. Could he and Cheryl ever have anything real, beyond the insane sex between them? He didn't know, but for the first time he wanted to try and do something that was unselfish. He didn't know what that meant, but he would be open enough to find out.

Meanwhile Cheryl had made an important decision to have her baby, but she would go away to do this. She was over her vanity about stretch marks, but she wasn't prepared to deal with all the questions and disdaining glares that her swelling stomach would surely attract. She had told Two about the baby, but she assured him that it was okay if he didn't go along with her decision to keep it. She accepted the fact that he wouldn't change.

Lamont and Marcia had lived together in his apartment for the past week and neither of them had any plans to change that arrangement. It was six months later when Lamont knew for sure and without any doubts that he wanted Marcia to be his wife. "So Marsh, how do you feel about the name Marcia Savage?" Lamont asked one night while they were relaxing casually watching a rented movie.

"What?" Marcia went into his arms and smothered him with kisses. "Oh Lamont are you proposing?"

"Maybe," he said coyly.

"Don't tease me."

"I won't and I guess that maybe I am."

She grabbed the top of his head and pulled it to her breast. "Yes yes

yes. Of course I'll marry you." Then she moved back and looked into his eyes. "You're sure?" She asked with nervous anticipation.

"I've never been more positive about anything in my life. My mother even likes you and that's a miracle in itself."

"I like her too; she's so feisty and frank. I like knowing where I stand with her and I do."

"Well even if she didn't, I like you enough for a whole horde of people."

"Lamont you make me feel so special."

"You are special, baby, and precious. I look forward to our life together. You're my friend, most trusted confidant, and spectacular lover. There little doubt about how I feel and what I must do. The thought of being married to you is so blissful"

Lamont never thought of Jane these days, except for the times that he had seen her forecasting the weather on television. So far Jane hadn't got that promotion to co-anchor, but he had no doubt that she would do whatever it took to get what she wanted. She was a real pit bull when she wanted something. She always had a scheme in play and wasn't about to accept less than what was promised to her. He suspected that she had tired of Greg and he was no longer in the picture, but it didn't matter.

Looking back, he couldn't figure out why he had ever dreamed that he loved someone that shallow, especially when some one as deep as Marcia was in his life the whole time. Marcia was a handful but she was honest and he loved that about her.

JJ has a new mysterious woman in his life and is very hush hush about her. No one had seen this new love interest, and after six months, JJ still refused to talk about her, or tell anyone her name. The good news is that he's not out partying so much these days, and is actually working at his job. Lamont hoped that this wasn't a temporary situation that would only last until he became bored with the job and the new girl.

"So JJ, what's this chick's name man. What girl could tame you and take you off the party circuit?" Lamont asked on one recent occasion.

"That's personal man," JJ had replied. "What my lady and I do is between me and my lady."

"Sorry, man, didn't mean no harm, just making conversation," Lamont had replied. Now he knew that any conversation about the new girl was strictly off limits. He could live with that, but he thought that it was odd that JJ wasn't bragging about the new girl like he always did with his other conquests.

Jake made a full recovery and Lamont had gladly relinquished his power of attorney.

"Glad you're back, Pop," Lamont said jokingly.

"Good to be back," Jake replied, and then added, "and by the way, I want you to have Peter's job and his office. You'll be my senior consultant and vice president."

"Jake you don't have to do that," Lamont started.

"I don't have to do anything that I don't want to," he said cutting Lamont off. "So I must want to do this, and you have to learn not to argue with me. I'm a double threat cause I'm your boss and your dad, so do what you're told or I'll have to spank you and fire you," Jake said lightly.

"Okay, then boss dad," Lamont said and they both laughed.

"You going to have a bright future here, Lamont and with you me and JJ working together, Cooper and Sons is going to shine and prosper."

"I believe you Jake, and," Lamont paused. "Did you say Cooper and Sons?"

Jake said nothing; he just observed Lamont's pleased expression with a smile. "Man this is.." Lamont couldn't form the words. "I got to go tell Marcia." He left Jake's office walking on air.

Lamont felt a genuine closeness to his father for the first time since he has known him. That's because they had worked together as a team and defeated the bad guys, while watching each other's back.

He sensed that the family bonding would come along slowly, but eventually it would be the deep bond that he sought. For now he was happy to accept what he had, because it was much more than he had before. He felt closure and completion, and Jake's dream was now his dream and he knew that there was lots of promise ahead. He was a part of Cooper Industries, the Cooper family, and he had found Marcia. Now he had contentment, purpose, and happiness in his life along with so many blessing to count daily.

The End